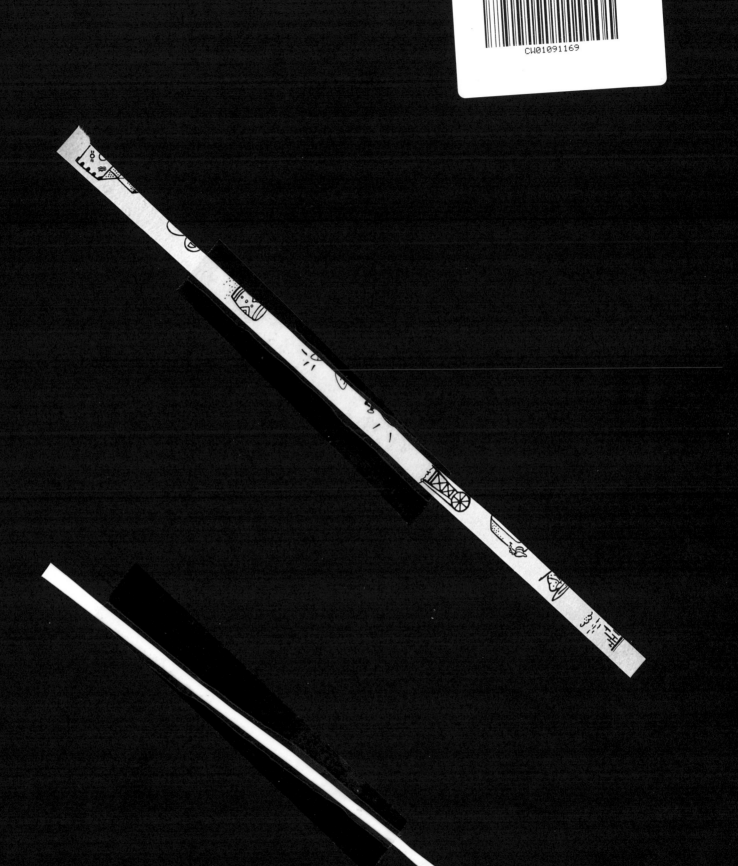

SEASON TO TASTE

FOR
Jan, my best friend
Vera Tomlin, my Mum

IN MEMORY OF
Liam Tomlin Snr, my Dad

SEASON TO TASTE

LIAM TOMLIN

Photography by Geoff Lung

First published in 2005 by Struik Publishers
(a division of New Holland Publishing (South Africa) (Pty) Ltd)
Cape Town • London • Sydney • Auckland
www.struik.co.za

Cornelis Struik House, 80 McKenzie Street, Cape Town 8001, South Africa
Garfield House, 86 – 88 Edgware Road, London W2 2EA, United Kingdom
14 Aquatic Drive, Frenchs Forest, NSW 2086, Australia
218 Lake Road, Northcote, Auckland, New Zealand

New Holland Publishing is a member of Johnnic Communications Ltd

10 9 8 7 6 5 4 3 2 1

Publishing Manager: Linda de Villiers
Editor: Janice Botha
Consulting Editor: Joy Clack
Art Director: Anne Barton
Photographer: Geoff Lung
Food styling: Liam Tomlin
Proofreader: Irma van Wyk

Reproduction by Hirt & Carter Cape (Pty) Ltd
Printed and bound by Kyodo Printing Co (Singapore) Pte Ltd

ISBN 1 77007 200 4

Log on to our photographic website – **www.imagesofafrica.co.za** –
for an African experience

CONTENTS

FOREWORD

Ireland has bred many literary and musical icons: Brendan Beehan, James Joyce, Patrick Kavanagh and, more recently, Van Morrison, Bono, Phil Lynott and Bob Geldoff. Its culture of friendly people, green pastures, great pubs, superb whiskeys and Guinness is legendary but a reputation for outstanding food eluded Ireland for many years. Recently this has changed with the emergence of several celebrated chefs, including Liam Tomlin, who can be added to Ireland's list of proud claims.

Liam and I both trained in Ireland and coincidentally spent time in the kitchens of Tim O'Sullivan in Renvyle House where we first experienced gourmet cuisine. Although we worked there at different times, we both realised that if we were to grow and mature in our chosen profession, we needed to travel the world.

Liam paid his dues in the great London kitchens, before heading for Australia with his beautiful wife, Jan. Little did Sydney know that the Irishman who'd arrived in Australia with his last week's pay cheque, a bundle of knives and a book of dog-eared recipes, would play a major part in the international culinary arts revival over the next 12 years.

Soon, Liam became one of the most talked-about chefs in Sydney for his modern French cuisine. Back in Ireland, I became aware of names like Gordon Ramsay and Marco Pierre White in London; big-name American chefs Charlie Trotter, Daniel Boulud and David Bouley; and in Sydney, Tetsuya Wakuda, Neil Perry and Liam Tomlin. Described as a visionary, a mild-mannered genius and a raving lunatic, what always followed was a very clear description of Liam's unforgettable food. Determined to experience it for myself, I flew to Sydney and had my first taste. I also met the chef himself. Neither disappointed; I close my eyes and can still remember each incredible dish. We instantly became friends and I have valued his advice and loved his cooking both in his restaurants and his home ever since.

Exceptional standards maintained over several years in the culinary capital of the world won Liam many awards and Australian Best Restaurant; Best Chef; Best Design and Best Wine List are just a few of the accolades garnered by this young man from Dublin.

Having left behind a legacy of signature dishes, Liam has chosen South Africa as his new challenge. He lives in Cape Town and I've no doubt is sorely missed in Australia by both peers and devoted patrons. His unwavering passion for his craft earned him the deepest respect and adoration of many talented young Australian chefs and restaurant managers who benefited from the privilege of working with Liam and in his kitchens.

A visionary and an entrepreneur, Liam has the ability to create inspired restaurant concepts and tantalising menus. His new cookbook bears testimony to his talent and is a tribute to his classic training. This book for cooks is the gift that he gives to me and to all serious foodies, and that no kitchen should be without.

Liam, I wish you great success with *Season To Taste* and look forward to enjoying lots more of your magnificent food and hospitality in the future.

Your friend,

Conrad Gallagher

Cape Town, South Africa, August 2005

INTRODUCTION

Throughout this book I have attempted to illustrate the methods and techniques used to prepare a selection of my favourite ingredients; from a simple vine-ripened tomato salad dressed with a quality extra virgin olive oil, aged balsamic vinegar, baby basil leaves and black olives, to the more complex and time-consuming carpaccio of pig's trotter stuffed with foie gras, calves sweetbreads and wild mushrooms with a truffle dressing. It's all about combining ingredients that complement each other, resulting in well-balanced dishes with great flavour and classic combinations such as champagne and berries, sweetcorn and basil, beef and foie gras, thyme and Riesling, celeriac and truffle, venison and black figs, to mention a few.

Great food begins with great ingredients. As a chef I surround myself with only those suppliers and producers who have the same pride and passion for what they do as I have for my profession; those who don't take any shortcuts; those who have an understanding for the demands of a busy, professional kitchen and the capability to keep up with its requirements for consistent and fresh products. I speak with suppliers on a daily basis and am guided by them as to what to include on the menu, and when to remove certain dishes. The menu is never changed for the sake of change; it reflects the seasons according to the availability and quality of ingredients.

With a wide choice of raw ingredients now available in the high-street supermarkets, shopping for food has become a whole new experience. The majority of our produce comes from small, individual, boutique producers, which in many cases are family-run businesses; producers who focus on quality rather than quantity; those who hand-feed squabs; hand-pick the vegetables that they grow and milk the goats for making the cheese with which they supply us. In other words, those who produce products and ingredients that cannot be bettered. So, I urge you to shop at, and support your local butchers, fishmongers and greengrocers as they can offer you a service that is much more personal and knowledgeable. They have selected and know the origin of the product that you are buying and these days the source of the food chain is crucial. Also, they are able to obtain the unusual for you, such as crepinette or fresh pig's blood. Take time to visit your local market and be aware of the fresh produce that your local growers are producing. Your eyes will be opened to a whole new variety of flavours and tastes.

I dislike food with too many layers and flavours – it's so unnecessary, because if you're working with the best raw ingredients, they really need very little done to them and I still think the best way to eat an oyster is freshly shucked with a squeeze of lemon; and it's hard to beat fresh asparagus spears, simply steamed, with a drizzle of olive oil and a sprinkling of sea salt and freshly ground pepper. However, I realise that when patrons visit a restaurant they expect a bit more than that, but I always look at a finished dish and think about what can be taken away from it rather than what can be added. So, I hope you enjoy my choice of ingredients and the recipes that I have created with them as much as the exquisite photography by Geoff Lung and the inspired art direction by Anne Barton. Remember, just keep it simple and season to taste.

Liam Tomlin
Sydney, Australia, June 2003
Dublin, Ireland, May 2004
Cape Town, South Africa, August 2005

BEFORE USING THESE RECIPES...

... it's important to consider the differences between the professional and domestic kitchen. The professional kitchen is designed with self-contained sections for different food preparation tasks, each with its own work surface, stove tops, ovens and refrigeration. Additional luxuries are plate warmers, hot lights, salamanders, slicing machines, blenders, electric mincers, and ice-cream machines. A selection of ovens set at different temperatures and modes accommodate a varied menu allowing for all types of dishes to be prepared in different ways, using several techniques and cooking methods. And then, there is the brigade of qualified chefs working in harmony with each other. All these factors conspire to function like a well-oiled machine. The domestic kitchen on the other hand may be equipped with many of these kitchen aids and appliances but not the manpower, so, concentrate on the flavour of the dish and serving it at the correct temperature rather than on precise presentation, which could result in cold food. Outlined below are a few simple guidelines to assist with the recipes in this book.

- Use heavy-based stainless steel saucepans and cast-iron pans. These give much better results than cheaper pots and pans, which tend to wear out quickly, buckle and distribute uneven heat, resulting in inconsistently cooked ingredients. Stainless steel and cast-iron pans have the advantage of being able to be used on the stove top to seal meat, fish and vegetables and can then be transferred directly to a hot oven, thereby maintaining the temperature for the duration of cooking. Good kitchen equipment and appliances collected over a period of time will make a significant difference to final results and if bought wisely, each piece should last a lifetime.

- Oven temperatures and cooking times may vary depending on the equipment being used.

- Read through the ingredients and method before starting a recipe to enable you to schedule enough time needed to make the dish. Always prepare the Basic Recipes first and familiarise yourself with the Basic Techniques. If a recipe calls for a stock, make double the quantity and freeze half for future use – you will soon build up a useful supply of basic ingredients such as stocks, flavoured oils, rendered duck fat, syrups and seasonings – saving time and labour when the same basic ingredient is required again.

- The introduction page to each chapter gives detailed information on the ingredient and possible varieties thereof, highlighted in that particular chapter.

- The glossary details information on the ingredients used in these recipes.

- Where an ingredient is measured by a teaspoon or tablespoon, this indicates a level spoonful.

- Refer to the Conversion Chart on page 9 if you are unfamiliar with the measurement given.

- No weights or measurements are given for seasonings such as salt, pepper or lemon juice – taste as you proceed.

- Use fresh herbs unless otherwise stated.

- Always wash and dry vegetables before using, except for mushrooms and courgette flowers. These need only be wiped with a damp cloth to remove any dirt that might be on, or in them.

- If blanching vegetables or pasta, do so in a large amount of salted, boiling water so as not to reduce the temperature once they are immersed. Have a bowl of iced water standing by, ready to refresh the ingredient, stop the cooking process and preserve the colour, texture and flavour (see glossary).

- For vegetable stocks, use water instead of chicken stock, which will render them suitable for vegetarians.

- Where butter is listed as an ingredient, use unsalted butter unless otherwise stated. Whole butter is used in sauces and pastry and should always be chilled and diced unless stated otherwise. Softened butter should be kept at room temperature.

- To reduce or limit the amount of butter or cream used, don't replace it with low-fat alternatives. Rather, replace it with a dressing like the Bois Boudran or a flavoured oil.

- Where alcohol is required, ensure it is reduced according to the recipe, which will remove the acidic taste that unevaporated alcohol imparts. Where wine is a required ingredient, choose one that you would drink yourself; it should be of good quality, just like the other raw ingredients.

- No quantities are given for vegetable oil for deep-frying. Fill the saucepan to two-thirds full and bring to the required temperature over a low heat before adding the food to be deep-fried. Cook in small batches so as to maintain the temperature and prevent the oil from spilling over.

- Although the number of servings for each recipe is specified below the title, in most instances plating is described for one portion only.

BEFORE SEASONING...

- Salt added to raw meat will draw out moisture, which is vital in the preparation of confit. Also, it will draw the juices of vegetables such as tomatoes and aubergines.

- Avoid salting delicate fish, e.g. John Dory and shellfish such as scallop, too far in advance of cooking. Only season just before or during cooking.

- If serving fish with the skin on, a little salt rubbed into the skin 15 minutes before cooking will draw moisture and result in a crisp skin.

- When reducing liquids, e.g. stocks and sauces, to concentrate their flavour, it's best to season them once reduced to prevent them becoming too salty.

- It's easy to rectify a bland sauce or dressing with a pinch of salt or sugar, a dash of vinegar or a squeeze of lemon.

- Use freshly ground white pepper to avoid unsightly specks of black pepper in pale-coloured sauces.

- Allow for the naturally high salt content in ingredients such as anchovy, pancetta, nam pla or soy sauce before adding additional seasoning.

- Maldon sea salt is a superior, delicate flake that can be easily ground between fingertips or with a pestle and mortar. It is also a good table salt.

- Gradually add citrus juice, alcohol, Tabasco, Worcestershire sauce, flavoured vinegars or pickled ginger juice to a sauce and taste after each addition as it's difficult to rectify without diluting the original flavours.

- Flavoured oils such as truffle, sesame, walnut or hazelnut must be used sparingly and added gradually as they have an intense flavour and can be overpowering. Flavoured oils are not usually served neat, but rather should be blended with other ingredients.

- Finally…taste food first. It may not require any additional seasoning. Always *Season To Taste*.

CONVERSION CHARTS

LIQUID MEASURES

Metric	Imperial	US
5 ml	3/16 fl oz	1 tsp
15 ml	1/2 fl oz	1 tbsp
60 ml	2 fl oz	4 tbsp (1/4 cup)
80 ml	2¾ fl oz	1/3 cup
125 ml	4½ fl oz	1/2 cup
200 ml	7 fl oz	3/4 cup
250 ml	9 fl oz	1 cup

DRY MEASURES

100 g	3½ oz
250 g	9 oz
500 g	1 lb
750 g	1¾ lb
1 kg	2¼ lb

MEASUREMENTS

5 mm	1/4 in
1 cm	1/2 in
2.5 cm	1 in
10 cm	4 in
15 cm	6 in
30 cm	12 in (1 ft)

OVEN TEMPERATURES

Gas	°C	°F	Oven Temperature
1/4	110	225	Very cool
1	140	275	Cool
3	160	325	Warm
4	180	350	Moderate
7	220	425	Hot
9	240	475	Very hot

It's difficult to beat the smell and flavour of a beautifully sun-ripened tomato. They're at their best during the warm summer months. The tomato is such a versatile ingredient that it always has a place on the menu.

There are many different varieties from which to choose and endless ways in which to prepare and serve them; from a simple tomato salad sprinkled with sea salt and dressed with quality olive oil and aged balsamic vinegar to a spicy tomato sorbet served with a chilled tomato consommé. Whenever possible, buy tomatoes that have been sun-ripened on the vine. Buy them on a daily basis and store on a kitchen shelf rather than in the fridge. If refrigerated, take them out an hour before serving, allowing them to reach room temperature, which will revive their flavour.

The most common varieties are used for salads, tomato concassée or they can be cut up, marinated and turned into consommé. The Ailsa Craig is the most

TOMATOES

flavoursome of these varieties, and grows to a good size and bright colour. Choose medium-sized tomatoes that are unblemished as large tomatoes are often dry, floury and lack flavour.

Cut plum or egg tomatoes lengthways, scoop out and discard the seeds with a teaspoon and slowly cook the flesh with fresh herbs and seasoning to make tomato confit for terrines. They are also suitable for tomato fondue and sauces. The water that is released can be decanted and used as stock for tomato risotto. Choose the San Marzano variety.

Red and yellow cherry tomatoes are full of flavour. When semi-dried, they can be stuffed with tapenade or anchovies to serve with fish. Warm and use as a garnish for tomato and tapenade tarts and also in the preparation of gazpacho. Tomato paste is excellent to colour and flavour stocks, shellfish bisque and tomato and crustacean oils (basic recipes 17 & 18, page 194). Tomato ketchup is used in dressings like Marie-Rose for shellfish and sauce Bois Boudran (basic recipe 4, page 191), which is served with grilled fish or steamed vegetables.

TOMATO AND BASIL CONSOMMÉ

Serves 4

1 kg	**Over-ripe, vine-ripened tomatoes**
1	**Shallot, sliced**
3	**Sprigs fresh chervil, roughly chopped**
3	**Sprigs fresh tarragon, roughly chopped**
1	**Small bunch fresh basil, roughly chopped**
10 ml	**White wine**
	Pinch Maldon sea salt
	Pinch sugar
80 g	**Tomato concassée (basic technique 9, page 217)**
20	**Picked baby basil leaves**
20	**Picked baby tarragon leaves**
24	**Slices black olive**
	Salt
	Freshly ground pepper

Core the tomatoes and roughly chop. Place in a bowl with the sliced shallot, roughly chopped herbs, white wine, sea salt, sugar and a twist of freshly ground pepper. Mix the ingredients together and cover with clingfilm. Refrigerate for 4 hours to allow the flavours to infuse. After 4 hours, transfer the contents of the bowl into a double-layer of muslin cloth and tie up as tightly as possible. Place in a sieve over a large bowl to catch the juice released from the tomatoes and return to the fridge for 12 hours.

The tomatoes will have released all their juice and the sediment will have settled at the bottom of the bowl. Carefully decant the consommé into a clean bowl through a coffee filter paper – take care not to disturb the sediment at the bottom of the bowl. Discard the sediment and tomato pulp.

The consommé can be served either hot or cold. If hot, place the consommé in a saucepan and gently warm over a very low heat. Lightly season the tomato concassée with salt and freshly ground pepper and spoon into a soup bowl. Pour over the consommé and garnish with the picked basil and tarragon leaves and slices of olive.

TOMATO TERRINE WITH BABY VEGETABLES AND TOMATO OIL

Makes 750 ml terrine/12 slices

TOMATO CONFIT

650 g	Tomato confit (basic technique 10, page 217)
25 ml	Extra virgin olive oil
1 tbsp	Julienne of flat-leaf parsley
1 tbsp	Julienne of basil
10 ml	Aged balsamic vinegar
10 ml	Basil oil (basic recipe 15, page 193)

GAZPACHO

250 g	Vine-ripened tomatoes, cored, halved and seeded
¼	Cucumber, peeled and seeded
½	Red capsicum, halved and seeded
1	Clove garlic, peeled
½	Small Spanish onion, peeled
6	Sprigs fresh basil
15 ml	Sherry vinegar
	Dash Tabasco Sauce to taste
4	Leaves gelatine
50 ml	Tomato water, released from the tomato confit
4	Vine-ripened tomatoes, blanched, quartered and de-seeded

BABY VEGETABLES (Serves 4)

8	Baby carrots, peeled and blanched
8	Baby leeks, trimmed and blanched
8	Baby beetroot, cooked and peeled (basic technique 7, page 216)
4	Green asparagus spears, peeled and blanched (basic technique 5, page 216)
4	White asparagus spears, peeled and blanched (basic technique 5, page 216)
8	Baby fennel, trimmed, blanched
2	Baby turnips, blanched
4	Baby globe artichokes, prepared and cooked (basic technique 6, page 216)
8	Broad beans, shelled and blanched
4	Cherry tomatoes
12	Slices black olive
20 ml	Extra virgin olive oil
20 ml	Tomato oil (basic recipe 17, page 194)
20 ml	Basil oil (basic recipe 15, page 193)
12	Picked chervil leaves
12	Picked baby basil leaves
12	Picked tarragon leaves
12	Chive tips
	Salt
	Freshly ground pepper

The tomato confit, gazpacho, basil and tomato oils can all be made 24 hours in advance of serving. When the terrine is made, refrigerate for at least 6 hours, but preferably overnight before turning out and slicing.

Prepare the gazpacho: Roughly chop the tomatoes, cucumber, red capsicum, garlic, Spanish onion and basil, place in a food processor and blend to a smooth purée. Pass the purée through a fine sieve and press down hard on the purée to extract as much flavour as possible. Discard the pulp. Add the sherry vinegar and Tabasco. Take care not to over-spice as this will overpower the finished dish. Season to taste with salt and freshly ground pepper. Cover the gazpacho with clingfilm and refrigerate until ready to use.

Remove the tomato confit from the muslin cloth and place in a bowl. Add 25 ml extra virgin olive oil, julienne of parsley and basil and stir through the tomato confit. Add the balsamic vinegar and 5 ml basil oil. Season to taste with salt and freshly ground pepper.

Soften the gelatine leaves in cold water, remove and squeeze dry. Warm 50 ml tomato water over a gentle heat, add the gelatine and stir until dissolved. Remove from the heat and allow to cool slightly before stirring into the gazpacho.

Square the 4 quartered tomatoes. Trim all 4 sides with a sharp knife and lightly season with salt and freshly ground pepper. Line a 750 ml terrine with clingfilm, leaving a 2.5 cm over-hang. Pour a thin layer of gazpacho to cover the base of the terrine and refrigerate for 3 minutes until the gelatine begins to set. Add a layer of tomato confit and smooth out with a palette knife. Pour a second thin layer of gazpacho over the tomato confit. Press the squared tomato quarters into the gazpacho and refrigerate for a further 3 minutes. Add a second layer of tomato confit and continue to layer the terrine until the terrine is full, finishing with a layer of tomato confit. Fold over the clingfilm to enclose the terrine. If the gazpacho begins to set while building the terrine, place over a very low heat to melt again.

To press the terrine, cut out a piece of cardboard the same size as the terrine and wrap with aluminium foil and then clingfilm. Place onto the terrine and set a 500 g weight evenly on top. Refrigerate for at least 6 hours or preferably overnight.

Remove the weight from the terrine, remove the cardboard and open the clingfilm covering the top of the terrine. Run the tip of a sharp knife around the edge of the terrine and invert onto the cut-out cardboard. Cut four 2 cm slices of the terrine and brush with extra virgin olive oil. Lightly season with salt and freshly ground pepper. Place a slice in the centre of 4 serving plates and allow to stand for 15 minutes to reach room temperature.

Place the blanched vegetables, cherry tomatoes and sliced olives into a bowl and add 20 ml extra virgin olive oil. Season to taste with salt and freshly ground pepper. Spoon the vegetables and sliced olives around the terrine. Drizzle the tomato and basil oils over and around the vegetables and garnish with the picked herbs.

TOMATO AND OLIVE TART

Serves 4

50 ml	**Cabernet Sauvignon vinegar**
50 ml	**Extra virgin olive oil**
	Pinch sugar
I	**Sprig fresh basil, roughly chopped**
I	**Small sprig fresh rosemary**
I	**Sprig fresh thyme**
I	**Bay leaf**
200 g	**Puff pastry (basic recipe 94, page 212)**
8	**Roma tomatoes, blanched and peeled**
120 g	**Tapenade (basic recipe 12, page 192)**
	Egg wash of I free-range egg and 10 ml milk
8	**Cherry tomatoes**
8	**Yellow teardrop tomatoes**
24	**Slices black olive**
12	**Baby basil leaves**
12	**Chive tips**
12	**Sprigs fresh chervil**
12	**Mâche leaves (lamb's lettuce)**
20 ml	**Tomato oil (basic recipe 17, page 194)**
20 ml	**Basil oil (basic recipe 15, page 193)**
	Salt
	Freshly ground pepper

Marinade for Roma tomatoes: Mix together the Cabernet Sauvignon vinegar, olive oil, sugar, chopped basil, rosemary, thyme and bay leaf in a bowl and lightly season with salt and freshly ground pepper. Allow to infuse at room temperature for I hour.

Lightly dust a work surface with flour and roll out the puff pastry to a thickness of 5 mm. Cut out 4 circles of pastry with a 10 cm pastry cutter. Place the pastry on a cold baking sheet and prick all over with a fork. Rest the pastry in the fridge for 30 minutes.

Cut the Roma tomatoes into 5 mm thick slices and place in a bowl. Pour the marinade over the sliced tomatoes and marinate at room temperature for 30 minutes. Drain the tomatoes on a wire rack. (Reserve the marinade for future use.)

Preheat the oven to 200°C. Remove the puff pastry circles from the fridge. Place an 8 cm pastry cutter in the centre of the pastry and spread 10 g tapenade inside the pastry cutter using a small palette knife. Brush the 2 cm pastry rim with the egg wash. Arrange eight overlapping slices of Roma tomato in a circle on top of the tapenade. Lightly season the tomato with salt and freshly ground pepper. Spray a cold baking sheet with water and transfer the tomato tarts onto it. Bake the tarts in the oven for 8 minutes until the pastry is crisp and golden.

While the tarts are cooking, cut the cherry and teardrop tomatoes in half and lightly season with salt and freshly ground pepper. Warm them under a salamander or in the oven for 2 minutes. Using two teaspoons, make four 15 g quenelles with the remainder of the tapenade.

Check that the pastry bases are cooked before removing from the oven. Place a tart in the centre of a warm plate and spoon the cherry and teardrop tomatoes and olive slices around it. Set a quenelle of tapenade in the centre of the tart and garnish with the basil, chive, chervil and mâche leaves. Drizzle a little of both the tomato and basil oils around the plate.

SALAD OF VINE-RIPENED TOMATOES WITH SHALLOTS, BASIL AND OLIVES

Serves 4 as a side dish

2	**Large, vine-ripened tomatoes**
1	**Large shallot, sliced**
30 ml	**Extra virgin olive oil**
25 ml	**Aged balsamic vinegar**
12	**Calamata olives**
8	**Picked baby basil leaves**
	Salt
	Freshly ground pepper

Core the tomatoes and cut into quarters. Cut each quarter into three even pieces and place in a bowl. Add the sliced shallots and season with salt and freshly ground pepper. Pour the olive oil and balsamic vinegar over the tomatoes and toss to evenly coat with the dressing. Allow the tomatoes to stand at room temperature for 15 minutes to absorb the flavours of the oil and vinegar.

Place a 10 cm pastry cutter in a bowl plate. Arrange overlapping tomato pieces in a circle against the side of the mould, with the skin facing outward. When the first layer is complete, spoon some of the sliced shallots and dressing over the tomato. Arrange a second layer in the same way, ending with the remaining shallots and dressing. Gently remove the pastry cutter. Garnish the salad with the olives and baby basil.

There is a wide selection of cultivated mushrooms all year round from which to choose. Some of the more common varieties are button, oyster, shiitake, chestnut, shimiji and enoki.

A vast choice of wild mushrooms with a range of different textures and flavours appear from late summer to late autumn. Of these, the more familiar are the morel, cep, saffron milk cap, horn of plenty, chanterelle and the most sought-after mushroom of all, the black Perigord truffle.

Select dry, fresh and plump specimens. Avoid any that appear slimy, shrivelled or have hollow stalks, as this is a sign that they have had worms through them. Buy only what you need, as mushrooms deteriorate and lose flavour immediately after they have been picked.

Never wash mushrooms, as they absorb water like sponges; simply clean with a damp cloth to remove any grit or sand. Remove the gills from capped

MUSHROOMS

mushrooms with the tip of a paring knife, cover with a damp cloth and refrigerate until ready to use.

Briefly sauté small batches of mushrooms in very hot olive oil to seal in the flavour. Season when cooked to prevent the salt from drawing water out of the mushrooms.

Mushrooms lose between 80 and 90 per cent of their weight when dried. This makes them very expensive to use, but a small amount goes a long way. Dried mushrooms, especially ceps and morels, have an intense flavour and can be used in sauces or ground with a little rock salt for seasoning meat, poultry, stocks and risotto.

Fresh truffles stored in sealed containers of raw arborio rice, polenta and fresh eggs impart their flavour to these ingredients, which can then be used in dishes such as truffle risotto, truffle-infused polenta terrine and creamed truffle eggs.

MUSHROOM CONSOMMÉ WITH TRUFFLE TORTELLINI

Serves 6

MUSHROOM CONSOMMÉ

100 g	Chicken, skin and fat removed, and minced
10 g	Julienne of leek
10 g	Julienne of celeriac
5 g	Dried cep mushrooms
6	Button mushrooms, roughly chopped
200 ml	Fresh free-range egg whites
1.5 ltr	Cold mushroom stock (basic recipe 21, page 195)

TRUFFLE TORTELLINI

60 g	Mushroom duxelle (basic recipe 57, page 204)
5 ml	Truffle oil
1 tsp	Chopped truffle
1 tsp	Sliced chives
200 g	Plain pasta dough (basic recipe 68, page 207)
	Egg wash of 1 free-range egg yolk and 15 ml water

GARNISH

18	Small morel mushrooms
18	Slices of truffle
12	Tarragon leaves
12	Chive tips
12	Sprigs fresh chervil
	Salt
	Freshly ground pepper

To clarify the mushroom stock: Place the chicken mince, leek, celeriac, dried cep mushrooms, button mushrooms and the egg whites into a bowl and beat together. Season lightly with salt and freshly ground pepper. Pour the cold mushroom stock into a heavy-based saucepan and beat the mince mixture into the stock. Bring to the boil, stirring frequently to prevent sticking to the bottom or around the sides of the saucepan. Reduce the heat to a simmer and stop stirring.

The mince, vegetables and egg white will float to the surface after 10–15 minutes, and will bring all the impurities in the stock with them, forming a crust. Continue to simmer for a further 15 minutes. Make a hole in the centre of the crust with a tablespoon. Remove from the heat and ladle out the clarified consommé through the hole, taking care not to break the crust. Pass the consommé through a fine sieve lined with a double layer of muslin cloth or a coffee filter paper into a clean stainless steel container. Taste the consommé and adjust the seasoning if necessary. Refrigerate until ready to use.

Prepare the truffle tortellini: Place the mushroom duxelle into a bowl, add the truffle oil, chopped truffle and sliced chives and mix together. Season to taste with salt and freshly ground pepper.

Cut the pasta dough into two pieces. Roll out both pieces with a rolling pin on a lightly floured work surface until they are 5 mm thick. Set a pasta machine on the thickest setting and feed through the first piece of pasta twice. Adjust the setting one notch and feed the pasta through twice again. Continue to roll the pasta until it is on the thinnest setting. Roll the second piece in the same way. When all the pasta is rolled, cut out 12 circles of pasta using an 8 cm plain pastry cutter. Place the pasta on a plate and cover with clingfilm to prevent it from drying out.

Prepare the tortellini one at a time: Spoon a teaspoon of mushroom duxelle into the centre of each circle of pasta. Brush the edge of each with the egg wash. Fold the pasta to make a semi-circle and press the edges together from one side to the other, pressing out any air from the pocket of pasta.

Hold the tortellini in your hand and curl the two tips around the index finger and press together; press the edges together again with your fingers to ensure that they are firmly joined. Repeat with the remaining tortellini. Blanche the tortellini in salted boiling water for 2 minutes and refresh in iced water. Drain well.

Reheat the consommé in a saucepan over a gentle heat; do not allow it to boil. Add the tortellini and morel mushrooms and poach in the consommé for 2 minutes. Add the sliced truffle and heat for a further 15 seconds. Adjust the seasoning if necessary. Lift the tortellini, morels and truffle from the consommé and divide between 6 warm soup bowls. Pour the consommé into the bowls and garnish with the tarragon, chives and chervil.

POLENTA TERRINE WITH SAUTÉED MUSHROOMS, ASPARAGUS AND PARMESAN CREAM

For 16 portions of terrine and 4 portions of garnish

POLENTA

500 ml	Mushroom stock (basic recipe 21, page 195)
150 ml	Milk
150 ml	Cream
4	Cloves garlic
4	Dried cep mushrooms
1	Sprig fresh thyme
1	Bay leaf
1	Sprig fresh rosemary
1	Shallot, sliced
350 g	Polenta
50 g	Parmesan cheese, freshly grated

MUSHROOM DUXELLE

20 g	Dried trompette des morts
220 g	Mushroom duxelle (basic recipe 57, page 204)
1	Large bunch chives, sliced
1	Small bunch flat-leaf parsley, chopped
25 ml	Clarified butter

TO SERVE (for 4 portions)

60 ml	Extra virgin olive oil
12	Button mushrooms
12	Small morel mushrooms
12	Small oyster mushrooms
24	Shimiji mushrooms
12	Asparagus spears, peeled and blanched (basic technique 5, page 216)
60 ml	Parmesan cream (basic recipe 39, page 200)
8	Slices of truffle
12	Chive tips
	Salt
	Freshly ground pepper

Line a terrine 32 cm long x 8 cm wide x 7 cm deep with clingfilm leaving a 2.5 cm over-hang. Place the mushroom stock, milk, cream, garlic, dried cep mushrooms, thyme, bay leaf, rosemary and sliced shallot into a heavy-based saucepan and bring to the boil. Reduce the heat and simmer for 10 minutes. Remove from the heat and allow to infuse for 1 hour.

Reconstitute the dried trompette des morts in warm water for 30 minutes. Lay a large double-folded sheet of clingfilm on a work surface and spoon the chopped mushroom duxelle onto it. Roll the mushroom duxelle in the clingfilm to form a cylinder 3 cm thick x 32 cm long and place in the freezer until firm but not frozen.

Lift the softened trompette des morts out of the water, squeeze to remove any excess water and chop very finely. Mix the chopped trompette des morts, chives and parsley in a bowl and season to taste with salt and freshly ground pepper. Lay this mix out on a tray. Remove the mushroom duxelle from the freezer and carefully remove the clingfilm. Brush with clarified butter and roll in the trompette des morts mix to completely cover. Return to the freezer until ready to use.

Pass the infused mushroom stock through a fine sieve into a heavy-based saucepan. Return to the heat, bring back to the boil and reduce the heat to a simmer. Pour in the polenta in a steady stream, stirring vigorously to prevent any lumps from forming. Continue to stir while cooking for 15–20 minutes – the polenta will come away from the sides of the saucepan when cooked. Season to taste with salt and freshly ground pepper and fold in the Parmesan cheese. Cook for a further minute and remove the polenta from the heat.

Half-fill the terrine with the warm polenta. Lay the cylinder of mushroom duxelle down the centre and cover with the remaining polenta to the top of the terrine. Smooth over with a palette knife. Fold the over-hanging clingfilm to cover the top of the polenta. Cut out a piece of cardboard the same size as the terrine and wrap first with aluminium foil and then with clingfilm. Place onto the terrine and set a 2 kg weight evenly on top. Refrigerate for at least 12 hours to set before turning out.

Run a sharp knife around the inside of the terrine and invert onto the cut-out cardboard. Cut a 5 mm thick slice off the end of the terrine to neaten. Slice four 2 cm wide slices. Heat 20 ml of the olive oil in a non-stick pan, reduce to a gentle heat, place the slices in the pan and cook for 4–5 minutes until golden brown. Gently turn the terrine slices with a palette knife and cook for a further 4–5 minutes until golden brown and warmed through. Lightly season with salt and freshly ground pepper.

Heat the remaining olive oil in a cast-iron pan and sauté the button, morel, oyster and shimiji mushrooms for 3–4 minutes until golden brown. Season with salt and freshly ground pepper. Add the asparagus spears and toss through the mushrooms to warm through without colouring. Drain the mushrooms and asparagus. Heat the Parmesan cream. Lift the terrine slices onto kitchen paper to absorb any excess oil and transfer to the centre of a warm plate. Spoon the mushrooms and asparagus around the terrine. Pour the Parmesan cream over and around the mushrooms and garnish with the sliced truffle and chive tips.

POTATO AND MUSHROOM TERRINE WITH MUSHROOM À LA GRECQUE

For 20 portions of terrine and 4 portions of garnish

5 kg	**Large Nicola potatoes, or similar waxy potatoes**
1 kg	**Mushroom duxelle (basic recipe 57, page 204)**
30 ml	**Truffle oil**
1 tsp	**Chopped curly parsley**
	Picked leaves of 1 large sprig fresh thyme
50 ml	**Clarified butter**

TO SERVE (for 4 portions)

20 ml	**Extra virgin olive oil**
120 g	**Mushroom à la Grecque (basic recipe 3, page 191)**
12	**Chive tips**
12	**Leaves flat-leaf parsley**
12	**Mâche leaves (lamb's lettuce)**
	Salt
	Freshly ground pepper

Wash the potatoes under cold running water, then cook in a steamer until tender. Allow to cool slightly, then peel and slice the potatoes into 1 cm thick slices. Place the mushroom duxelle into a bowl and mix with the truffle oil, parsley and thyme. Season to taste with salt and freshly ground pepper.

Line a terrine 32 cm long x 8 cm wide x 7 cm deep with clingfilm leaving a 2.5 cm over-hang. Trim the potatoes on four sides into even blocks to fit neatly into the terrine. Lightly season the potatoes with salt and freshly ground pepper. Cover the base of the terrine with a layer of potatoes. Brush the potatoes with clarified butter and spoon in a 1 cm deep layer of mushroom duxelle, smoothing it over with a palette knife. Place a second layer of potato onto the mushroom duxelle and continue to build the terrine, ending with a layer of potato. The finished terrine will have three layers of mushroom duxelle and four layers of potato. Cover the potato with the over-hang of clingfilm.

To press the terrine, cut out a piece of cardboard the same size as the terrine and wrap with aluminium foil and then clingfilm. Place onto the terrine and set a 2 kg weight evenly on top. Refrigerate for 12 hours.

Remove the weight and cardboard from the terrine and peel back the clingfilm. Run a sharp knife around the inside of the mould, invert the terrine onto the cut-out cardboard and remove the clingfilm. Cut four 1 cm thick slices of the terrine with a sharp knife. Brush the slices with the olive oil and lightly season with salt and freshly ground pepper. Allow to stand for 10–15 minutes to reach room temperature. Place the slices in the centre of four plates and spoon the mushroom à la Grecque around them. Spoon a little of the à la Grecque vinaigrette over the mushrooms and garnish with the chive tips, parsley and mâche leaves.

WILD MUSHROOM RAVIOLI WITH ASPARAGUS SPEARS AND CEP CREAM SAUCE

Serves 4

200 g	**Mushroom duxelle** (basic recipe 57, page 204)
5 ml	**Truffle oil**
I tbsp	**Chopped truffle**
I tbsp	**Sliced chives**
200 g	**Plain pasta dough** (basic recipe 68, page 207)
	Egg wash of I free-range egg yolk and I5 ml water
8	**White asparagus spears, peeled and blanched** (basic technique 5, page 216)
8	**Green asparagus spears, peeled and blanched** (basic technique 5, page 216)
100 ml	**Cep cream sauce** (basic recipe 34, page 199)
40 ml	**Extra virgin olive oil**
160 g	**Mixed wild mushrooms**
12	**Sprigs fresh chervil**
	Salt
	Freshly ground pepper

Place the mushroom duxelle into a bowl and add the truffle oil, chopped truffle and sliced chives. Mix together and season to taste with salt and freshly ground pepper.

Cut the pasta dough into two pieces. Roll out both pieces with a rolling pin on a lightly floured surface until they are 5 mm thick. Set a pasta machine on the thickest setting and feed through the first piece of pasta twice. Adjust the setting one notch and feed the pasta through it twice again. Continue to roll the pasta until it is on the thinnest setting. Roll the second piece in the same way. When all the pasta is rolled, cut out eight circles of pasta using a 9 cm plain pastry cutter. Place the pasta on a plate and cover with clingfilm to prevent it from drying out.

Make the ravioli one at a time: Lightly dust a work surface with flour and place a circle of pasta on it. Spoon 50 g mushroom duxelle into the centre of the pasta and lightly brush the edge of the pasta with the egg wash. Place another circle of pasta over the top and tightly mould it over the filling, pressing out any air between the filling and the pasta (this prevents them from bursting when cooking). Work the two circles of dough together with your fingertips. Place the blunt side of a 6 cm pastry cutter over the filling and lightly press down to ensure that the two sheets of pasta are firmly joined. Cut out the ravioli with an 8 cm pastry cutter for even-sized and neat ravioli. Make the other three ravioli in the same way.

Bring a large pot of salted water to the boil and blanche the ravioli for 2 minutes. Refresh in iced water, drain and refrigerate until ready to use.

Cut the tips off the asparagus, reserving the stalks for another use. Reheat the cep cream sauce. Heat the olive oil in a heavy-based pan and sauté the wild mushrooms until golden brown. Add the asparagus tips to warm through and season to taste with salt and freshly ground pepper. Reheat the ravioli in lightly salted simmering water for 3 minutes, drain and lightly season with salt and freshly ground pepper.

Arrange the mushrooms and asparagus in the centre of a warm bowl plate and spoon over a little cep cream sauce. Set a ravioli on top and spoon over more sauce. Garnish with sprigs of chervil.

Asparagus has a relatively short season. However, it is cultivated in every corner of the globe and, with modern hygiene, packaging, transport methods and regulations, it is now available almost all year round. The best quality asparagus is grown in Europe, America and Australia. Avoid asparagus produced in Asia, which is often too thin, limp and light in both colour and flavour.

Asparagus is an expensive vegetable due to the way it is grown and harvested. Once the bed of asparagus is sown it will only produce its first edible crop in the third year and will continue to produce from the same bed for a few short seasons only. Asparagus beds require a lot of maintenance and the crop is hand harvested. White asparagus requires even more work as the beds have to be built up to protect the spears from exposure to light. They, too, are hand harvested once they surface.

ASPARAGUS

Whether green or white, choose medium-sized asparagus spears that are firm with tight tips. If they are limp or flowering it is a sign of old age and should be avoided. Snap the base of the asparagus and small pearls of sap will appear. If the asparagus are dry, this is another sign of old age. Pick asparagus that are the same length and thickness to ensure even cooking.

Cut 2–3 cm off the woody base with a sharp, heavy knife and discard. Peel the asparagus; begin 1 cm below the tips and work down towards the base in even strokes until all the peel has been removed. Many recipes suggest that the peel be saved to make stock for soup. They can be bitter, however, so rather use the peeled stalks for this, reserving the tips for garnishing.

To blanche asparagus (basic technique 5, page 216) bring a large pot of salted water to the boil and cook the asparagus for 2–3 minutes until tender, depending on their thickness. Plunge into iced water to stop the cooking process and to retain their colour.

SALAD OF ASPARAGUS AND ARTICHOKE WITH SAUCE BOIS BOUDRAN

Serves 4

100 g	**Tomato concassée** **(basic technique 9, page 217)**
100 ml	**Sauce Bois Boudran** **(basic recipe 4, page 191)**
1 tsp	**Chopped herbs of equal** **quantities chives, chervil** **and tarragon**
28	**Green asparagus spears,** **peeled and blanched** **(basic technique 5, page 216)**
12	**Baby artichoke hearts, prepared** **and cooked** **(basic technique 6, page 216)**
12	**Sprigs fresh chervil**
12	**Chive tips**
12	**Tarragon leaves**
12	**Baby basil leaves**
	Salt
	Freshly ground pepper

Place the tomato concassée in a bowl and pour over the sauce Bois Boudran. Allow to stand for 15 minutes for the flavours to infuse. Fold the chopped herbs through the sauce and season to taste with salt and freshly ground pepper. Season the asparagus spears and artichoke hearts with salt, freshly ground pepper and a small amount of oil from the sauce Bois Boudran and gently mix to coat the vegetables.

Arrange the asparagus in the centre of a plate and spoon the artichokes and sauce Bois Boudran around the asparagus. Garnish with the chervil, chive tips, tarragon and baby basil leaves.

WHITE ASPARAGUS WITH TWICE-COOKED EGG AND TRUFFLE VINAIGRETTE

Serves 4

4	**Free-range eggs**
50 ml	**White wine vinegar**
3 tbsp	**Plain flour, sieved and seasoned**
	Egg wash of 1 free-range egg and 10 ml milk
50 g	**Fresh breadcrumbs, sieved and seasoned**
1	**Small head curly endive salad**
	Vegetable oil, for deep-frying the eggs
20 ml	**Clarified butter**
16	**White asparagus spears, peeled and blanched (basic technique 5, page 216)**
8	**Slices of truffle**
16	**Sprigs fresh chervil**

TRUFFLE VINAIGRETTE

½ tsp	**Dijon mustard**
15 ml	**Sherry vinegar**
50 ml	**Truffle oil**
25 ml	**Extra virgin olive oil**
	Salt
	Freshly ground pepper

Poach the eggs: Have a large bowl of iced water ready to refresh the eggs. Bring a large saucepan of water to the boil and add the white wine vinegar. Reduce the heat to a simmer. Break the eggs into individual cups and pour them, one at a time, into the water, keeping them apart from each other. Poach the eggs for 4–5 minutes until the whites have set but the yolks remain soft. Remove the eggs from the water with a slotted spoon and refresh in the iced water to stop the cooking process. Remove the eggs from the water and drain on a clean kitchen cloth. Take an appropriate-sized pastry cutter and trim the edges to create neat, round eggs.

Place the flour, egg wash and breadcrumbs into three separate shallow bowls. Lightly season the eggs with salt and freshly ground pepper. Pass the eggs through the flour, egg wash and then the breadcrumbs. Repeat the process of the egg wash and breadcrumbs so that the eggs are double-crumbed. Refrigerate the eggs until ready to deep-fry.

Prepare the truffle vinaigrette: Place the Dijon mustard in a bowl, add the sherry vinegar and whisk together. Add the truffle and olive oils in a slow, steady stream, whisking continuously. Season the vinaigrette to taste with salt and freshly ground pepper. If the dressing is too thick, thin with warm water.

Remove the stalk from the curly endive. Strip back and discard all the bitter, dark green outer leaves to reveal the lighter leaves of the heart. Wash these leaves in lightly salted, cold water, drain and dry in a clean kitchen cloth and place in a bowl until ready to dress.

Heat the vegetable oil to 180°C. Heat the clarified butter in a heavy-based pan large enough to hold the 16 asparagus spears. Warm through in the butter, then remove the pan from the heat. Add 20 ml truffle vinaigrette to the pan and roll the asparagus spears in it to coat. Lightly season with salt and freshly ground pepper. Julienne four slices of truffle.

Lower the crumbed eggs into the heated vegetable oil and cook for 1–1½ minutes until golden. Remove the eggs from the oil with a slotted spoon and drain on kitchen paper to absorb the excess oil. Lightly season with salt and freshly ground pepper. Dress the curly endive with half the truffle vinaigrette, add the julienne of truffle and lightly season with salt and freshly ground pepper.

Place four asparagus spears in the centre of a warm plate. Arrange the curly endive and chervil sprigs onto the asparagus. Set an egg on top of the salad and garnish with a slice of truffle. Drizzle the remaining truffle vinaigrette around the plate.

ASPARAGUS SPEARS WITH FRIED QUAIL EGGS AND TRUFFLE

Serves 4

24	**Small morel mushrooms**
8	**Quail eggs**
40 ml	**Clarified butter**
16	**White asparagus spears,**
	peeled and blanched
	(basic technique 5, page 216)
50 ml	**Morel cream sauce**
	(basic recipe 35, page 199)
20 ml	**Extra virgin olive oil**
24	**Slices of truffle**
24	**Sprigs fresh chervil**
	Salt
	Freshly ground pepper

Wash the morels in several changes of cold water to extract any sand. Drain, and pat dry on a clean kitchen towel. Set aside. Cut through the shells of the quail eggs with a sharp paring knife and pour each egg into individual spoons.

Heat 20 ml clarified butter in a heavy-based pan large enough to hold the 16 asparagus spears. Place the asparagus in the pan, warm through in the butter and lightly season with salt and freshly ground pepper. Remove the asparagus from the pan and keep warm while the rest of the dish is prepared.

Heat the remaining clarified butter over a low heat in a large non-stick pan. Spoon the eggs into the butter and fry for 15–25 seconds until the egg whites have set but the yolks are still soft. Remove the pan from the heat to prevent the eggs from over-cooking. Lift the eggs from the pan with a palette knife, place on a warm plate and lightly season with salt and freshly ground pepper. Take an appropriate-sized pastry cutter and trim the edges of the eggs to give them a neat, round shape. Reheat the morel cream sauce.

Heat the olive oil in a heavy-based pan and sauté the morel mushrooms for 2 minutes. Season with salt and freshly ground pepper, remove them from the pan and drain.

Place four asparagus spears on a warm plate. Set two fried quail eggs onto the asparagus and arrange the morels and sliced truffle over and around them. Spoon the morel sauce over the asparagus and garnish with the sprigs of chervil.

GOAT'S CHEESE TORTELLINI WITH ASPARAGUS AND BABY BEETROOT SALAD

Serves 4

100 g	**Soft goat's cheese**
20 g	**Shallot confit**
	(basic recipe 50, page 203)
1 tsp	**Sliced chives**
100 g	**Plain pasta dough**
	(basic recipe 68, page 207)
	Egg wash of 1 free-range
	egg yolk and 15 ml water
8	**White asparagus spears, peeled**
	and blanched
	(basic technique 5, page 216)
8	**Green asparagus spears, peeled**
	and blanched
	(basic technique 5, page 216)
8	**Baby beetroot, cooked**
	(basic technique 7, page 216)
8	**Golden beetroot, cooked**
	(basic technique 7, page 216)
1	**Head baby fennel, blanched**
25 ml	**Extra virgin olive oil**
50 ml	**Beetroot vinaigrette**
	(basic recipe 7, page 192)
8	**Sprigs fresh chervil**
8	**Chive tips**
	Salt
	Freshly ground pepper

Place the goat's cheese into a bowl and beat until soft. Add the shallot confit and sliced chives and mix through the cheese. Season to taste with salt and freshly ground pepper. Cover the cheese with clingfilm and refrigerate until ready to use.

Roll out the pasta dough with a rolling pin on a lightly floured work surface, until it is 5 mm thick. Set the pasta machine on the thickest setting and feed through the pasta twice. Adjust the setting one notch and feed the pasta through twice again. Continue to roll the pasta until it is on the thinnest setting. When all the pasta is rolled, cut out four circles of pasta using a 10 cm plain pastry cutter. Place the pasta on a plate and cover with clingfilm to prevent it from drying out.

Prepare the tortellini one at a time: Spoon 30 g goat's cheese mix into the centre of each circle of pasta. Brush the edge of the pasta with egg wash. Fold the pasta to make a semi-circle and press the edges together from one side to the other, pressing out any air from the pocket of pasta.

Hold the tortellini in your hand and curl the two tips around the index finger and press together; then press the edges together again to ensure that they are firmly joined. Repeat with the remaining tortellini. Blanche the tortellini in salted boiling water for 2 minutes and refresh in iced water. Drain well.

Reheat the vegetables in a steamer, remove and dress with the extra virgin olive oil. Season to taste with salt and freshly ground pepper.

Reheat the tortellini in salted boiling water for 1 minute, lift out and drain well. Lightly season with salt and freshly ground pepper. Arrange the vegetables in a warm bowl and drizzle the beetroot vinaigrette over and around them. Set the tortellini on top and garnish with the sprigs of chervil and chive tips.

Oysters are the most prolifically cultivated of all molluscs. This is done in two different ways: the first is 'intertidally', which allows the oysters to move in and out of the water depending on tidal movement. The sea water is filtered and the oysters are able to extract nourishment from it. This exposes the oysters to all the natural elements that make them extremely hardy, tough-shelled and full of flavour. The second way is 'subtidally', where the oysters are constantly submerged beneath the water. They remain unexposed to the elements, which results in softer-shelled oysters.

Rock, Pacific and Angasi are probably the three species of oyster that are commercially common and of these, Rock oysters are available all year round. Each region has an off-season that depends on the spawning periods, which are determined by rainfall, flooding and water pollution. Pacific oysters are best during the cold winter months as they spawn during the warmer months, which gives the oyster flesh a creamy texture, making them unpleasant to eat. Angasi oysters are also harvested during the colder months. These are a strong-flavoured species that are much sought-after by oyster connoisseurs.

OYSTERS

Some of the more famous species from around the world are the Natives of Ireland; the Pyfleet oysters of Colchester; New Zealand's Bluff oysters; Sydney Rock oysters from Wallis Lake in New South Wales; the American Cape oyster; the French Belon and those classified as Fine de Claires.

Buy live, unshucked oysters that feel heavy and full. Avoid those where the shells are not clamped tightly together. Open oysters with an oyster knife (basic technique 3, page 216).

Cover oysters with a damp cloth and refrigerate. Their lids should face upwards to prevent any seepage, which allows them to sit in their own juice.

In recipes where oysters are cooked, they are simmered in a flavoured stock or sauce and gently warmed through for a matter of seconds. When deep-fried, the batter should be crisp and golden and the oysters slightly warmed.

VICHYSSOISE OF OYSTERS WITH OYSTER BEIGNETS AND SAUCE GRIBICHE

Serves 4

OYSTER BEIGNETS (makes 12 beignets)

125 g	**Plain flour, sifted**
30 ml	**Cold water**
110 ml	**Warm beer**
30 ml	**Olive oil**
1	**Free-range egg yolk**
14	**Unshucked oysters**
	Vegetable oil for deep-frying oysters
2	**Free-range egg whites**
	Plain flour, sifted for dusting oysters
	Maldon sea salt

VICHYSSOISE (makes 1 ltr)

25 g	**Unsalted butter**
175 g	**Potatoes, peeled and cut into small, even-sized pieces**
150 g	**Onions, finely sliced**
300 g	**Leeks, white part only, finely sliced**
25 ml	**Noilly Prat**
750 ml	**Chicken stock (basic recipe 22, page 195) or water**
125 ml	**Cream**

TO SERVE

1	**Lemon**
80 ml	**Sauce gribiche (basic recipe 11, page 192)**
8	**Lemon segments**
8	**Sprigs fresh chervil**
	Salt
	Freshly ground pepper

Prepare the first stage of the beignet batter: Whisk together the flour, water, warm beer, olive oil and egg yolk to form a smooth batter. Clean down the sides of the bowl and cover with clingfilm to prevent a skin forming. Allow the batter to stand at room temperature for 1 hour.

Shuck the oysters (basic technique 3, page 216) and remove from the shells, reserving the oyster juice for the vichyssoise. Pick out the eight largest oysters and lay them on a clean, dry kitchen cloth. Refrigerate while preparing the vichyssoise, leaving the remaining six oysters in the reserved oyster juice.

Prepare the vichyssoise: Melt the butter in a heavy-based pan until foaming, add the potatoes, onions and leeks and sweat without colouring over a medium heat for 8–10 minutes. Add the Noilly Prat and continue to cook until it has evaporated. Pour in the chicken stock or water and bring to the boil. Reduce the heat and simmer for 20 minutes until the potato pieces are tender. Add the cream and bring the soup back to the boil. Reduce the heat and simmer for a further 5 minutes.

Pour the soup into a food processor, blend until smooth and pass through a fine sieve into a clean stainless steel container. Press down hard on the vegetables to extract as much flavour as possible. Add the oyster juice and six oysters to the vichyssoise in stages and blend with a hand-held blender. Taste from time to time to check whether less oysters and juice are required than is suggested in the recipe. After blending the oysters, taste the vichyssoise and adjust the seasoning if necessary. Once again, pass the vichyssoise through a fine sieve into a clean saucepan.

Heat the vegetable oil to 180°C. Whisk the egg whites to soft peaks in a clean bowl and fold through the batter. Lightly season the flour with salt and freshly ground pepper. Dust the remaining eight oysters with the flour, drop them into the batter, and gently work with your fingertips until each oyster is coated. Allow the excess batter to drain off, place the oysters in the oil and deep-fry until the batter is crisp. Turn the oysters with a fork and continue to cook until golden. Remove the oysters from the oil with a slotted spoon and drain on kitchen paper. Lightly season the beignets with Maldon salt, freshly ground pepper and a squeeze of lemon.

Place a 5 cm pastry ring onto a plate, spoon the sauce gribiche into it and spread evenly. Gently remove the pastry ring. Set two beignets onto the sauce gribiche. Garnish with two lemon segments and two sprigs of chervil. Pour the vichyssoise into small warmed soup cups and place next to the beignets.

NAGE OF OYSTERS AND CUCUMBER

Serves 4

NAGE BASE (makes 150 ml)

200 ml	Cream
15 g	Whole unsalted butter, diced
2	Shallots, finely chopped
1	Clove garlic, crushed
1	Sprig fresh thyme
75 ml	Noilly Prat
75 ml	Dry white wine
100 ml	Fish stock (basic recipe 24, page 196)

NAGE OF OYSTERS

12	Freshly shucked oysters and their juice (basic technique 3, page 216)
150 ml	Nage base (as above)
150 ml	Fish stock (basic recipe 24, page 196)
1	Lemon
100 g	Peeled cucumber, cut into julienne on a mandolin
20 g	Caviar (see glossary)
4	Sprigs fresh chervil
	Salt
	Freshly ground pepper

Prepare the nage base: Place the cream into a heavy-based saucepan over a low heat and reduce by half. Remove from the heat and set aside until ready to use.

Melt the butter in a heavy-based pan and add the shallots, garlic and thyme and sweat without colouring for 3 minutes. Pour the Noilly Prat and white wine over the shallots and reduce until all the liquid has evaporated. Pour over the 100 ml fish stock and reduce by half. Add the reduced cream and bring back to the boil. Remove from the heat and pass through a fine sieve.

Strain the juice off the oysters. Bring the nage base, oyster juice and 150 ml fish stock to the boil in a heavy-based saucepan. Season to taste with salt, freshly ground pepper and a squeeze of lemon. Pass the nage through a fine sieve into a clean saucepan. Warm the julienne of cucumber in the nage over a low heat, add the oysters and warm through for 30 seconds.

Place a mound of the cucumber in the centre of a warm soup bowl. Spoon three oysters around the cucumber and gently pour the nage over the oysters. Spoon the caviar on top of the cucumber and garnish with the sprigs of chervil.

FRESHLY SHUCKED OYSTERS WITH VIETNAMESE DRESSING

Serves 4

12	**Unshucked oysters**
	Maldon sea salt
150 ml	**Vietnamese dressing**
	(basic recipe 9, page 192)
50 g	**Julienne of spring onion**
50 g	**Deep-fried shallots**
	(basic recipe 49, page 203)
25 g	**Baby coriander**
4	**Lime cheeks**

Shuck the oysters (basic technique 3, page 216), keeping them in their shells, and reserving all their juice. Arrange three small mounds of Maldon salt on each plate and press an oyster into each mound. Stir the Vietnamese dressing and spoon over the oysters. Mix together the julienne of spring onion, deep-fried shallots and baby coriander and place a small mound on top of each oyster. Set a lime cheek on the side.

OYSTERS WITH CUCUMBER JELLY, SOUR CREAM AND CAVIAR

Serves 4

12	**Unshucked oysters**
I	**Cucumber, peeled and roughly chopped**
200 ml	**Lemon-and-lime-infused gin**
¼	**Lime, juiced**
35 ml	**Verjuice**
I	**Leaf gelatine**
120 g	**Brunoise of cucumber (see glossary)**
	Maldon sea salt
60 g	**Sour cream**
50 g	**Caviar (see glossary)**
12	**Sprigs fresh chervil**
	Salt
	Freshly ground pepper

Shuck the oysters (basic technique 3, page 216) and remove from the shells. Drain off the oyster juice, reserve and refrigerate until ready to use. Sterilise the shells by boiling them for 10 minutes, then cooling them under cold running water. Drain and wipe dry. Reserve the shells for the presentation of the dish.

Blend the oyster juice, cucumber, gin, lime and verjuice to a fine purée. Adjust the acidity with lime juice and verjuice if necessary and season to taste.

Pour the cucumber purée into a double layer of muslin cloth suspended over a bowl to catch the juice and refrigerate for 2 hours. Pass the cucumber juice through a fresh double layer of muslin cloth into a clean bowl. Soften the gelatine in cold water. Gently heat 25 ml cucumber juice in a small saucepan. Squeeze the water from the gelatine, add to the warmed cucumber juice and stir until dissolved. Stir into the remaining chilled cucumber juice and allow to set in the fridge.

Break up the jelly with a fork and fold through the brunoise of cucumber and fresh oysters. Season to taste with salt and freshly ground pepper.

Arrange three small mounds of Maldon salt on each plate and place an oyster shell on top of each one. Spoon an oyster and some of the cucumber jelly into each shell. Make a small quenelle of sour cream using 2 teaspoons and set onto each oyster. (If the sour cream is not firm, then thicken by gently folding through a pinch of salt and a squeeze of lemon.) Top with the caviar and garnish with a sprig of chervil.

The scallop season begins in spring and continues through until autumn. Scallops vary in size from the Small Bay or Queen scallop, to the larger plump, sweet King scallop. My preference is for King Diver scallops that are hand-picked from the ocean bed. They are very expensive but guarantee ultimate freshness.

Another way of harvesting scallops is by dredging them, whereby large nets are dragged across the ocean bed, picking up everything in their path. This disturbs the sand and grit, which is pushed into the scallops. If scallops have sand in them, plunge the scallop meat into sparkling mineral water for 30 seconds. This will help to open the pores and release the sand. Lay them on a kitchen towel to absorb any excess moisture.

Buy scallop meat from a reputable fishmonger and avoid unscrupulous processors who pump water into scallops to increase their weight. This water is released when the scallops are cooked and they end up boiling in their own

SCALLOPS

juices, losing colour, flavour and texture. Likewise, frozen scallop meat should be avoided at all costs as half their weight could possibly be water.

Scallops have a rounded, ribbed shell that should be tightly closed. To open, insert the tip of a long, thin-bladed knife between the shells and run it along the roof of the scallop. Cut through the muscle that attaches the scallop meat to the shell. Separate the shells and gently remove the scallop with a spoon. Remove the coral and black shirt and lay the scallop meat on a clean kitchen cloth to absorb any moisture. The coral can be dried and ground into a powder and used as a seasoning or added to butter for finishing fish sauces.

Scallop meat is very gelatinous and is able to absorb a lot of liquid, which makes it ideal for making delicate mousse. Or, simply slice and marinate in citrus juice, olive oil and spices. Pan fry scallops in a little olive oil, add a knob of butter, a squeeze of lemon and lightly season with salt and freshly ground pepper. Or, gently poach in a flavoured stock. Take care not to mask scallops with big flavours as they are sweet and delicate.

SEARED SCALLOPS AND CRISP CHICKEN WINGS WITH SWEETCORN

Serves 4

CHICKEN WING CONFIT

8	Chicken wings, tips removed
45 g	Maldon sea salt
1	Star anise
10	Coriander seeds, crushed
10	White peppercorns, crushed
¼	Stick cinnamon
1	Bay leaf
2	Sprigs fresh thyme
2	Cloves garlic
1 litre	Rendered duck fat (basic technique 1, page 215)

TO SERVE

8 x 30 g	Fresh scallops with muscles removed
25 ml	Water
25 g	Unsalted butter
160 g	Sweetcorn, removed from cob, blanched and refreshed
100 ml	Sweetcorn and basil sauce (basic recipe 37, page 199)
10 ml	Olive oil
1	Lemon
1	Large shallot, sliced and deep-fried (basic recipe 49, page 203)
1 tsp	Julienne of basil
	Salt
	Freshly ground pepper

Prepare the chicken wings: Grind the Maldon salt, star anise, crushed coriander seeds, peppercorns and cinnamon stick with a pestle and mortar. Transfer the ground spices to a bowl and add the bay leaf, thyme and garlic. Rub the spice mix into the chicken wings, cover with clingfilm and refrigerate for 3 hours.

Preheat the oven to 120°C. Wipe the salt mix from the chicken wings, place in a heavy-based saucepan, and pour over the rendered duck fat. Bring to simmering point over a low heat, cover with a lid and transfer the saucepan to the oven. Cook for 2½–3 hours. The chicken wings are cooked when the bones are easily removed. Lift the wings from the duck fat and place on a tray. Allow them to cool sufficiently to handle and then extract the bones and cartilage. Place on a greaseproof paper-lined tray and cover with a second sheet of greaseproof paper. Place a second tray on top with enough weight to press the wings. Refrigerate until ready to use. Strain the duck fat through a fine sieve and refrigerate in a sealed container for future use.

Place the scallops on a clean kitchen cloth to soak up any moisture. Ensure that the scallops are dry before cooking or they will poach in their own juices rather than caramelise. Refrigerate the scallops until ready to cook.

Increase the oven temperature to 180°C. Melt a teaspoon of duck fat in a cast-iron pan. Add the chicken wings, skin side down, and transfer to the oven. Cook the chicken wings for 3–4 minutes until the skin is crisp and brown and season with freshly ground pepper. Remove the wings from the pan and keep warm while preparing the rest of the dish.

Bring 25 ml water to the boil in a saucepan, add the butter and bring back to the boil until the butter has melted. Add the sweetcorn, reheat and lightly season with salt and freshly ground pepper. Strain the corn and keep warm. Gently reheat the sweetcorn and basil sauce and adjust the seasoning if necessary. Pass the sauce through a fine sieve.

Heat the olive oil until almost smoking in a heavy-based frying pan. Add the scallops and sear for 30 seconds on both sides until golden brown, keeping them under-cooked in the centre. Remove from the pan and drain on a clean kitchen cloth. Lightly season with salt, freshly ground pepper and a squeeze of lemon.

Place a 12 cm square mould in the centre of a plate, spoon the sweetcorn into it and press down with the back of the spoon. Gently remove the mould. Spoon over a little of the sweetcorn and basil sauce. Sprinkle the deep-fried shallot and julienne of basil over the sweetcorn. Place two chicken wings and two scallops onto the sweetcorn. Froth the sweetcorn and basil sauce with a hand-held blender and spoon around the chicken wings and scallops.

CARAMELISED SCALLOPS WITH SAUTÉED CEP MUSHROOMS

Serves 4

12 x 30 g	Fresh scallops with muscles removed
300 g	Mushroom duxelle (basic recipe 57, page 204)
120 ml	Cep cream sauce (basic recipe 34, page 199)
30 ml	Extra virgin olive oil
12 x 25 g	Slices cep mushroom
25 g	Whole, unsalted butter
1	Lemon
20	Baby mâche leaves (lamb's lettuce)
	Salt
	Freshly ground pepper

Place the scallops on a clean kitchen cloth to soak up any moisture. Ensure that the scallops are dry before cooking or they will poach in their juices rather than caramelise. Refrigerate the scallops until ready to cook.

Place the mushroom duxelle in a heavy-based saucepan and add 20 ml cep cream sauce. Warm over a low heat, check the seasoning and adjust if necessary. Heat 15 ml olive oil in a heavy-based frying pan, add the sliced cep mushrooms and cook on each side until golden brown. Add the butter and baste the cep mushrooms. Lightly season with salt and freshly ground pepper. Remove the cep mushrooms from the pan and drain on a clean kitchen cloth. Gently reheat the remaining cep cream sauce, adjust the seasoning if necessary and pass through a fine sieve. Keep the sauce warm while cooking the scallops.

Heat the remaining olive oil until almost smoking in a heavy-based frying pan. Add the scallops and sear for 30 seconds on both sides until golden brown, keeping them under-cooked in the centre. Remove from the pan and place onto kitchen paper. Season lightly with salt, freshly ground pepper and a squeeze of lemon.

Place a 7.5 cm square mould in the centre of a warm plate. Spoon a quarter of the mushroom duxelle into it and smooth with the back of the spoon. Arrange three overlapping scallops on top of the duxelle and gently remove the pastry ring. Place three slices of cep mushroom around the scallops. Froth the cep cream sauce with a hand-held blender and spoon over and around the scallops and cep mushrooms. Garnish with the baby mâche leaves.

SCALLOP MOUSSE WITH ROAST SCAMPI TAIL, CHAMPAGNE VELOUTÉ AND CAVIAR

Serves 4

200 g	**Fresh scallop meat with muscles removed**
100 g	**Fresh prawn meat, peeled and deveined**
1	**Large leek**
10 g	**Softened, unsalted butter**
1	**Baby leek, finely sliced and washed in several changes of cold water**
4	**Scampi tails, peeled and deveined**
1	**Free-range egg white**
5 ml	**Pernod reduction (basic recipe 44, page 201)**
300 ml	**Chilled cream**
5 ml	**Olive oil**
15 g	**Whole, unsalted butter**
½	**Lemon**
100 ml	**Fish velouté (basic recipe 32, page 198)**
20 ml	**Champagne**
20 g	**Caviar (see glossary)**
4	**Sprigs fresh chervil**
	Salt
	Freshly ground pepper

Chill the bowl of a food processor in the freezer for 15 minutes before preparing the scallop mousse. Place the scallop and prawn meat on a clean kitchen cloth to extract any moisture.

Prepare the leek: Remove the root and thick outer leaves from the leek and cut through to the centre, from top to tail. Separate each layer of leek into broad, flat sheets. Blanche the sheets of leek for 30 seconds in salted boiling water and refresh in iced water. Drain the leek and lay flat on a clean kitchen cloth to extract any excess water. When dry, cut into sheets 20 cm long × 4.5 cm wide. Scrape the back of the leek with a sharp knife to remove any stringy bits, leaving thin transparent pieces of leek. Liberally brush 4 pastry rings, 4 cm × 4.5 cm deep with the softened butter and line each one with a sheet of blanched leek, ensuring that the ends overlap. If necessary, trim the leek to the top of the pastry rings with a sharp knife. Place each ring on a square of buttered greaseproof paper and refrigerate until ready to use. Blanche the sliced baby leek in salted boiling water for 45 seconds and refresh in iced water. Drain the leek and dry on a clean kitchen cloth to absorb any excess water. Refrigerate until ready to use.

Roll the scampi tails from the tail to the head and tie with a piece of butcher's twine. Refrigerate until ready to use. Preheat the oven to 200°C.

Prepare the scallop mousse: Dice the scallop and prawn meat, place into the chilled food processor with a pinch of salt and freshly ground pepper and blend until smooth. Add the egg white, Pernod reduction and the chilled cream in a slow, steady stream. When the cream is fully incorporated, transfer the mousse to a clean stainless steel bowl and refrigerate for 30 minutes before passing the mousse through a fine drum sieve.

Test the mousse to check the consistency and seasoning (basic technique 11, page 217). Spoon the mousse into a piping bag fitted with a 2 cm nozzle and fill each leek-lined pastry ring to the top. Refrigerate the mousse for 30 minutes before cooking in a steamer for 8 minutes.

Lightly season the scampi tails with salt and freshly ground pepper. Heat the olive oil in a heavy-based pan and cook the scampi tails for 2 minutes until golden brown. Turn the scampi over and cook for a further minute. Add the whole butter and, as it melts, squeeze the lemon over the scampi. Baste the scampi with the butter and lemon for 1 minute, remove from the pan and allow the scampi to rest for 2 minutes before removing the butcher's twine. Warm the fish velouté and add 20 ml champagne. Reheat the blanched, sliced baby leek in a saucepan with sufficient champagne velouté to cover.

After 8 minutes, check whether the scallop mousse is cooked by inserting the tip of a knife into the centre; the knife should come away clean but, if not, steam the mousse for a further 2 minutes before testing again.

Remove the mousse from the steamer, place in the centre of a warm plate and lift off the pastry ring. Spoon a small mound of creamed leek beside the mousse. Top the leek with a scampi tail and spoon a teaspoon of caviar onto the scampi. Garnish with a sprig of chervil. Froth the champagne velouté with a hand-held blender, and spoon it onto the mousse.

OPEN SAFFRON RAVIOLI OF SCALLOP AND MARRON TAILS WITH THYME AND RIESLING SAUCE

Serves 4

200 g	**Saffron pasta dough** **(basic recipe 69, page 207)**
10 ml	**Olive oil**
200 ml	**Thyme and Riesling sauce** **(basic recipe 33, page 198)**
8 x 60 g	**Marron tails, removed from** **the shell**
12 x 40 g	**Fresh scallops with muscles** **removed**
8	**Baby leeks, blanched**
8	**Green asparagus spears, peeled** **and blanched** **(basic technique 5, page 216)**
40 ml	**Fennel purée** **(basic recipe 53, page 203)** **Picked leaves of 1 sprig** **fresh thyme** **Salt** **Freshly ground pepper**

Cut the saffron pasta dough into two pieces. Roll out both pieces with a rolling pin on a lightly floured surface until they are 5 mm thick. Set a pasta machine on the thickest setting and feed through the first piece of pasta twice. Adjust the setting one notch and feed the pasta through twice again. Continue to roll the pasta until it is on the thinnest setting. Roll the second piece in the same way. When all the pasta is rolled, cut into 6 cm squares. Blanche the pasta squares in salted boiling water for 45 seconds and refresh in iced water. Drain the pasta, lightly brush each square with olive oil and cover with clingfilm until ready to use.

Gently warm the thyme and Riesling sauce in a heavy-based saucepan large enough to hold the scallops and marron tails. Place the marron tails in the sauce and poach for 2½ minutes. Add the scallops and poach for a further 30 seconds. Add the baby leeks and asparagus and poach for a further minute. Drain the shellfish and vegetables and lightly season with salt and freshly ground pepper. Pass the sauce through a fine sieve and keep warm. Heat the fennel purée over a low heat. Reheat the pasta in salted boiling water for 30 seconds, drain and lightly season with salt and freshly ground pepper.

Spoon half a teaspoon of fennel purée into the centre of a warm bowl plate and place a square of pasta onto it. Spoon the fennel purée onto the pasta and arrange the marron tails, scallops, baby leeks and asparagus tips onto it. Froth the thyme and Riesling sauce with a hand-held blender and spoon it over the shellfish and vegetables. Set a second square of pasta on top and spoon over more sauce. Sprinkle with the picked thyme leaves.

Prawns are the most popular, widespread and easily available of all crustaceans. They thrive in both cold and warm waters and are available all year round. Prawn aquaculture is a rapidly growing industry, making fresh prawns more readily accessible. Most prawns are caught in deep water on large factory trawlers that can remain at sea for weeks at a time and have on-board facilities to process their catch. To maintain freshness before landing them, the prawns are often kept in ice-slurries or in sea water at 0°C. In some instances, they are cooked on board in sea water and kept in large chillers and are often processed, blast-frozen and packed on board.

Of the cold-water varieties, the Dublin Bay prawn (also known as langoustine or scampi), is the most sought-after and expensive. Of the warm-water varieties, look for the Giant, Black Tiger, Banana, King or Endeavor prawns.

Whenever possible, choose prawns that are alive, or at least fresh in the shell with the head attached to the body. They should be sweet smelling, firm, plump, translucent, with eyes protruding, and feel heavy in relation to their size.

PRAWNS

Avoid prawns that are discoloured, whose eyes have collapsed or give off a noticeable ammonia smell; these are signs that the prawns are inedible. Frozen prawns, when defrosted, rapidly deteriorate and can become mushy and difficult to peel.

Prawns have a short shelf-life and oxidise fast because they don't tolerate change in temperature or exposure to the air. Peel prawns immediately, reserving the shells. Twist and pull the head from the tail section and pinch the rings, one after another, snapping the shell and pulling away without tearing the meat. Remove the intestinal tract and refrigerate the meat between damp cloths until ready to use.

Prawns are very versatile and can be cooked by various methods, such as pan-frying, poaching, steaming and grilling. The reserved fresh shells and heads are full of flavour; slowly roast until deep red and brittle and use to make shellfish stock (basic recipe 25, page 196), bisque, sauces, flavoured butters and crustacean oil (basic recipe 18, page 194). Prawns can be substituted with lobster, crayfish, marron or yabbies.

ESCABÈCHE OF PRAWN, SCALLOP AND YABBY WITH CITRUS AND CAVIAR

Serves 4

ESCABÈCHE (see glossary)

I tsp	Coriander seeds, crushed
2	Shallots, finely sliced
I	Baby fennel, thinly sliced
	Zest of ½ lemon
	Zest of ½ orange
	Juice of ½ orange
15 ml	Pernod
45 ml	White wine vinegar
45 ml	Olive oil
	Pinch saffron threads

TO SERVE

20 ml	Extra virgin olive oil
8 x 30 g	Fresh scallops with muscles removed
8	Yabbies, blanched and peeled
4	Green prawns, peeled, deveined and cut in half lengthways
8	Pink grapefruit segments
8	Orange segments
8	Lime segments
8	Asparagus spears, peeled, blanched and sliced (basic technique 5, page 216)
40 g	Tomato concassée, large dice (basic technique 9, page 217)
24	Mâche leaves (lamb's lettuce)
12	Sprigs fresh chervil
20 g	Caviar (see glossary)
	Salt
	Freshly ground pepper

Prepare the escabèche: Place the coriander seeds, shallots, fennel, zests, orange juice, Pernod, white wine vinegar, olive oil and saffron threads into a heavy-based saucepan. Bring to the boil, reduce the heat and cook for 7–10 minutes or until the vegetables are tender. Allow the escabèche to cool for 15 minutes.

Heat the olive oil in a heavy-based pan and sear the scallops, yabbies and prawns for 15 seconds ensuring that they remain under-cooked. Drain and lay the shellfish in a deep tray. Lightly season with salt and freshly ground pepper and allow to cool. Pour the escabèche over the shellfish and refrigerate to allow the flavours to infuse for at least 30 minutes, but no more than 3 hours. Lift the shellfish out of the escabèche and dry on a clean kitchen cloth. Arrange the shellfish in a bowl plate and reserve the escabèche for dressing.

Mix the citrus segments, asparagus and tomato concassée in a bowl, lightly season with salt and freshly ground pepper and spoon over and around the shellfish. If necessary, add more olive oil to slightly thicken the escabèche and drizzle it over and around the shellfish. Garnish with the mâche leaves and chervil sprigs. Spoon the caviar onto the escabèche.

SQUID INK RAVIOLI OF PRAWN AND SCALLOP WITH SAUCE VIERGE

Serves 4

RAVIOLI

220 g	Fresh prawn meat
100 g	Fresh scallop meat with muscles removed
	Grated zest of ½ lemon
1 tsp	Julienne of flat-leaf parsley
1	Lemon
200 g	Squid ink pasta dough (basic recipe 70, page 207)

SAUCE VIERGE

4	Asparagus spears, peeled, blanched and refreshed (basic technique 5, page 216)
40 g	Tomato concassée (basic technique 9, page 217)
1	Small shallot, sliced
40 ml	Extra virgin olive oil
120 g	Squid, julienned
40 ml	Dry white wine
1	Lemon
	Baby coriander to garnish
	Salt
	Freshly ground pepper

Prepare the ravioli filling: Dice the prawn and scallop meat, place in a bowl and mix through the grated lemon zest and julienne of parsley. Season with salt, freshly ground pepper and a squeeze of lemon. Divide the mix into four and mould each one into a neat mound in a 6 cm pastry ring, making it easier to enclose in the pasta.

Cut the squid ink pasta dough into two pieces. Roll out both pieces with a rolling pin on a lightly floured surface until they are 5 mm thick. Set a pasta machine on the thickest setting and feed through the first piece of pasta twice. Adjust the setting one notch and feed the pasta through twice again. Continue to roll the pasta until it is on the second thinnest setting. Roll the second piece in the same way. When all the pasta is rolled, cut out eight circles of pasta using a 9 cm plain pastry cutter. Place the pasta on a plate and cover with clingfilm to prevent it from drying out.

Make the ravioli one at a time: Lightly dust a work surface with flour and place a circle of pasta on it. Place a mound of ravioli filling in the centre of the pasta. Lightly brush the edge of the dough with water. Place another circle of pasta over the top and tightly mould it over the filling, pressing out any air between the filling and pasta (this prevents them from bursting when cooking). Work the two circles of dough together with your fingertips. Place the blunt side of a 6 cm pastry cutter over the filling and lightly press down to ensure that the two sheets of pasta are firmly joined. Cut out the ravioli with an 8 cm pastry cutter for even-sized and neat ravioli. Make the other three ravioli in the same way. Bring a large pot of salted water to the boil and cook the ravioli for 9 minutes.

Prepare the sauce vierge while the ravioli cooks. Cut off the asparagus tips, slice the stalks at an angle, and place in a saucepan. Add the tomato concassée, sliced shallots and 30 ml olive oil and mix together. Place over a low heat and, when warmed through, remove from the heat. Heat the remaining oil in a heavy-based saucepan, add the squid and sauté without colouring for 30 seconds. Add the white wine and a squeeze of lemon to halt the cooking process. Transfer to the saucepan with the asparagus and gently mix through. Season to taste with salt, freshly ground pepper and more lemon juice if necessary.

Drain the ravioli and season with salt and freshly ground pepper. Spoon a small amount of sauce vierge into the centre of a bowl plate and set the ravioli onto it. Spoon the remaining sauce over the top of the ravioli and garnish with a small bunch of baby coriander.

PANCETTA-WRAPPED PRAWNS WITH MUD CRAB AND SPRING ONION RISOTTO

Serves 4

8	**Medium tiger prawns, peeled and deveined**
8	**Thin slices pancetta**
450 ml	**Shellfish stock (basic recipe 25, page 196)**
60 g	**Whole unsalted butter, diced**
2	**Small shallots, finely chopped**
I	**Clove garlic, crushed**
200 g	**Arborio rice**
25 ml	**Cream**
200 g	**Mud crab meat, cooked and picked (basic technique 4, page 216 and see glossary)**
3	**Spring onions, sliced**
½	**Lemon**
10 ml	**Vegetable oil**
I tsp	**Sliced chives**
	Salt
	Freshly ground pepper

Lay each prawn flat on a work surface and insert a wooden skewer through each one lengthways to prevent them from curling up during cooking. Lightly season the prawns with salt and freshly ground pepper. Tightly roll each prawn in a slice of pancetta and refrigerate until ready to use.

Preheat the oven to 200°C. Bring the shellfish stock to the boil and reduce the heat to a simmer.

Melt 25 g diced butter in a heavy-based saucepan, add the shallots and garlic and sweat without colouring for 2 minutes. Add the rice and seal without colouring for a further 2 minutes. Add a ladle of shellfish stock and reduce the heat to a simmer. Continuously stir until the stock is absorbed and to prevent the rice from sticking. Continue to add the stock, one ladle at a time, and cook until absorbed and the rice is *al dente*. This will take 18–20 minutes.

To finish the risotto, add the cream and stir through the rice. Add 25 g diced butter and stir until incorporated into the rice. Stir in the mud crab and 35 g spring onion, and season to taste with salt, freshly ground pepper and a squeeze of lemon. Remove and discard the garlic clove.

Heat the vegetable oil in a heavy-based frying pan, add the prawns and cook over a gentle heat for 2 minutes until the pancetta is crisp. Turn the prawns, transfer to the oven and continue to cook for a further 2 minutes. Add 10 g butter and a squeeze of lemon to the pan and baste the prawns for a further minute.

Spoon the mud crab risotto into a warm bowl plate. Remove the skewers from the prawns and place two prawns onto the risotto. Sprinkle over the remaining spring onion and sliced chives.

STEAMED PRAWNS WITH BABY LEEKS, CAVIAR AND CHAMPAGNE VELOUTÉ

Serves 4

12	**Prawns, peeled**
16	**Baby leeks, blanched and refreshed**
100 ml	**Fish velouté (basic recipe 32, page 198)**
20 ml	**Champagne**
50 g	**Caviar (see glossary)**
20	**Sprigs fresh chervil**
12	**Chive tips**
	Salt
	Freshly ground pepper

Make an incision down the back of each prawn, from the base of the head to the tip of the tail, exposing the intestinal tract. Open up the prawn and remove the tract with the tip of a knife.

Lightly season the prawns with salt and freshly ground pepper and wrap each one in clingfilm. Cook the prawns in a steamer for 2–3 minutes until opaque. Add the baby leeks to the steamer to reheat for the last minute.

Remove the prawns from the steamer, unwrap them and reserve the juices that are released from the prawns. Add the prawn juices and the champagne to the fish velouté and warm over a low heat.

Lightly season the baby leeks with salt and freshly ground pepper. Spoon the caviar into the prawn cavity from which the intestinal tract was removed. Pass the champagne velouté through a fine sieve, season to taste with salt and freshly ground pepper and pour into four warm bowl plates. Place three prawn tails into each and garnish with the baby leeks, sprigs of chervil and chive tips.

Salmon is one of the most beautiful and versatile fish available and salmon farming has turned into a major industry, accounting for most of the salmon consumed today.

Wild salmon is a migratory fish; born in a river, living in the sea and finally, swimming thousands of miles to return to the river of its birth to spawn. This tones the flesh and develops the muscles that give wild salmon its superior texture and colour when compared with the farmed salmon, which has less flavour and flesh, and can be flabby and tasteless from lack of exercise.

Glossy, smooth skin, bright red gills, protruding eyes and firm flesh indicate the freshness of a salmon. Choose salmon that weigh between 2.5 kg and 3 kg, yielding eight to ten portions. Remove the scales of the salmon before cooking.

SALMON

Grip the fish firmly by the tail with a damp cloth and, using the back of a slightly inclined knife, scrape from the tail to the head to remove the scales. Rinse the fish under cold water and pat dry with a cloth before filleting. When filleted, trim the fillet, removing the thin belly-flap. Using fish tweezers, remove the line of pin bones that run down the centre of the flesh from the head to two-thirds of the way down the fillet. Reserve the bones for stock, which can be flavoured and reduced to make a savoury jelly or clarified for consommé.

There are numerous ways of preparing and serving salmon; raw as sashimi or tartare, smoked, marinated, confit, poached, grilled, pan-fried, mousse and brandade. Cook salmon skin side down in a pan, turning it over three-quarters of the way through cooking, keeping the centre pink.

TERRINE OF SMOKED SALMON WITH CRAB AND BABY CORIANDER SALAD

16–18 portions

TERRINE OF SMOKED SALMON

175 g	**Unsalted butter**
50 g	**Marinated anchovy fillets**
	Zest of 1 lemon, finely grated
	Juice of ½ lemon
2 tbsp	**Chopped flat-leaf parsley**
1 tbsp	**Sliced chives**
2	**Small shallots, finely chopped**
1–1.5 kg	**Smoked salmon, thinly sliced**
10 ml	**Lemon oil (basic recipe 16, page 193)**

CRAB SALAD (4 portions)

80 g	**Crab meat, cooked and picked (basic technique 4, page 216)**
1	**Small shallot, sliced**
40 g	**Tomato concassée (basic technique 9, page 217)**
	Juice of 1 lemon
10 ml	**Lemon oil (basic recipe 16, page 193)**
	Baby coriander to garnish
	Salt
	Freshly ground pepper

Line a 1.4 kg terrine with clingfilm, allowing a 2.5 cm over-hang. Beat the butter with an electric mixer until light and airy. Dice the anchovies, stir into the butter and add the lemon zest, lemon juice, parsley, chives and shallots. Season to taste with salt and freshly ground pepper.

Cover the base of the terrine with a layer of smoked salmon, ensuring that there are no gaps. Spread a thin layer of the butter over the smoked salmon with a palette knife, covering the entire surface. Continue to build the terrine with alternating layers of smoked salmon and butter until all the ingredients have been used or the terrine is full. Finish with a layer of smoked salmon.

Cover the top of the terrine with the over-hang of clingfilm and place a 1 kg weight evenly on top. Refrigerate overnight to allow the butter to set.

Turn out onto a clean chopping board and slice with a very sharp knife. Cut all the way through the clingfilm which will help the slices of terrine retain their original shape. Remove the clingfilm and brush the slices of terrine with lemon oil.

Place a slice of terrine onto a plate and allow it to stand for 15 minutes to reach room temperature and for the butter to soften slightly. Gently mix together the crab meat, sliced shallots and tomato concassée. Season to taste with salt, freshly ground pepper and lemon juice and bind with more lemon oil. Spoon a small mound of crab salad at either end of the slice of terrine and drizzle with the remaining lemon oil. Garnish the crab salad with a small bunch of baby coriander.

MARINATED SALMON WITH CRAB AND LIME CRÈME FRAÎCHE

Serves 4

400 g	**Fresh salmon fillet**
1½ tbsp	**Maldon sea salt**
10	**Coriander seeds**
10	**White peppercorns**
1 tbsp	**Sugar**
	Grated zest and juice of 1 lime
100 g	**Crab meat, cooked and picked (basic technique 4, page 216)**
20 ml	**Crème fraîche**
1	**Lime**
60 g	**Brunoise of peeled and seeded cucumber (see glossary)**
60 g	**Brunoise of red onion (see glossary)**
60 g	**Brunoise of peeled and seeded red capsicum (basic technique 8, page 217)**
60 g	**Brunoise of blanched and seeded tomato (basic technique 9, page 217)**
5 ml	**Extra virgin olive oil**
48	**Chervil leaves**
20 ml	**Basil oil (basic recipe 15, page 193)**
	Salt
	Freshly ground pepper

Remove the skin, bloodline and pin bones from the salmon. Crush the sea salt, coriander seeds and peppercorns to a coarse powder with a pestle and mortar. Add the sugar, lime zest and juice and mix together. Evenly spread the marinade over the salmon. Wrap the salmon in clingfilm and refrigerate to marinate for 6 hours. Wash off the marinade under cold water and dry the salmon on a clean kitchen cloth.

Bind the crab meat with the crème fraîche. Season to taste with salt, freshly ground pepper and a squeeze of fresh lime.

Thinly slice the marinated salmon. Place an 11 cm pastry ring in the centre of a chilled plate and arrange overlapping slices of marinated salmon into it to create a neat round. Mix together the cucumber, red onion, capsicum and tomato brunoise with the extra virgin olive oil and lightly season with salt and freshly ground pepper. Spoon the vegetables over the entire surface of the marinated salmon.

Divide the crab meat into four portions and form into quenelles using 2 tablespoons. Place a quenelle of crab meat onto the vegetables and garnish with the picked chervil. Drizzle the basil oil around the marinated salmon.

ROAST FILLET OF SALMON WITH SAUTÉED YABBY TAILS AND CRUSTACEAN OIL

Serves 4

12	**Live yabbies**
8	**Green asparagus spears, peeled and blanched (basic technique 5, page 216)**
25 ml	**Olive oil**
4 x 160 g	**Salmon fillet portions, skin on and pin bones removed**
50 g	**Unsalted butter**
1	**Lemon**
150 ml	**Crustacean oil (basic recipe 18, page 194)**
2	**Shallots, finely sliced**
	Freshly picked leaves of 1 sprig thyme
200 g	**Tomato concassée (basic technique 9, page 217)**
1 tsp	**Sliced chives**
1 tsp	**Finely chopped flat-leaf parsley**
12	**Sprigs fresh chervil**
	Salt
	Freshly ground pepper

Blanche the yabbies in salted boiling water for 1 minute and refresh in iced water. Remove the shells and the intestinal tract. Cut off the asparagus tips, and slice the stalks at an angle into 3 cm pieces. Set aside. Preheat the oven to 200°C.

Heat the olive oil in a large heavy-based frying pan over a medium heat. Lightly season the salmon with salt and freshly ground pepper and place in the pan, skin-side down. Cook for 2 minutes and transfer the salmon to the oven for a further 4–5 minutes depending on the thickness of the fillets – keep them pink in the centre. Remove the salmon from the oven, add the butter to the pan and baste the salmon with it. Lightly season with salt, freshly ground pepper and a squeeze of lemon. Remove the salmon from the pan and keep warm.

Warm 100 ml crustacean oil in a saucepan, add the yabby tails and sauté until golden brown. Add the shallots, asparagus and thyme, reduce the heat and continue to cook until the shallots have softened. Add the remaining crustacean oil, tomato concassée, chives and parsley. Season to taste with salt, freshly ground pepper and a squeeze of lemon.

Place the salmon in the centre of a warm plate and spoon the garnish around it in neat mounds. Drizzle the crustacean oil from the pan over and around the salmon. Garnish with sprigs of chervil.

ROAST FILLET OF SALMON WITH SHALLOT AND PARSLEY SALAD AND BONE MARROW JUS

Serves 4

2	Small shallots, sliced
1 tbsp	Julienne of parsley
1½ tbsp	Capers, rinsed and dried
	Grated zest of ¼ lemon
1	Lemon
15 ml	Extra virgin olive oil
160 g	Bone marrow, after being extracted from 4 cm long bones
25 ml	Olive oil
4 x 160 g	Salmon fillet portions, skin on and pin bones removed
50 g	Unsalted butter
120 ml	Red wine jus (basic recipe 27, page 197)
80 g	Tomato concassée (basic technique 9, page 217)
12	Leaves flat-leaf parsley
	Salt
	Freshly ground pepper

Preheat the oven to 200°C. Mix the sliced shallots, julienne of parsley, capers and grated lemon zest in a bowl. Season to taste with salt, freshly ground pepper and a squeeze of lemon, and add enough extra virgin olive oil to coat the shallots. Keep at room temperature until ready to use.

Extract the bone marrow from the bones by gently pushing it out with your thumb. Slice the bone marrow into 1 cm thick pieces and lightly season with salt and freshly ground pepper. Keep at room temperature until ready to use.

Heat the olive oil in a heavy-based pan over a medium heat. Lightly season the salmon with salt and freshly ground pepper and place skin-side down in the pan. Cook for 2 minutes and transfer to the oven for a further 4–5 minutes depending on the thickness of the fillets – keep them pink in the centre. Remove the salmon from the oven, add the butter to the pan and baste the salmon with it. Lightly season with salt, freshly ground pepper and a squeeze of lemon. Remove the salmon from the pan and keep warm.

Warm the red wine jus over a low heat and add the tomato concassée and bone marrow. Immediately remove from the heat and allow the tomato and bone marrow to warm through in the jus. Do not allow the jus to boil as the marrow will melt and the fat will float to the surface.

Place an 8 cm pastry ring in the centre of a plate and spoon the shallot salad into it. Smooth with the back of the spoon and gently remove the pastry ring. Set the salmon, skin-side up, onto the shallot salad and spoon the jus around the plate. Garnish with flat-leaf parsley.

There are many varieties of dory; Silver, Mirror and King, but the John Dory or Saint-Pierre, as it is also known, is superior. It is easily recognised by its large head in comparison with the rest of its thin body. John Dory has a prominent mouth with retractable jaws used for catching prey and also has a large thumb-sized dark mark on both sides of its body. The dorsal fin is long and sharp and should be removed before filleting. Because the size of the head and bone structure accounts for two thirds of its weight, the John Dory is an expensive fish.

Choose a whole fish weighing around 2 kg that will yield four portions. The John Dory has two fillets; each one made up of three smaller fillets, which separate if the skin is removed. When serving whole fillets, cook the fish with the skin on and remove it only when cooked.

JOHN DORY

To fillet the fish use a sharp, flexible filleting knife. Cut through the skin around the base of the head and run the knife down the belly of the fish towards the tail. Remove the flesh as close to the bone as possible with the tip of the knife held at an angle. Gently ease back the flesh, making it easier to guide the knife. When the first fillet has been removed, turn the fish and repeat the process on the other side. Reserve the bones of the John Dory for fish stock (basic recipe 24, page 196).

John Dory has firm flesh with good texture and is full of flavour. It doesn't need much cooking, requires simple preparation and is tastiest when pan-fried and basted with butter and a squeeze of lemon. Like scallops, John Dory is very gelatinous and can absorb a lot of liquid, making it suitable for delicate mousse.

Sole is an excellent substitute for John Dory. It is prepared and cooked in the same way and can be used in the same recipes. Although it differs in shape, the flesh is as firm in texture as the John Dory and the flavour is equally good.

PAN-FRIED JOHN DORY AND SCALLOPS WITH CRUSHED POTATO, BABY LEEKS AND LIME JUS

Serves 4

LIME JUS

60 g	Whole unsalted butter, diced
2	Shallots, finely chopped
1	Tomato, seeded and chopped
1	Clove garlic, crushed
	Pinch sugar
5 ml	Sherry vinegar
50 ml	Port
150 ml	Noilly Prat
100 ml	Chicken stock (basic recipe 22, page 195)
150 ml	Veal stock (basic recipe 23, page 196)
1	Stalk parsley
	Juice of 1 lime

CRUSHED POTATO

500 g	Crushed potato (basic recipe 63, page 206)
1 tsp	Sliced chives

TO SERVE

50 ml	Olive oil
8 x 50 g	John Dory portions, skinned
25 g	Unsalted butter
1	Lemon
8	Baby leeks, blanched
10 g	Julienne of trompette des morts
12 x 30 g	Fresh scallops with muscles removed
12	Lime segments at room temperature
8	Sprigs fresh chervil
12	Chive tips
	Salt
	Freshly ground pepper

Prepare the lime jus: Melt 20 g butter in a heavy-based saucepan, add the shallots and sweat for 5 minutes without colouring. Add the tomato and garlic and cook for a further 3 minutes. Sprinkle with the sugar and stir until the sugar has dissolved. Pour in the sherry vinegar and reduce until the vinegar and sugar have caramelised. Add the Port and Noilly Prat and reduce by three-quarters. Pour in both stocks and bring to the boil. Add the parsley stalk and reduce by a third. Pass the sauce through a fine sieve into a clean saucepan, return to the heat and reduce by half. Whisk the remaining 40 g butter into the sauce and season to taste with salt, freshly ground pepper and lime juice. Once more, pass through a fine sieve into a clean saucepan.

Warm the crushed potato and add the sliced chives at the last minute to prevent them from discolouring. Season to taste with salt and freshly ground pepper.

Heat 30 ml olive oil in a large heavy-based frying pan over a medium heat. Lightly season the John Dory with salt and freshly ground pepper and cook for 3 minutes until golden brown. Turn the fish over and cook for a further 2 minutes. Add the butter to the pan and baste the fish with it. Again, lightly season the fish with salt, freshly ground pepper and a squeeze of lemon. Drain the fish on kitchen paper to absorb any excess oil and keep warm.

Lightly season the blanched baby leeks and trompette des morts with salt and freshly ground pepper. Place on buttered greaseproof paper and steam for 2 minutes.

Heat the remaining olive oil until almost smoking in a cast-iron frying pan. Add the scallops and sear for 30 seconds on both sides until golden brown – keep them under-cooked in the centre. Remove from the pan and place on kitchen paper with the John Dory. Lightly season the scallops with salt, freshly ground pepper and a squeeze of lemon.

Place an 8 cm pastry ring in the centre of a plate and spoon the potato into it, smoothing it over with the back of the spoon. Gently remove the pastry ring and lay the baby leeks across the potato. Arrange three scallops and three lime segments around the potato and leeks. Set two pieces of John Dory onto the leeks and spoon the lime jus over and around the fish. Garnish with the julienne of trompette des morts, chervil and chive tips.

PAN-FRIED JOHN DORY WITH PEA RISOTTO, SEMI-DRIED TOMATOES AND TOMATO OIL

Serves 4

200 g	Fresh peas, blanched and refreshed
24	Pieces semi-dried tomatoes (basic recipe 46, page 202)
80 ml	Tomato oil (basic recipe 17, page 194)
1 ltr	Chicken stock (basic recipe 22, page 195)
55 ml	Olive oil
1	Clove garlic, crushed
½	Small onion, finely chopped
250 g	Arborio rice
65 g	Whole unsalted butter, diced
8 x 50 g	John Dory portions, skinned
1	Lemon
24	Broad beans, shelled, blanched and refreshed
24	Baby basil leaves
	Salt
	Freshly ground pepper

Crush the blanched peas with the back of a fork. Allow the semi-dried tomatoes and tomato oil to reach room temperature.

Bring the chicken stock to the boil and reduce to a simmer. Heat 25 ml olive oil in a heavy-based saucepan, add the crushed garlic clove and onion and sweat without colouring for 2 minutes. Add the rice and seal without colouring for a further 2 minutes. Add a ladle of chicken stock and reduce the heat to a simmer. Continuously stir until the stock is absorbed and to prevent the rice from sticking. Add the stock, one ladle at a time, and cook until absorbed and the rice is *al dente*. This will take about 18–20 minutes. To finish the risotto, add 40 g diced butter and stir into the rice until fully incorporated. Add the crushed peas and fold through the risotto. Remove and discard the garlic clove. Season to taste with salt and freshly ground pepper. Keep warm while preparing the rest of the dish.

Heat the remaining olive oil in a heavy-based frying pan over a medium heat. Lightly season the John Dory with salt and freshly ground pepper and cook for 3 minutes until golden brown. Turn the fish over and cook for a further 2 minutes. Add the remaining butter to the pan and baste the fish with it. Again, lightly season the fish with salt, freshly ground pepper and a squeeze of lemon. Drain on kitchen paper to absorb any excess oil and keep warm. Reheat the broad beans in a little salted boiling water, drain and lightly season with salt and freshly ground pepper.

Place an 8 cm pastry ring in the centre of a plate and spoon a quarter of the pea risotto into it, pressing down with the back of the spoon so that it holds together. Gently remove the pastry ring and set two pieces of John Dory onto the risotto. Arrange six pieces of semi-dried tomato and six broad beans around the risotto. Spoon the tomato oil over the John Dory, allowing it to run down and over the tomatoes and broad beans. Garnish with the baby basil leaves.

FILLET OF JOHN DORY WITH COURGETTE FLOWER, CRAB MOUSSE AND FENNEL EMULSION

Serves 4

1x2.2 kg	**Whole John Dory**
60 g	**Crab meat, cooked and picked (basic technique 4, page 216)**
120 g	**Scallop mousse (basic recipe 75, page 208)**
4	**Baby courgettes with flowers attached**
1	**Head baby fennel, sticks separated and blanched**
8 strips	**Red capsicum, 1 x 4 cm, blanched (basic technique 8, page 217)**
8	**Baby leeks, blanched**
1	**Vine-ripened tomato, blanched, seeded and quartered (basic technique 9, page 217)**
4	**White asparagus spears, peeled and blanched (basic technique 5, page 216)**
4	**Green asparagus spears, peeled and blanched (basic technique 5, page 216)**
4	**Baby artichokes, prepared and cooked (basic technique 6, page 216)**
4	**Kipfler potatoes, or similar waxy potato, cooked in the skin, cooled, peeled and sliced**
20 ml	**Extra virgin olive oil**
1	**Lemon**
16	**Calamata olives**
100 ml	**Fennel emulsion (basic recipe 38, page 200)**
4	**Slices lemon à la Grecque (basic recipe 2, page 191)**
12	**Sprigs fresh chervil**
12	**Baby basil leaves**
	Salt
	Freshly ground pepper

Fillet and skin the John Dory and trim the sides of the fillets, both of which have three sections. Cut the larger section away for one portion and leave the other two smaller sections intact for the second portion. Repeat the process with the second fillet to yield four portions from the John Dory. Refrigerate until ready to cook.

Fold the picked crab meat through the scallop mousse and spoon into a piping bag with a 2 cm nozzle attached. Carefully open the courgette flowers without breaking them or snapping them from the courgette. Check that the insides of the flowers are clean and pipe the scallop and crab mousse into them. Close over the tops of the flowers to enclose the mousse. Carefully wrap each flower in clingfilm to protect the mousse from moisture during cooking. Refrigerate until ready to cook.

Place the fennel, red capsicum, baby leeks, tomato, white and green asparagus, artichokes and kipfler potatoes onto lightly buttered greaseproof paper and lightly season with salt and freshly ground pepper.

Cook the stuffed courgette flowers in a steamer for 5 minutes. After 2 minutes add the vegetables and steam for the last 3 minutes. While the courgette flowers and vegetables steam, cook the John Dory.

Heat the olive oil in a heavy-based pan over a medium heat. Lightly season the fish with salt and freshly ground pepper and cook for 3 minutes until golden brown. Carefully turn over the fillets and cook for a further 2 minutes. Remove the fish from the pan, drain on kitchen paper to absorb any excess oil and squeeze a little lemon over the fish.

Remove the courgette flowers and vegetables from the steamer. Unwrap the flowers and place on warm plates. Arrange the vegetables and olives beside the flowers and spoon the fennel emulsion over and around the vegetables. Set the John Dory onto the vegetables taking care not to cover the courgette flower. Garnish the John Dory with a slice of lemon à la Grecque, chervil and basil.

FILLET OF JOHN DORY MAZARIN

Serves 4

4	**Leeks, white part only,** **20 cm long and 4.5 cm wide**
15 g	**Softened, unsalted butter**
3 tbsp	**Plain flour, sifted and seasoned** **Egg wash of 1 free-range egg** **and 10 ml milk**
50 g	**Fresh breadcrumbs, sifted and** **seasoned**
12 x 40 g	**John Dory portions, skinned**
300 g	**Scallop mousse** **(basic recipe 75, page 208)**
100 ml	**Clarified butter**
50 ml	**Sauce Perigeux** **(basic recipe 31, page 198)**
2	**Baby courgettes, sliced into** **rounds**
4	**Slices of truffle** **Salt** **Freshly ground pepper**

Prepare the leek: Remove the root and thick outer leaves from the leek and cut through to the centre, from top to tail. Separate each layer of leek into broad, flat sheets. Blanche the sheets of leek for 30 seconds in salted boiling water and refresh in iced water. Drain the leek and lay flat on a clean kitchen cloth to extract any excess water. When dry, cut into sheets 20 cm long x 4.5 cm wide. Scrape the back of the leeks with a sharp knife to remove any stringy bits, leaving thin transparent sheets of leek. Liberally brush 4 pastry rings, 4 cm x 4.5 cm deep with the softened butter and line each one with a sheet of blanched leek, ensuring that the ends overlap. If necessary, trim the leek to the top of the pastry rings with a sharp knife. Place each ring on a square of buttered greaseproof paper and refrigerate until ready to use.

Place the flour, egg wash and breadcrumbs into three separate shallow bowls. Lightly season the egg with salt and freshly ground pepper. Lightly season the John Dory with salt and freshly ground pepper. Pass the John Dory through the flour, egg wash and the breadcrumbs. Repeat the process of the egg wash and breadcrumbs so that the fish is double crumbed.

Spoon the scallop mousse into a piping bag fitted with a 2 cm nozzle and fill each leek-lined pastry ring to the top. Refrigerate the mousse for 30 minutes and then cook for 8 minutes in a steamer. Check that the scallop mousse is cooked by inserting the tip of a knife into the centre. The knife should come away clean, but if not, steam the mousse for a further 2 minutes before testing again.

Heat the clarified butter in a heavy-based pan large enough to hold the John Dory. Cook the fish portions for 2 minutes on each side until golden brown. (Have extra clarified butter ready in case the breadcrumbs soak it all up and the pan becomes dry, causing the breadcrumbs to burn.) Lift the John Dory from the pan and drain on kitchen paper to absorb any excess butter. Reheat the sauce Perigeux.

Cook the sliced courgettes in salted boiling water for 45 seconds, drain and season with salt and freshly ground pepper. Remove the mousse from the steamer and place on a warm plate. Gently lift the pastry ring off the mousse and place a slice of truffle onto it. Arrange three small stacks of courgette around the mousse and set a piece of John Dory on top of each one. Spoon the sauce Perigeux between each piece of John Dory.

Swordfish is a deep-sea predator with a large sword-shaped bill that is usually removed by the fishermen at sea. The fish has been recorded to grow as long as five metres and to weigh in excess of 400 kilograms, so it's unlikely that you will see a whole swordfish on your fishmonger's slab. It is usually sold off the bone, either as steaks or cutlets.

Swordfish is similar to tuna in relation to where it breeds, the size to which it grows, body structure and the way it is prepared. The differences between these fish are the colour of the flesh – tuna is a deep red and swordfish is white with a slight pink tinge; swordfish is not as lean and muscular as tuna; swordfish has a thick layer of blubber-like fat that needs to be trimmed and discarded as it is tough and inedible; and swordfish has thick leather-like skin that needs to be removed before cooking.

SWORDFISH

Like tuna, swordfish has dense flesh with a full, rich flavour, and can be prepared and cooked the same way. This makes both fish perfect substitutes for each other.

When choosing a piece of swordfish, gently press the flesh with the tip of your finger. The flesh should bounce back to its original shape. If it feels soft or spongy or the flesh is dull, these are signs that it is past its best. Pick a mid-cut or tailpiece as they are easier to handle; avoid the upper part, which is too broad to cook evenly.

Trim the fish, removing any sinew or congealed blood and shape it into an even, round piece. Tightly wrap it in several layers of clingfilm and refrigerate for 12 hours before cutting it into 140 g portions. The trimmings can be diced, seasoned and served raw as tartare. Like tuna, swordfish dries out very quickly and should not be cooked beyond medium-rare.

CEVICHE OF SWORDFISH WITH OYSTER BEIGNET

Serves 4

OYSTER BEIGNETS (makes 4 beignets)

60 g	**Plain flour, sifted**
15 ml	**Cold water**
55 ml	**Warm beer**
15 ml	**Olive oil**
½	**Free-range egg yolk**
4	**Unshucked oysters**
	Vegetable oil for deep-frying oysters
1	**Free-range egg white**
	Plain flour, sifted and seasoned for dusting oysters
	Maldon sea salt
1	**Lemon**

CEVICHE OF SWORDFISH

240 g	**Swordfish fillet**
50 ml	**Vietnamese dressing (basic recipe 9, page 192)**
20 g	**Deep-fried shallots (basic recipe 49, page 203)**
10 g	**Deep-fried chilli (basic recipe 48, page 203)**
12	**Lime segments at room temperature**
	Baby coriander to garnish
	Salt
	Freshly ground pepper

Prepare the first stage of the batter for the beignets: Whisk together the flour, water, warm beer, olive oil and egg yolk to form a smooth batter. Clean down the sides of the bowl and cover with clingfilm to prevent a skin forming. Allow the batter to stand at room temperature for 1 hour.

Shuck the oysters (basic technique 3, page 216), removing them from their shells, and refrigerate in their juice until ready to use.

Prepare the swordfish: Remove the skin and bloodline from the underside of the fish with a sharp, thin-bladed knife and cut into thin slices. Lay the sliced fish onto a tray and lightly season on both sides with salt and freshly ground pepper. Brush the slices with the Vietnamese dressing.

Place a 10 cm pastry ring in the centre of a chilled plate and arrange overlapping slices of swordfish in a neat circle inside the ring. Sprinkle over the deep-fried shallots and chilli and arrange three lime segments on the swordfish. Garnish with the baby coriander.

Prepare the beignets: Heat the vegetable oil to 180°C. Whisk the egg white to soft peaks in a clean bowl and fold through the prepared batter mixture. Drain the oysters from their juice (reserve the juice for another use) and dry on a clean kitchen cloth. Dust the oysters with the seasoned flour, drop into the batter, and gently work with your fingertips until each oyster is coated. Remove the oysters and allow the excess batter to drain off. Place into the oil and deep-fry until the batter is crisp. Turn the oysters with a fork and continue to cook until golden. Remove the oysters from the oil with a slotted spoon and drain on kitchen paper. Lightly season with Maldon salt, freshly ground pepper and a squeeze of lemon.

Place an oyster beignet in the centre of the ceviche and spoon over a little more Vietnamese dressing. Serve immediately so that the oysters, shallots and chilli all remain crisp.

SEARED AND TARTARE OF SWORDFISH WITH LEMON À LA GRECQUE

Serves 4

600 g	**Tail piece of swordfish, skin and sinew removed**
I tsp	**Chopped tarragon**
I tsp	**Chopped flat-leaf parsley**
I tsp	**Chopped chervil**
I tsp	**Sliced chives**
25 ml	**Olive oil**
I tsp	**Wholegrain mustard**
	Lemon à la Grecque, from peel of I lemon (basic recipe 2, page 191)
3	**Cherry tomatoes**
I	**Red capsicum, blanched (basic technique 8, page 217)**
I	**Spanish onion, peeled**
2	**Green asparagus spears, peeled, blanched and refreshed (basic technique 5, page 216)**
I	**Stick baby fennel**
20	**Calamata olives**
25 ml	**Extra virgin olive oil**
I	**Lemon**
20	**Picked baby basil leaves**
	Salt
	Freshly ground pepper

Prepare the swordfish several hours before serving: Trim the swordfish into a neat 400 g cylinder using a long, thin-bladed knife. Tightly wrap in several layers of clingfilm and refrigerate until ready to use. Cut the remaining outer layer of the swordfish into 5 mm dice. Cover with clingfilm and refrigerate until ready to use.

Mix together the tarragon, parsley, chervil and chives in a bowl and spread out on a small tray. Unwrap the cylinder of swordfish and lightly season with salt and freshly ground pepper. Heat the olive oil until almost smoking in a cast-iron pan. Add the swordfish and sear quickly and evenly – keep it rare inside. Remove the swordfish from the pan and allow to cool before brushing with a thin layer of grain mustard. Roll the swordfish in the herb mixture so that the entire piece is coated. Roll the herbed swordfish in several layers of clingfilm and refrigerate while preparing the remainder of the dish.

Drain the lemon peel from the lemon à la Grecque. Cut the cherry tomatoes into quarters. Cut the red capsicum and Spanish onion into 5 mm dice. Remove the tips of the asparagus and slice each one in half lengthways. Cut the asparagus stalks and fennel into thin slices at an angle. Place all the vegetables into a bowl and add the olives and lemon peel. Dress with 20 ml of the extra virgin olive oil and season to taste with salt and freshly ground pepper.

Season the diced swordfish with salt and freshly ground pepper and add the lemon à la Grecque vinaigrette to taste. Let it stand at room temperature for 10 minutes to allow the tartare to marinate and for the flavours to penetrate the fish.

Unwrap the seared swordfish and slice into 16 neat medallions using a sharp knife. Brush each slice with the remaining extra virgin olive oil and lightly season with salt, freshly ground pepper and a squeeze of lemon.

Place a rectangular mould, 8.5 cm long x 5.5 cm wide x 3.5 cm deep, into the centre of a chilled plate and spoon a quarter of the tartare into it, pressing down with the back of the spoon so that it holds together. Gently remove the mould. Place four overlapping slices of the seared swordfish onto the tartare. Spoon the vegetables neatly around the swordfish. Garnish with the baby basil leaves.

PAN-FRIED SWORDFISH WITH CELERY CRUSHED POTATO AND SAUCE BOIS BOUDRAN

Serves 4

100 ml	**Sauce Bois Boudran** **(basic recipe 4, page 191)**
8	**Baby artichokes, prepared and cooked** **(basic technique 6, page 216)**
16 x 2 cm	**Pieces baby leeks, blanched**
100 g	**Tomato concassée** **(basic technique 9, page 217)**
500 g	**Celery crushed potato** **(basic recipe 64, page 206)**
1 tsp	**Sliced chives**
1	**Lemon**
4 x 140 g	**Swordfish portions**
25 ml	**Olive oil**
1 tsp	**Equal quantities chopped chives, chervil and tarragon**
16	**Chive tips**
16	**Sprigs fresh chervil**
	Salt
	Freshly ground pepper

Have the sauce Bois Boudran prepared. Cut the baby artichokes in half and add to the sauce together with the blanched baby leeks and tomato concassée.

Warm the celery crushed potato and add the sliced chives at the last minute to prevent them discolouring. Season to taste with salt, freshly ground pepper and a squeeze of lemon.

Lightly season the swordfish with salt and freshly ground pepper. Heat the olive oil in a heavy-based pan and cook the fish for 2 minutes on both sides until golden brown – keep the fish medium-rare inside. Drain the fish on kitchen paper to absorb any excess oil and keep warm. Season with a squeeze of lemon.

Warm the Bois Boudran sauce over a gentle heat – take care not to cook the tomatoes. Add the chopped herbs to the sauce and adjust the seasoning if necessary.

Place a 10 cm pastry ring in the centre of a warm plate, spoon the potato into it and smooth with the back of the spoon. Gently remove the pastry ring. Spoon the sauce Bois Boudran, artichokes, baby leeks and tomato concassée around the potato and garnish with the chive tips and sprigs of chervil. Place the swordfish onto the potato.

GRILLED SWORDFISH NIÇOISE WITH TAPENADE BEURRE BLANC

Serves 4

12	**Small kipfler potatoes or similar waxy potatoes**
100 ml	**Pesto (basic recipe 13, page 193)**
1	**Lemon**
6	**Marinated anchovy fillets**
12	**Pieces semi-dried tomatoes (basic recipe 46, page 202)**
6	**Quail eggs, boiled for 2 minutes, refreshed and peeled**
50 g	**Tapenade (basic recipe 12, page 192)**
150 ml	**Beurre blanc (basic recipe 40, page 200)**
4 x 140 g	**Swordfish portions**
25 ml	**Extra virgin olive oil**
80 g	**French beans, topped, tailed and blanched**
30 g	**Calamata olives, sliced**
12	**Flat-leaf parsley leaves**
12	**Baby basil leaves**
	Salt
	Freshly ground pepper

Preheat the oven to 140°C. Heat a grill plate over a high heat. Scrub the kipfler potatoes under cold, running water and cook in salted water for 20 minutes or until tender. Peel the potatoes while still hot and place in a bowl. Crush the potatoes with a fork and add the pesto to taste – colouring the potatoes a deep green. Season to taste with salt, freshly ground pepper and a squeeze of lemon. Cover with clingfilm and keep warm while preparing the remainder of the dish.

Cut the anchovies in half and lay a piece inside each of the semi-dried tomatoes. Fold over the tomatoes to enclose the anchovy, exposing the skin side of the tomato.

Cut the quail eggs in half and lightly season with salt and freshly ground pepper. Warm the quail eggs and semi-dried tomatoes in the oven. Whisk the tapenade into the beurre blanc to taste – colouring the sauce charcoal. Check the seasoning and adjust if necessary with salt, freshly ground pepper and a squeeze of lemon.

Season the swordfish with salt and freshly ground pepper and brush with extra virgin olive oil. Cook the swordfish on the grill plate for 2–3 minutes on both sides, turning the fish at a 90° angle to achieve lattice grill marks. Keep the swordfish medium-rare as it will start to dry out if cooked longer.

Reheat the French beans in salted boiling water, drain and season to taste with salt, freshly ground pepper and a drizzle of extra virgin olive oil. Spoon them into the centre of a warm plate. Make three quenelles of pesto potato using 2 teaspoons and place around the French beans. Set three pieces of semi-dried tomato and three halves of quail eggs between the potato quenelles. Spoon the olive slices around the plate and the tapenade beurre blanc over and around the garnish.

Lift the fish from the grill, brush with extra virgin olive oil, season with a squeeze of lemon and set onto the beans. Garnish with the flat-leaf parsley and baby basil leaves.

Pork is best bought from a specialist pork butcher who sells an outdoor-reared breed such as the Saddleback and Tamworth. These are fatter, meatier and more flavoursome than pigs that have been reared indoors and fed on meal, which results in disappointingly lean animals. The butcher will also be able to provide fresh charcuterie, sausages, pancetta, pig's blood, caul, ears, heads, trotters and skin for crackling.

Pig's trotters are one of the least used yet tastiest parts of the pig. Choose hind trotters with the shank still attached as these are meatier than the front trotters. They will also provide a larger piece of skin, which becomes a 'wrapper' to enclose stuffings and fillings, to roll the trotter back into its original shape. Boning and braising causes a lot of shrinkage, so the larger the trotter, the better. Inspect the skin for punctures as this could cause the filling to seep out or allow liquid to get in and break down the filling during cooking.

PIG'S TROTTERS

To prepare trotters for braising, wash in cold running water before singeing any remaining hair over a low, open flame or with a blowtorch. Ensure that the trotters are well chilled before de-boning as the meat will be firm and easier to work with.

De-bone the shank bone by making an incision down the back of the trotter from the top down to where the shank bone and toe joints meet. Keep the blade as close to the bone as possible and follow the curve of the bone, releasing the meat and skin from the bone in one piece – take care not to puncture the skin. When the meat and skin are free of the bone, cut through the bone joint and remove the shank bone. Leave the small toe bones in – they are easier to extract when the trotter has been braised.

Soak the trotters in cold water to remove all traces of blood before slowly braising in stock for 3 hours until tender (basic technique 12, page 217). Cool and remove the remaining bones from the toes. Allow the trotters to reach room temperature, making them more pliable, before stuffing them.

CARPACCIO OF PIG'S TROTTER WITH CELERIAC AND TRUFFLE RÉMOULADE

Serves 4

FILLING FOR TROTTERS

20 g	**Unsalted butter**
50 g	**Calves sweetbreads from the pancreas, blanched, peeled and diced (basic technique 2, page 215)**
1 x 225 g	**Chicken breast, skin and sinew removed**
1	**Free-range egg white**
200 ml	**Cream, chilled**
50 g	**Pig's tongue, braised and diced (basic technique 12, page 217)**
50 g	**Ham hock, braised and diced (basic technique 12, page 217)**
20 g	**Dried trompette des morts, softened in warm water for 30 minutes and drained**
1 tsp	**Chopped flat-leaf parsley**
4	**Braised pig's trotters and braising liquid (basic technique 12, page 217)**

TO SERVE

40 g	**Pork rind**
5 ml	**Vegetable oil**
40 g	**Julienne of celeriac**
30 ml	**Sauce gribiche (basic recipe 11, page 192)**
	Mesclun leaves to garnish
5 ml	**Extra virgin olive oil**
30 ml	**Truffle dressing (basic recipe 8, page 192)**
8	**Chive tips**
8	**Leaves fresh tarragon**
8	**Sprigs fresh chervil**
8	**Leaves flat-leaf parsley**
	Salt
	Freshly ground pepper

Melt the butter until it begins to froth in a heavy-based frying pan. Add the diced sweetbreads and sauté until evenly browned. Season with salt and freshly ground pepper, transfer to a tray and allow to cool.

Dice the chicken breast and blend in the chilled bowl of a food processor for 1 minute. Add the egg white and continue to blend until thoroughly mixed. Pour in the cream in a slow, steady stream. Season with salt and freshly ground pepper. Transfer the chicken mousse to a clean bowl and chill for 30 minutes before passing through a fine drum sieve. Chill for a further 15 minutes before testing the mousse (basic technique 11, page 217).

Fold the tongue, hock, sweetbreads, trompette des morts and parsley through the chicken mousse and season with salt and freshly ground pepper.

Lay a double square of clingfilm on a work surface. Open out the trotters and lay each on a square of clingfilm. Lightly season the trotters with salt and freshly ground pepper. Fill each trotter with the mousse and gently roll into its original shape. Firmly roll each trotter in clingfilm and tightly secure the ends; then roll each in a sheet of aluminium foil and refrigerate for 2 hours for the mousse to firm up before poaching.

To poach the trotters, bring the braising liquid back to the boil and reduce the heat to a simmer. Place the trotters into the liquid and poach for 12 minutes. Remove and refrigerate overnight.

Preheat the oven to 200°C. Remove excess fat from under the pork rind with a sharp knife. Cut the rind into julienne, sprinkle with salt and allow to stand for 20 minutes to extract moisture from the rind, which will to help create crisp crackling.

Heat the vegetable oil in a heavy-based pan, add the pork rind and seal. Transfer the pan to the oven and, occasionally stirring the rind, cook until crisp and golden – 10–15 minutes. Remove the crackling from the pan and drain on kitchen paper to absorb any excess oil. Lightly season with salt and freshly ground pepper.

Remove the foil and clingfilm from the chilled trotters and trim the ends. Carve each trotter into 32 thin slices.

As a guide, place a 2 cm pastry ring in the centre of a cold plate and arrange overlapping slices of pig's trotter around the outside of the pastry ring to create a neat circle. Mix the sauce gribiche through the julienne of celeriac and season to taste with salt and freshly ground pepper. Spoon the celeriac into the pastry ring and press down with the back of the spoon. Gently remove the pastry ring. Lightly dress the mesclun with the extra virgin olive oil and season with salt and freshly ground pepper. Arrange the mesclun and pork crackling onto the celeriac. Brush the pig's trotter with truffle dressing and drizzle the remaining dressing around the plate. Garnish the mesclun with the chives, tarragon, chervil and flat-leaf parsley.

PAN-FRIED BLOOD PUDDING WITH FRIED PIG'S EAR AND SAUTÉED MUSHROOMS

Makes 20 portions blood pudding and 4 portions garnish

PIG'S TROTTERS AND EARS

2	Braised pig's trotters and braising liquid (basic technique 12, page 217)
2	Braised pig's ears (basic technique 12, page 217)
3 tbsp	Plain flour, sifted and seasoned
	Egg wash of 1 free-range egg and 10 ml milk
50 g	Fresh breadcrumbs, sifted and seasoned

BLOOD PUDDING

1 ltr	Fresh pig's blood
20 ml	Rendered duck fat (basic technique 1, page 215)
1	Onion, finely chopped
3	Cloves garlic, peeled and finely chopped
12	Leaves fresh marjoram, finely chopped
	Pinch five spice
	Pinch ground cinnamon
	Pinch garam masala
150 g	Polenta
1	Granny Smith apple, peeled, cored and diced
75 g	Sultanas
125 g	Pork back-fat, 1 cm dice

TO SERVE

150 ml	Clarified butter
32	Pieces sautéed potatoes (basic recipe 66, page 206)
24	Lardons of pancetta (see glossary)
60 ml	Red wine jus (basic recipe 27, page 197)
16	Mâche leaves (lamb's lettuce)
12	Chive tips
	Salt
	Freshly ground pepper

Prepare the pig's trotters and ears: Cut the trotters into 1 cm dice and refrigerate until ready to use. Cut the ears into strips 5 mm wide x 6 cm long.

Preheat the oven to 120°C. Place the flour, egg wash and breadcrumbs into separate shallow bowls. Lightly season the egg wash with salt and freshly ground pepper. Pass the strips of pig's ear through the flour, egg wash and then the breadcrumbs. Repeat the process of the egg wash and breadcrumbs so that the pig's ears are double-crumbed. Refrigerate until ready to cook.

Prepare the blood pudding: Line a terrine, 32 cm long x 8 cm wide x 7 cm deep, with clingfilm with a 2.5 cm over-hang. Blend the pig's blood with a hand-held blender for 2 minutes until smooth. Heat the duck fat in a heavy-based saucepan over a low heat. Add the onion and garlic and sweat for 3 minutes without colouring. Add the remaining ingredients except the pork back-fat. Continue to cook for 10–15 minutes until the mix starts to thicken but remains moist. Continuously stir to prevent it from sticking. Remove from the heat and stir in the diced pork back-fat and diced trotters. Season the blood pudding to taste with salt and freshly ground pepper. Pour into the lined terrine and close over with the clingfilm. Put into a deep roasting tray and pour in water to come three-quarters the way up the side of the terrine, creating a *bain-marie*. Place in the oven and cook for 45 minutes. To check whether the blood pudding is cooked, insert the tip of a sharp knife into the centre and leave it in for 30 seconds. If the knife comes away clean, the blood pudding is ready. If not, allow it to cook for a further 10 minutes before testing again. Remove the terrine from the *bain-marie*.

To press the terrine, cut out a piece of cardboard the same size as the terrine, wrap with aluminium foil and then with clingfilm. Place onto the terrine and set a 2 kg weight evenly on top. Refrigerate for at least 12 hours to set before turning out. Run the tip of a sharp knife around the inside of the terrine and invert onto the foil-covered cardboard. Remove the clingfilm and cut a 5 mm slice off the end of the terrine to neaten. Cut four 1 cm wide slices of the terrine.

Heat 40 ml clarified butter in a cast-iron pan and reduce the heat. Place the slices of terrine into the pan and cook for 3–4 minutes. Gently turn the slices with a palette knife and cook for a further 3–4 minutes until warmed through. Lightly season the terrine with salt and freshly ground pepper. Remove from the pan and keep warm while preparing the garnish.

Heat 50 ml clarified butter in a large cast-iron pan and add the potatoes. Season with salt and freshly ground pepper and sauté for 6 minutes, tossing frequently until tender. Add the lardons, continue to sauté until brown, then drain. Adjust the seasoning if necessary. Heat the remaining clarified butter in a heavy-based pan large enough to hold the pig's ears. Add the ears and cook for 2–3 minutes until evenly browned. (Have extra clarified butter ready in case the breadcrumbs soak it all up and the pan becomes dry, causing the breadcrumbs to burn.) Lift the ears from the pan and drain on kitchen paper to absorb any excess butter. Reheat the red wine jus.

Place a slice of terrine in the centre of a warm plate. Spoon the potatoes, lardons and fried pig's ear around the terrine and garnish with the mâche leaves and chive tips. Drizzle the red wine jus over and around the garnish.

BACON AND EGGS WITH COLCANNON

Serves 4

FILLING FOR THE TROTTERS

20 g	**Unsalted butter**
50 g	**Calves sweetbreads from the pancreas, blanched, peeled and diced (basic technique 2, page 215)**
1 x 225 g	**Chicken breast, skin and sinew removed**
1	**Free-range egg white**
200 ml	**Cream, chilled**
50 g	**Pig's tongue, braised and diced (basic technique 12, page 217)**
50 g	**Ham hock, braised and diced (basic technique 12, page 217)**
20 g	**Dried trompette des morts, softened in warm water for 30 minutes and drained**
1 tsp	**Chopped flat-leaf parsley**
4	**Braised pig's trotters and braising liquid (basic technique 12, page 217)**

TO SERVE

4	**Thin slices pancetta (see glossary)**
3 tbsp	**Plain flour, sifted and seasoned**
	Egg wash of 1 free-range egg and 10 ml milk
50 g	**Fresh breadcrumbs, sifted and seasoned**
200 g	**Colcannon (basic recipe 62, page 206)**
100 ml	**Clarified butter**
4	**Quail eggs**
100 ml	**Red wine jus**
	Salt
	Freshly ground pepper

Melt the butter until it begins to froth in a heavy-based frying pan. Add the diced sweetbreads and cook until evenly browned. Season with salt and freshly ground pepper, transfer to a tray and allow to cool.

Dice the chicken breast and blend in a chilled food processor for 1 minute. Add the egg white and continue to blend until thoroughly mixed. Pour in the cream in a slow, steady stream. Season with salt and freshly ground pepper. Transfer the chicken mousse to a clean bowl and chill for 30 minutes before passing through a fine drum sieve. Chill for a further 15 minutes before testing the mousse (basic technique 11, page 217).

Fold the tongue, hock, sweetbreads, trompette des morts and parsley through the chicken mousse and season with salt and freshly ground pepper.

Lay a double square of clingfilm on a work surface. Open out the trotters and lay each on a square of clingfilm. Lightly season the trotters with salt and freshly ground pepper. Fill each trotter with the mousse and gently roll into its original shape. Firmly roll each trotter in clingfilm and tightly secure the ends; then roll each in a sheet of aluminium foil and refrigerate for 2 hours for the mousse to firm up before poaching.

To poach the trotters, bring the braising liquid back to the boil and reduce the heat to a simmer. Place the trotters into the liquid and poach for 12 minutes. Remove the trotters and refrigerate overnight.

Preheat the oven to 180°C. Unwrap the trotters and trim the ends with a sharp knife, leaving a 6 cm piece of each trotter. Lay the sliced pancetta on a tray and cook in the oven for 4–5 minutes until crisp. Remove from the tray and drain on kitchen paper to absorb any excess fat.

Place the flour, egg wash and breadcrumbs into separate shallow bowls and lightly season the egg wash with salt and freshly ground pepper. Pass the trotters through the flour, egg wash and then the breadcrumbs. Repeat the process of the egg wash and breadcrumbs so that the trotters are double-crumbed.

Gently reheat the colcannon. Heat 60 ml clarified butter in a heavy-based pan, add the crumbed trotters and cook for 4 minutes until evenly brown. (Have extra clarified butter ready in case the breadcrumbs soak it all up and the pan becomes dry, causing the breadcrumbs to burn.) Transfer the trotters to the oven and cook for a further 3 minutes. Remove the trotters and drain on kitchen paper to absorb any excess butter.

Cut through the shells of the quail eggs with a sharp paring knife and pour the eggs into individual spoons. Heat the remaining clarified butter in a large non-stick pan over a low heat. Spoon the eggs into the butter and fry for 15–25 seconds until the egg whites have set but the yolks remain soft. Remove the pan from the heat to prevent the eggs from over cooking. Lift the eggs from the pan with a palette knife, place on a warm plate and lightly season with salt and freshly ground pepper. Trim the edges of the eggs to give a neat shape using an appropriate-sized pastry cutter.

Make a quenelle of the colcannon using 2 tablespoons and place on a warm plate. Arrange a slice of crisp pancetta onto the colcannon. Cut each trotter into two and place both pieces beside the colcannon. Set a fried quail's egg on top of the trotter and drizzle with the red wine jus.

BRAISED PIG'S TROTTERS À LA PARISIENNE

Serves 4

FILLING FOR THE TROTTERS

20 g	**Unsalted butter**
50 g	**Calves sweetbreads from the pancreas, blanched, peeled and diced (basic technique 2, page 215)**
1 x 225 g	**Chicken breast, skin and sinew removed**
1	**Free-range egg white**
200 ml	**Cream, chilled**
50 g	**Pig's tongue, braised and diced (basic technique 12, page 217)**
50 g	**Ham hock, braised and diced (basic technique 12, page 217)**
20 g	**Dried trompette des morts, softened in warm water for 30 minutes and drained**
1 tsp	**Chopped flat-leaf parsley**
4	**Braised pig's trotters and braising liquid (basic technique 12, page 217)**

GARNISH

320 g	**Potato purée (basic recipe 61, page 205)**
120 g	**Lyonnaise onions (basic recipe 56, page 204)**
100 ml	**Red wine jus (basic recipe 27, page 197)**
24	**Pieces pre-cooked snails in brine (basic recipe 19, page 194)**
50 g	**Herb butter (basic recipe 42, page 201)**
16	**Leaves flat-leaf parsley**
16	**Chive tips**
	Salt
	Freshly ground pepper

Melt the butter until it begins to froth in a heavy-based frying pan. Add the diced sweetbreads and cook until evenly brown. Season with salt and freshly ground pepper, transfer to a tray and allow to cool.

Dice the chicken breast and blend in a chilled food processor for 1 minute. Add the egg white and continue to blend until thoroughly mixed. Pour in the cream in a slow, steady stream. Season with salt and freshly ground pepper. Transfer the chicken mousse to a clean bowl and chill for 30 minutes before passing through a fine drum sieve. Chill for a further 15 minutes before testing the mousse (basic technique 11, page 217).

Fold the tongue, hock, sweetbreads, trompette des morts and parsley through the chicken mousse and season with salt and freshly ground pepper.

Lay a double square of clingfilm on a work surface. Open out the trotters and lay each on a square of clingfilm. Lightly season the trotters with salt and freshly ground pepper. Fill each trotter with the mousse and gently roll into its original shape. Firmly roll each trotter in clingfilm and tightly secure the ends; then roll each in a sheet of aluminium foil and refrigerate for 2 hours for the mousse to firm up before poaching.

To poach the trotters, bring the braising liquid back to the boil and reduce the heat to a simmer. Place the trotters into the liquid and poach for 12 minutes. Remove from the heat and leave the trotters in the braising liquid while preparing the rest of the dish.

Gently heat the potato purée, Lyonnaise onions and red wine jus in separate saucepans. Warm the snails in the brine over a low heat – do not boil, as they will become rubbery. Melt the herb butter in a small saucepan. Drain the snails from the brine and add them to the melted butter. Lightly season with freshly ground pepper.

Place a 6 cm pastry ring onto a warm plate and spoon the Lyonnaise onions into it. Smooth with the back of the spoon and remove the pastry ring. Make a quenelle of potato purée using 2 tablespoons and set beside the Lyonnaise onions. Unwrap the pig's trotter and place onto the Lyonnaise onions. Spoon the snails and red wine jus over and around the pig's trotter and drizzle a little herb butter over each snail. Garnish with the flat-leaf parsley and chive tips.

Veal is the meat of a young unweaned calf, four to 12 weeks old and is available all year round, but is best during winter and spring. The calves are milk-fed, keeping the meat white and lean. If veal is dark, it is a sign that the animal has been fed solids. Unlike beef, veal is not improved by ageing, but should be eaten as fresh as possible.

Veal is graded into three classes: Bob Veal, which is less than four weeks old; Grain-fed Veal, which are calves reared on milk for six weeks and then grain-fed for a further six weeks and thirdly, Mild-fed Veal, which are calves reared on a program of milk-based feed.

Veal is a versatile meat with many cuts especially good for roasting and, due to its low fat content, is suitable for braising and poaching. Veal bones and hooves are extremely gelatinous and, after cooking for at least eight hours to release their natural jellies, produce a superior veal stock (basic recipe 23, page 196) used as the base for many sauces.

Calves sweetbreads come from two parts of the animal; the throat where the thymus gland is located and the stomach where the pancreas or 'heartbreads'

VEAL

are located. The latter are larger, meatier and have less fat and gristle attached, making them preferable to the thymus gland.

Soak calves sweetbreads under cold running water to remove all traces of blood before briefly blanching in a court bouillon (basic technique 2, page 215). This will firm the sweetbreads slightly and preserve their colour. Also, it will make it easier to peel off the thin membrane that surrounds them.

Veal tongue should also be soaked under cold running water and the roots of the tongue removed before braising in water or chicken stock (basic recipe 22, page 195) with mirepoix for 3 hours or until the thick skin covering the tongue peels away easily.

Calves liver and kidneys have a delicate flavour and the liver has a smoother texture than that of ox or pig's liver. The kidneys are encased in a thick layer of suet that can be rendered down and used as lard or in suet pastry for pies. Calves liver is covered in a thin layer of membrane that must be removed as it will cause shrinkage during cooking.

POACHED VEAL TONGUE WITH PARSLEY PURÉE AND TRUFFLE DRESSING

Serves 4

1 x 620 g	**Veal tongue, roots removed**
1 x 750 g	**Ham hock, on the bone and skin on**
1	**Onion, chopped**
2	**Carrots, peeled and chopped**
2	**Sticks celery, chopped**
1	**Small leek, chopped and washed in several changes of cold water**
2	**Cloves garlic, crushed**
4 ltr	**Chicken stock (basic recipe 22, page 195)**
12	**White peppercorns, crushed**
2	**Bay leaves**
2	**Sprigs fresh thyme**
180 g	**Parsley purée (basic recipe 54, page 204)**
20 g	**Chopped truffle**
50 ml	**Truffle dressing (basic recipe 8, page 192)**
20	**Slices of truffle**
20	**Leaves flat-leaf parsley**
	Salt
	Freshly ground pepper

Preheat the oven to 140°C. Soak the veal tongue and the ham hock under cold running water for 30 minutes. Drain and place in a large heavy-based saucepan with the onion, carrots, celery, leek and garlic. Cover with the chicken stock and slowly bring to the boil. Reduce the heat and continuously skim the stock until all the impurities are removed. Only then add the white peppercorns, bay leaves and thyme. Cover the pot with a lid, transfer to the oven and braise the meats slowly, barely simmering, for 2½–3 hours.

When the tongue and ham hock are cooked, the skin covering the tongue will easily peel away and the ham hock meat will come away from the bone without resistance. If the meats require additional cooking, return them to the oven and check again after a further 15 minutes. When the meats are ready, remove from the oven and allow to cool in the cooking liquid.

Lift the meats out of the cooking liquid. Peel the skin off the veal tongue. Remove the ham hock bone and the thick layer of skin from the meat. (A 750 g ham hock will yield approximately 200 g meat.) Pass the cooking liquid through a fine sieve and reserve for future use. Dice 50 g of the ham hock and mix through the parsley purée with the chopped truffle. Taste and adjust the seasoning if necessary.

Slice the veal tongue lengthways into 16 thin slices. Brush the slices with the truffle dressing and lightly season with salt and freshly ground pepper. Lay four overlapping slices of the tongue on a plate. Make a quenelle of parsley purée using 2 tablespoons and set in the centre of the tongue. Garnish with the sliced truffle and flat-leaf parsley. Drizzle the remaining truffle dressing over and around the tongue.

ROASTED CALVES SWEETBREADS WITH LYONNAISE TART AND SAUCE SOUBISE

Serves 4

200 g	**Puff pastry** **(basic recipe 94, page 212)**
60 g	**Lyonnaise onions** **(basic recipe 56, page 204)**
	Egg wash of 1 free-range egg **and 10 ml milk**
4 x 100 g	**Calves sweetbreads from** **the pancreas, blanched** **and peeled** **(basic technique 2, page 215)**
80 ml	**Sauce Soubise** **(basic recipe 36, page 199)**
25 ml	**Vegetable oil**
20 g	**Whole, unsalted butter**
1	**Clove garlic, crushed**
1	**Sprig fresh thyme**
16	**Slices of truffle**
60 ml	**Red wine jus** **(basic recipe 27, page 197)**
	Salt
	Freshly ground pepper

Lightly dust a work surface with flour and roll out the puff pastry to a thickness of 5 mm. Cut out four squares, 8 cm x 8 cm, place them on a cold baking sheet and prick with a fork. Refrigerate for 30 minutes.

Place a square pastry cutter 4 cm x 4 cm in the centre of each pastry square. Spoon a thin layer of Lyonnaise onions into it and spread evenly over the pastry with the back of the spoon. Remove the pastry cutter and brush the pastry border with egg wash. Refrigerate for a further 30 minutes.

Preheat the oven to 200°C. Lightly spray a second baking sheet with water and transfer the Lyonnaise tarts onto it. Bake in the oven for 8 minutes or until the pastry is crisp and golden. While the tarts are baking, finish cooking the sweetbreads.

Warm the sauce Soubise over a gentle heat. Heat the vegetable oil in a heavy-based cast-iron pan. Lightly season the sweetbreads with salt and freshly ground pepper, place in the pan and fry for 4–5 minutes until brown. Turn and cook for a further 2–3 minutes. Add the whole butter, garlic and thyme to the pan and baste the sweetbreads with it for a further 2 minutes. The outside of the sweetbreads should be brown and crisp while the inside should remain soft and creamy. Remove the sweetbreads from the pan and keep warm.

Spoon 20 ml sauce Soubise into the centre of a warm plate and spread with the base of the spoon to form a neat circle. Place a Lyonnaise tart in the centre of the sauce Soubise. Garnish each sweetbread with four slices of truffle and set in the centre of the Lyonnaise tart. Drizzle the red wine jus over the sweetbreads and around the sauce Soubise.

ROESTI POTATOES WITH CALVES LIVER AND LIME JUS

Serves 4

LIME JUS

60 g	**Unsalted butter**
2	**Shallots, finely chopped**
I	**Tomato, de-seeded and chopped**
I	**Clove garlic, crushed**
	Pinch sugar
5 ml	**Sherry vinegar**
50 ml	**Port**
150 ml	**Noilly Prat**
100 ml	**Chicken stock** **(basic recipe 22, page 195)**
150 ml	**Veal stock** **(basic recipe 23, page 196)**
I	**Stalk parsley**
I	**Lime, juiced**

ROESTI POTATOES

4 x 250 g	**Roesti potatoes, made in a**
	     28 cm pan
	     (basic recipe 65, page 206)

CALVES LIVER

12	**Pieces garlic confit** **(basic recipe 51, page 203)**
12	**Spring onion bulbs, blanched** **and refreshed**
4	**Baby leeks, blanched, cut into** **2 cm pieces**
4 x 120 g	**Slices calves liver, 5 mm thick**
3 tbsp	**Plain flour, sifted and seasoned**
60 ml	**Clarified butter**
12	**Lime segments**
12	**Sprigs fresh chervil**
12	**Chive tips**
	Salt
	Freshly ground pepper

Prepare the lime jus: Melt 20 g butter in a heavy-based saucepan, add the shallots and sweat for 5 minutes without colouring. Add the tomato and garlic and cook for a further 3 minutes. Sprinkle with sugar and stir until the sugar has dissolved. Pour in the sherry vinegar and reduce until the vinegar and sugar have caramelised. Add the Port and Noilly Prat and reduce by three-quarters. Pour in both stocks and bring to the boil. Add the parsley stalk and reduce by a third. Pass the sauce through a fine sieve into a clean saucepan, return to the heat and reduce by half. Whisk the remaining 40 g butter into the sauce and season to taste with salt, freshly ground pepper and lime juice. Once more, pass through a fine sieve into a clean saucepan.

Preheat the oven to 220°C. Reheat the roesti potatoes in the oven for 10 minutes. Warm the garlic confit, spring onion bulbs and baby leeks in the lime jus over a low heat.

Lightly season the calves liver with salt and freshly ground pepper and pass through the flour, shaking off any excess. Heat the clarified butter in a large, heavy-based pan and add the liver. Cook for 1½ minutes on both sides – keep the liver pink inside. Place the calves liver on kitchen paper to absorb any excess butter.

Place a roesti potato in the centre of a warm plate and set a slice of calves liver onto it. Spoon the garlic, spring onion bulbs and baby leeks over the liver. Drizzle the lime jus over the liver and garnish with the lime segments, sprigs of chervil and chive tips.

FILLET OF VEAL ZURICHOISE

Serves 4

10 g	**Dried trompette des morts**
2 x 320 g	**Veal fillets**
40 ml	**Vegetable oil**
4	**Roesti potatoes made in a 12 cm pan (basic recipe 65, page 206)**
100 ml	**Morel cream sauce (basic recipe 35, page 199)**
50 ml	**Cream**
200 g	**Mixed wild mushrooms**
10 g	**Deep-fried shallots (basic recipe 49, page 203)**
1 tsp	**Sliced chives**
	Salt
	Freshly ground pepper

Prepare the veal fillets 24 hours in advance of serving: Preheat the oven to the lowest setting and place the trompette des morts on a tray in the oven to dry. The mushrooms will take between 45–60 minutes to dry. When the mushrooms are brittle, remove from the oven, place in a food processor and grind to a powder. Pass the powder through a fine sieve.

Trim the veal fillets of all sinew and fat. Place the mushroom powder on a tray and roll the veal fillets in it to completely cover. Shake off any excess mushroom powder and tightly roll the fillets in several layers of clingfilm. Refrigerate to allow the mushroom flavour to penetrate the meat.

Preheat the oven to 200°C. Unwrap the veal fillets and lightly season with salt and freshly ground pepper. Heat 20 ml vegetable oil in a heavy-based pan and evenly seal the meat for 4 minutes. Transfer to the oven and cook the meat for a further 4 minutes – keep it medium-rare. Remove from the oven and allow the fillets to rest for 15 minutes. Place the roestis into the oven to warm through.

Reheat the morel cream sauce over a low heat. Whip the cream to soft peaks and refrigerate until ready to use. Thoroughly trim and clean the wild mushrooms. Heat the remaining vegetable oil in a heavy-based pan and sauté the mushrooms until golden brown. Season to taste with salt and freshly ground pepper and drain into a sieve to remove any excess oil. Carve both fillets into four neat medallions and lightly season with salt and freshly ground pepper.

Place a roesti potato in the centre of a warm plate and set two medallions of veal onto it. Spoon the sautéed mushrooms around the roesti. Make a quenelle of the whipped cream using 2 teaspoons and place on top of the veal. Sprinkle with the deep-fried shallots and sliced chives. Spoon the morel cream sauce over and around the mushrooms.

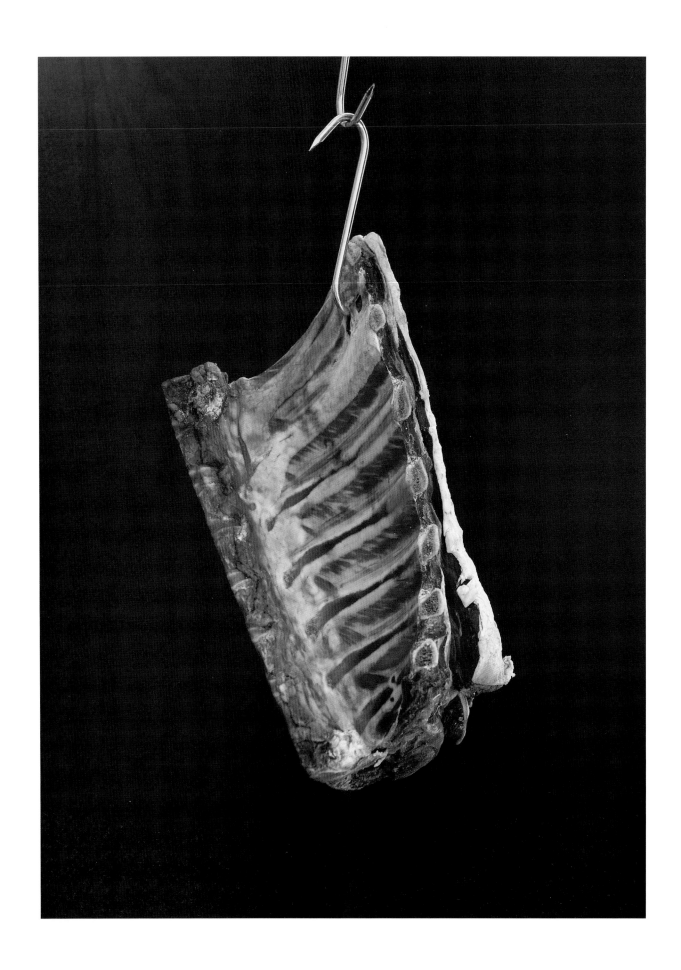

Most cattle produced for beef are cross-breeds of beef cattle that are still good quality but are leaner, with less fat than the pure breeds such as Angus, Hereford or Wagyu. Beef that has been reared naturally, on lush pastures in a stress-free growing environment, free of hormone and growth-promotants, have been reared to give maximum flavour. Finished off on a special diet of barley and oats for approximately 100 days to fatten them and create enough intermuscular fat or marbling throughout the meat, results in a juicy and tender product.

In countries like Australia, Japan and America the animals are all chiller-accessed. This entails stringent grading and quality checks, which require that the product complies with minimum fat, colour and marbling requirements. This guarantees a perfect product every step along the chain from grower to end-user.

When choosing beef, avoid vacuum-packed, pre-portioned meat from the supermarket shelves. Instead, buy it from a reputable butcher. Beef benefits from being hung for lengthy periods in cold storage of up to, and over,

BEEF

40 days to develop its flavour and increase tenderness, and a good butcher will do this automatically.

During this time the meat will lose moisture, resulting in loss of weight. Taking this into consideration, and that a pure breed has excess fat, will dictate a higher price for a good piece of meat. Well-hung meat will have a dry, dull and dark outer layer and the fat will have a yellow tinge, but when cut the meat will reveal a rich red colour and a good marbling of fat running through it. All these factors are signs of a quality and flavoursome piece of meat.

As meat cooks, particularly larger cuts, the heat cooks it from the outside in, driving the moisture into the centre. The heat also causes the fibres in the meat to tense, so it is important to allow it time to rest after cooking and before carving. The meat juices will evenly redistribute through the meat and cause the fibres to relax, resulting in a tender piece of meat. The larger the piece of meat, the longer the resting time and it may need to be returned to the oven for a short period to bring its temperature back up before serving.

FILLET OF BEEF ROSSINI

Serves 4

4 x 160 g	Beef fillet portions
80 g	Foie gras trimmings
10 g	Chopped truffle
4	Thin slices prosciutto, 15 cm long
20 ml	Vegetable oil
50 ml	Sauce Perigeux
	(basic recipe 31, page 198)
200 g	Creamed spinach
	(basic recipe 58, page 204)
4	Potato gallettes
	(basic recipe 67, page 207)
4 x 25 g	Slices of foie gras
4	Slices of truffle
	Salt
	Freshly ground pepper

Prepare the beef: Make an incision in the side of each piece of beef to form a small, deep pocket. Mix the foie gras trimmings with the chopped truffle and lightly season with salt and freshly ground pepper. Spoon the foie gras and truffle mixture into the pockets. Wrap a slice of prosciutto around each piece of beef to hold the foie gras and truffle in place during cooking. Secure with a piece of butcher's twine. Preheat the oven to 200°C.

Heat the oil in a heavy-based frying pan. Season the beef with salt and freshly ground pepper, evenly sear and cook for 6–8 minutes depending on the thickness of the meat – keep it medium-rare. (If you cook the meat past medium-rare, the foie gras will render down and seep out during cooking.) Remove the beef from the pan and allow to rest in a warm place for 10 minutes before serving.

Gently warm the sauce Perigeux over a low heat. Reheat the creamed spinach. Place the potato gallettes into the oven and warm through. Heat a non-stick frying pan over a high heat. Season the slices of foie gras with salt and freshly ground pepper, and evenly sear for 10–15 seconds depending on the thickness – keep the centres pink. Remove the foie gras with a spatula, place a slice on top of each piece of beef and garnish with a slice of truffle.

Place an 8 cm pastry ring in the centre of a warm plate and spoon the creamed spinach into it, pressing down with the back of the spoon. Gently remove the pastry ring. Lightly season the potato gallette with salt and freshly ground pepper and place onto the spinach. Set the beef on top of the potato gallette and spoon the sauce Perigeux over and around the beef.

MINUTE STEAK FORESTIÈRE WITH DEEP-FRIED HERB BUTTER

Serves 4

4 x 120 g	**Beef fillet portions**
50 ml	**Clarified butter**
16	**Pieces sautéed potato**
	(basic recipe 66, page 206)
1	**Clove garlic, crushed**
1	**Sprig fresh thyme**
20	**Lardons of pancetta**
25 g	**Whole butter**
25 ml	**Olive oil**
120 g	**Mixed wild mushrooms**
100 g	**Lyonnaise onions**
	(basic recipe 56, page 204)
	Vegetable oil for deep-frying
	the butter
4	**Pieces deep-fried butter**
	(basic recipe 43, page 201)
25 ml	**Vegetable oil**
12	**Leaves flat-leaf parsley**
	Salt
	Freshly ground pepper

Prepare the beef: Place each piece of beef between double-folded sheets of clingfilm. Evenly bat out the meat to a 13 cm diameter using a meat mallet. Place a 12 cm pastry ring in the centre of the meat. Trim around the pastry ring with a sharp knife to produce a neat 12 cm round of meat.

Heat the clarified butter in a large cast-iron pan and add the potatoes, garlic and thyme. Lightly season with salt and freshly ground pepper and sauté the potatoes, tossing frequently, for 6 minutes. Add the lardons and continue to sauté until brown. Add the whole butter and sauté for a further 2 minutes. Drain the potatoes and lardons. Remove and discard the garlic and thyme. Check the seasoning and adjust if necessary.

Heat the olive oil in a heavy-based pan and sauté the mushrooms for 3–4 minutes until golden brown. Season to taste with salt and freshly ground pepper. Drain the mushrooms, mix through the potatoes and lardons and keep warm while preparing the remainder of the dish. Reheat the Lyonnaise onions over a low heat.

Heat the vegetable oil to 180°C and deep-fry the herb butter until golden. Drain on kitchen paper to absorb any excess oil.

Heat 25 ml vegetable oil until almost smoking in a heavy-based pan. Season the beef with salt and freshly ground pepper and sear on both sides for 30 seconds. Remove the beef from the pan and rest for 1 minute.

Place a 12 cm pastry ring in the centre of a plate. Spoon a thin layer of the Lyonnaise onions into it and spread with the back of the spoon. Gently remove the pastry ring. Set a piece of beef on top of the Lyonnaise onions and spread a second thin layer of the Lyonnaise onions onto the surface of the beef. Spoon the potatoes, lardons and mushrooms over the Lyonnaise onions and top with the deep-fried butter. Garnish with the flat-leaf parsley.

BRAISED OXTAIL AND CARAMELISED CALVES SWEETBREADS WITH ROOT VEGETABLES

Serves 6

1 x 1.6 kg	**Piece of oxtail on the bone**
1 x 200 g	**Carrot**
200 g	**Piece pancetta, skin removed**
2	**Large Savoy cabbage leaves, blanched and refreshed**
750 ml	**Red wine**
300 ml	**Port**
25 ml	**Vegetable oil**
100 g	**Carrots, chopped**
100 g	**Onions, chopped**
100 g	**Celery, chopped**
6	**Cloves garlic, crushed**
2 ltr	**Veal stock (basic recipe 23, page 196)**
1	**Sprig fresh thyme**
2	**Fresh bay leaves**
1	**Sprig fresh rosemary**
320 g	**Potato purée (basic recipe 61, page 205)**
50 ml	**Clarified butter**
18 x 25 g	**Pieces calves sweetbreads from the pancreas, blanched and peeled (basic technique 2, page 215)**
18	**Baby carrots, peeled, blanched and refreshed**
18	**Baby turnips, blanched and refreshed**
	Salt
	Freshly ground pepper

Prepare the oxtail 24 hours in advance of serving: De-bone the oxtail in one piece or have a butcher do it – reserve the bones. The deboned oxtail will weigh approximately 1.2 kg. Chop the bones into small pieces and set aside until ready to use. Peel the carrot, cut in half lengthways and cut each half into four strips, the full length of the carrot. Slice the pancetta into strips the same length as the carrot. Trim the Savoy cabbage leaves to cover the entire surface of the oxtail.

Preheat the oven to 140°C. Lay the oxtail flat on a work surface, skin side down and season with salt and freshly ground pepper. Cover the oxtail with the Savoy cabbage leaves. Lay the carrot and pancetta down the centre of the cabbage and tightly roll up the oxtail to form a long cylinder. Secure with butcher's twine, working from one end of the oxtail to the other, to prevent the filling from falling out during cooking. Season the oxtail with salt and freshly ground pepper. Pour the red wine and Port into a heavy-based saucepan and reduce to 500 ml over a medium heat. Set aside until ready to use.

Heat the vegetable oil in a large cast-iron pan over a medium heat. Add the oxtail and the chopped bones and render the fat, frequently turning the oxtail and the bones until both are caramelised. As the fat renders, pour it from the pan and reserve for another use. Remove the oxtail and bones and return the pan to the heat. Add the chopped carrots, onions, celery and crushed garlic and sauté until golden brown. Pour the reduced red wine and Port over the vegetables to deglaze the pan.

Transfer the vegetables and alcohol into a large heavy-based pot. Add the roasted oxtail bones, lay the oxtail onto them and cover with the veal stock. Return to the heat and bring to the boil. Reduce the heat to a simmer and skim the surface to remove any scum that floats to the top. Add the thyme, bay leaves and rosemary, cover with a lid and transfer to the oven. Braise slowly for 3 hours until the oxtail is tender.

Carefully lift the oxtail from the stock and place on a tray. Pass the stock through a fine sieve and refrigerate to solidify any fat that may rise to the surface. Remove the string when the oxtail is cool enough to handle. Tightly roll the oxtail in several layers of clingfilm and refrigerate. Remove and discard the fat from the chilled oxtail stock, place the stock into a heavy-based pot and reduce by half over a medium heat. Pass through a fine sieve and season to taste with salt and freshly ground pepper. Unwrap the oxtail, carve into six even-sized medallions and place them into the reduced oxtail stock. Gently poach for 15 minutes over a low heat.

Prepare the garnish while the oxtail is poaching: Warm the potato purée. Heat 30 ml clarified butter in a heavy-based pan over a medium heat. Lightly season the sweetbreads with salt and freshly ground pepper. Cook for 2–3 minutes until brown and crisp – keep the insides creamy – and drain on kitchen paper. Add the remaining clarified butter to the pan and sauté the carrots and baby turnips until lightly coloured. Season the vegetables with salt and freshly ground pepper, drain and keep warm.

Remove the oxtail from the reduced stock, drain and pass the stock through a fine sieve. Place the oxtail in the centre of a warm plate and arrange the sweetbreads and vegetables around it. Make a quenelle of the potato purée using 2 tablespoons and set beside the oxtail. Spoon the sauce over and around the oxtail.

FILLET OF BEEF WITH WILD MUSHROOMS, WHITE ASPARAGUS AND TRUFFLE HOLLANDAISE

Serves 4

25 ml	**Vegetable oil**
4 x 140 g	**Beef fillet portions**
80 ml	**Olive oil**
200 g	**Mixed wild mushrooms**
200 g	**Truffle gnocchi** **(basic recipe 71, page 207)**
80 g	**Unsalted butter**
12	**Spears white asparagus,** **peeled, blanched and cut into** **9 cm lengths** **(basic technique 5, page 216)**
150 ml	**Truffle hollandaise** **(basic recipe 41, page 201)**
12	**Sprigs fresh chervil**
80 ml	**Sauce Perigeux** **(basic recipe 31, page 198)**
	Salt
	Freshly ground pepper

Preheat the oven to 180°C. Heat the vegetable oil in a heavy-based frying pan. Season the beef with salt and freshly ground pepper, evenly sear and cook for 6–8 minutes, depending on the thickness of the meat – keep it medium-rare. Remove the beef from the pan and allow to rest in a warm place for 10 minutes before serving.

Heat two heavy-based pans and add 40 ml olive oil to both. Add the mushrooms to one pan and the truffle gnocchi to the other and sauté both for 3–4 minutes until golden brown. Season to taste with salt and freshly ground pepper. Add 20 g butter to both pans and toss through the mushrooms and gnocchi until melted. Drain, mix together in a bowl and keep warm until ready to use.

Heat the remaining butter until foaming in a heavy-based pan. Add the asparagus and sauté in the butter until lightly coloured. Season to taste with salt and freshly ground pepper and drain on kitchen paper to absorb any excess butter.

Place three asparagus spears onto a warm plate and spoon over the truffle hollandaise, leaving the tips exposed, and garnish with the chervil. Spoon the mushrooms and gnocchi beside the asparagus and set a piece of beef on top. Drizzle the sauce Perigeux over and around the beef.

All game needs to be hung. Wild duck such as Mallard, Widgeon and Teal benefit from hanging by their necks for two to three days to develop their flavour, to help tenderise the meat and soften the feathers for plucking. The birds should be dry-plucked with the feathers pulled in the direction in which they lie to prevent the skin from tearing. Cut off the wing tips, feet and neck. Remove the innards and separate the livers, gizzard and heart.

Duck is ready for the table after three to four months. If using a farmed breed, choose a free-range bird that has been reared on a healthy diet. The French breed, Barbary, and the English breed, Gressingham, which is a cross-breed of Pekin and Wild Mallard, contain less fat than other breeds and are very meaty. Gressingham has a gamier flavour than Barbary.

Fresh duck liver needs to be trimmed before using to remove any sinew and bile, a very bitter green fluid secreted by the liver and stored in the gall bladder. To rid the liver of bile, soak it in cold milk with a large bunch of fresh thyme and a sliced clove of garlic, and refrigerate for a few hours; the liver will absorb the flavours of the garlic and thyme. Drain and dry on a clean kitchen cloth when ready to use. Use in stuffing or sear in clarified butter in a very

DUCK

hot pan – keeping the centre pink; or transform into a smooth parfait with the addition of eggs and softened butter and flavour with reduced Madeira, Port and Cognac, and cook in a terrine set in a *bain-marie*.

The gizzard is a second stomach that the duck uses to grind food. It needs to be slit from top to bottom to reveal the inside, which is usually full of grain. Remove it by peeling away the tough skin and sinew. Salt the gizzard for 3 hours, then slowly confit in duck fat for 2 hours until tender (basic technique 1, page 215). Allow to cool before thinly slicing and pan-frying in a little duck fat. Serve with salads or as a garnish with duck.

Like most poultry, the legs are tough and sinewy. They benefit from braising in a flavoured stock or cooked as confit (basic technique 1, page 215), rather than being roasted on the bird, as they require longer cooking than the breasts. Roasting duck breasts on the bone contributes to the flavour. Remove the wishbone to make it easier to carve. Score the skin, taking care not to cut into the flesh, and seal on both sides in a heavy-based pan for 4–6 minutes. The fat will render down and the skin will become crisp. Drain off the rendered fat. Use the carcass, wing bones and neck for stocks, sauces and consommé.

RILLETTE OF DUCK AND FOIE GRAS WITH ARMAGNAC JELLY

Serves 8

RILLETTE OF DUCK

275 g	**Picked duck confit, skin and bones removed (basic technique 1, page 215)**
25 ml	**Rendered duck fat (basic technique 1, page 215)**
2 tsp	**Sliced chives**
2 tsp	**Julienne of flat-leaf parsley**
30 g	**Gherkins, chopped**
30 g	**Cocktail onions, chopped**
1 tsp	**Grated fresh horseradish**
40 ml	**Sauce Perigeux (basic recipe 31, page 198)**
15 ml	**Cognac**
80 g	**Foie gras, diced**
8	**Slices of truffle, julienned**
400 ml	**Armagnac jelly of pouring consistency (basic recipe 45, page 202)**

GARNISH

2	**Small shallots, sliced**
80 g	**Artichokes, prepared, cooked and sliced (basic technique 6, page 216)**
5	**Pieces duck gizzard confit, cut into 40 slices (basic technique 1, page 215)**
40 g	**Walnuts, roughly chopped**
40 ml	**Blackberry and walnut vinaigrette (basic recipe 6, page 191)**
	Mesclun leaves
40	**Chive tips**
40	**Tarragon leaves**
	Salt
	Freshly ground pepper

Prepare the rillette of duck: Shred the duck confit into a large bowl. Melt the duck fat and mix through the shredded duck confit. Add the sliced chives, flat-leaf parsley, gherkins, cocktail onions and the horseradish to taste and fold through the duck confit – take care not to overwork the mixture. Add the sauce Perigeux and Cognac and season to taste with salt and freshly ground pepper.

Line a tray with silicon paper and place 8 ring moulds, 7 cm wide x 1.5 cm deep, onto it. Divide the rillette between the moulds to three-quarters full and evenly spread using a palette knife. Refrigerate for 15 minutes to allow the duck fat to set. When the rillette is firm, spoon the diced foie gras and julienne of truffle over the top. Pour the Armagnac jelly to fill the moulds to the top and refrigerate.

Check the level of the jelly after 15 minutes. If the rillette is not packed tightly into the moulds, some of the jelly may seep through into it and will require topping-up with more jelly. Refrigerate until the jelly is set before unmoulding. Set the remaining jelly in a small, deep, clingfilm-lined tray; turn out onto a clean chopping board and cut into 5 mm cubes. Refrigerate until ready to use.

Garnish: Place the sliced shallots, artichokes, duck gizzard confit, chopped walnuts and 25 ml blackberry and walnut vinaigrette into a bowl and mix together. Lightly season with salt and freshly ground pepper. Run the tip of a thin-bladed knife around the inside of the rillette moulds and gently remove – take care not to break the jelly. Place a rillette in the centre of a plate and surround with the dressed shallots, artichoke, gizzard and walnuts. Spoon the cubed Armagnac jelly around the garnish. Dress the mesclun with the remaining blackberry and walnut vinaigrette, lightly season with salt and freshly ground pepper and arrange around the rillette. Garnish with the chive tips and tarragon leaves.

WARM SALAD OF CRISP DUCK CONFIT AND SEARED FOIE GRAS, GREEN BEANS, SHALLOTS AND BLACKBERRY AND WALNUT VINAIGRETTE

Serves 4

2	**Pieces duck gizzard confit (basic technique 1, page 215)**
20 ml	**Rendered duck fat (basic technique 1, page 215)**
4	**Pressed legs of duck confit (basic technique 1, page 215)**
40 g	**Fine green beans, topped, tailed and blanched**
1	**Shallot, sliced**
15 g	**Walnuts, chopped**
4 x 40 g	**Slices of foie gras**
40 ml	**Blackberry and walnut vinaigrette (basic recipe 6, page 191)**
60 g	**Mesclun leaves**
12	**Chive tips**
12	**Sprigs fresh chervil**
12	**Picked tarragon leaves**
	Salt
	Freshly ground pepper

Preheat the oven to 200°C. Slice both pieces duck gizzard confit into six even slices. Heat the duck fat in a heavy-based pan and place the legs of duck confit into the pan, skin side down. Heat in the oven for 4–5 minutes until the skin is crisp and brown. Turn the legs over and cook for a further 2 minutes. Remove the duck legs from the pan and lightly season with salt and freshly ground pepper. Keep warm until ready to use. Add the sliced gizzards to the pan and warm through in the heat, turning once. Lightly season with salt and freshly ground pepper.

Split the green beans in half lengthways. Place in a bowl with the sliced shallot and the chopped walnuts and keep at room temperature until ready to use.

Heat a heavy-based non-stick pan over a high heat. Season the foie gras on both sides with salt and freshly ground pepper and sear for 10–15 seconds, depending on the thickness – keep the centres pink. Transfer the foie gras from the pan to a plate and keep warm while the remainder of the dish is being prepared. Reserve any fat from the pan in which the foie gras has been cooked and stir into the blackberry and walnut vinaigrette.

Add the gizzards to the green beans with half the dressing. Season to taste with salt and freshly ground pepper and toss gently. Divide the gizzards and beans between four warm plates and place a duck leg onto them. Top with a slice of seared foie gras.

In a separate bowl mix the mesclun, chive tips, chervil and tarragon, add the remaining dressing and adjust the seasoning if necessary. Arrange a small mound of salad on top of each slice of foie gras.

ROAST BREAST AND CONFIT OF DUCK WITH SEARED FOIE GRAS AND SAUCE SOUBISE

Serves 4

2 x 200 g	**Barbary duck breasts, with skin on**
15 ml	**Vegetable oil**
20 ml	**Rendered duck fat (basic technique 1, page 215)**
4	**Pressed legs of duck confit (basic technique 1, page 215)**
80 ml	**Sauce Soubise (basic recipe 36, page 199)**
4 x 20 g	**Slices of foie gras**
8	**Batons roasted parsnip (basic recipe 60, page 205)**
8	**Slices of truffle**
50 ml	**Sparkling Shiraz jus (basic recipe 29, page 197)**
	Salt
	Freshly ground pepper

Preheat the oven to 200°C. Trim the duck breasts of excess fat, score the skin with the tip of a sharp knife and season with salt and freshly ground pepper. Heat the vegetable oil in a heavy-based pan over a medium heat. Place the duck breasts into the pan, skin side down, and cook for 4 minutes. As the duck breasts cook, some of the fat from the skin will render down. Pour the fat out of the pan to prevent the skin from becoming too crisp. Turn the duck breasts over and seal the flesh side. Transfer the pan to the oven and cook for a further 3–4 minutes, depending on the thickness of the duck breasts – keep the insides pink. Remove the pan from the oven, baste the duck with the pan juices and rest them, skin side down, while preparing the remainder of the dish.

Heat the duck fat in a heavy-based pan and place the legs of duck confit, skin side down, into the pan and heat through in the oven for 3–4 minutes until the skin is crisp and brown. Turn the legs and cook for a further 2 minutes. Remove from the pan and lightly season with salt and freshly ground pepper. Carve each duck breast at an angle into 12 even slices and lightly season with salt and freshly ground pepper. Gently heat the sauce Soubise in a small saucepan.

Heat a heavy-based non-stick pan over a high heat. Season the foie gras on both sides with salt and freshly ground pepper and sear for 10–15 seconds, depending on the thickness – keep the centres pink. Remove from the pan and keep warm.

Spoon 20 ml sauce Soubise into the centre of a plate and spread with the back of the spoon to form a neat circle. Place two batons of roasted parsnip onto the sauce Soubise and lay a piece of duck confit across them. Arrange six overlapping slices of duck breast onto the duck confit and top with a slice of seared foie gras. Garnish the foie gras with two slices of truffle. Drizzle the sparkling Shiraz jus over the foie gras and around the sauce Soubise.

ROAST DUCK BREAST WITH SWEETCORN AND PARSNIP PURÉE

Serves 4

200 g	Fresh duck livers
2	Pieces duck gizzard confit (basic technique 1, page 215)
2 x 200 g	Barbary duck breasts, with skin on
30 ml	Vegetable oil
25 ml	Clarified butter
4	Duck and sweetcorn herbed pancakes (basic recipe 73, page 208)
120 ml	Parsnip purée (basic recipe 55, page 204)
60 ml	Sparkling Shiraz jus (basic recipe 29, page 197)
1	Clove garlic, crushed
1	Small sprig fresh rosemary
1	Small shallot, thinly sliced
20 ml	Cabernet Sauvignon vinegar
4 x 20 g	Slices of foie gras
12	Chive tips
12	Leaves shiso
	Salt
	Freshly ground pepper

Preheat the oven to 200°C. Cut the duck livers into 12 even-sized pieces and both pieces of gizzard confit into six even slices. Refrigerate until ready to use.

Trim the duck breasts of excess fat and score the skin with the tip of a sharp knife. Season with salt and freshly ground pepper. Heat 15 ml of the vegetable oil in a heavy-based pan over a medium heat. Place the duck breasts, skin side down, into the pan and cook for 4 minutes. Pour any rendered fat out of the pan to prevent the skin from becoming too crisp. Turn the ducks breasts over and seal the flesh side. Transfer to the oven and cook for a further 3−4 minutes, depending on the thickness of the breasts − keep the insides pink. Remove the pan from the oven, baste the duck with the pan juices and rest, skin side down, for 10 minutes.

Reduce the oven temperature to 180°C. Heat the clarified butter in a heavy-based pan over a low heat. Place the duck and sweetcorn-filled pancakes into the pan on the folded side to seal for 2 minutes. Remove the pancakes from the pan, place onto lightly buttered sheets of greaseproof paper 4 cm x 12 cm and wrap into parcels to prevent them from drying out. Place the pancake parcels on a baking tray and into the oven for 5−6 minutes to reheat. Remove from the oven and unwrap the parcels. Heat the parsnip purée and Shiraz jus in separate saucepans over a low heat.

Heat the remaining vegetable oil in a heavy-based pan over a medium heat. Season the duck livers with salt and freshly ground pepper and add to the pan with the crushed garlic clove and sprig of rosemary. Sauté the livers for 30 seconds, add the sliced gizzards and shallot and continue to sauté for a further minute until the shallot begins to break down and soak up some of the pan juices. Add the Cabernet Sauvignon vinegar and toss the pan to evenly coat the livers, gizzards and shallot. Immediately pour the contents of the pan into a bowl to stop the cooking process − keep the duck livers pink. Discard the garlic and rosemary and lightly season the contents of the bowl with salt and freshly ground pepper.

Carve each duck breast at an angle into 10 even slices and lightly season with salt and freshly ground pepper. Heat a heavy-based non-stick pan over a high heat. Season the foie gras with salt and freshly ground pepper and sear for 10−15 seconds, depending on the thickness − keep the insides pink. Remove the foie gras from the pan and keep warm.

Spoon 30 ml parsnip purée into the centre of a warm plate and spread with the back of the spoon to form a neat circle. Place a pancake in the centre of the purée and arrange five overlapping slices of duck breast on top of it. Set a slice of seared foie gras onto the duck breast. Spoon three pieces of both the duck livers and gizzards around the parsnip purée and spoon the shallots onto the duck livers. Drizzle the Shiraz jus over the duck, foie gras, duck livers and gizzards. Garnish the duck livers and gizzard with the chive tips and shiso leaves.

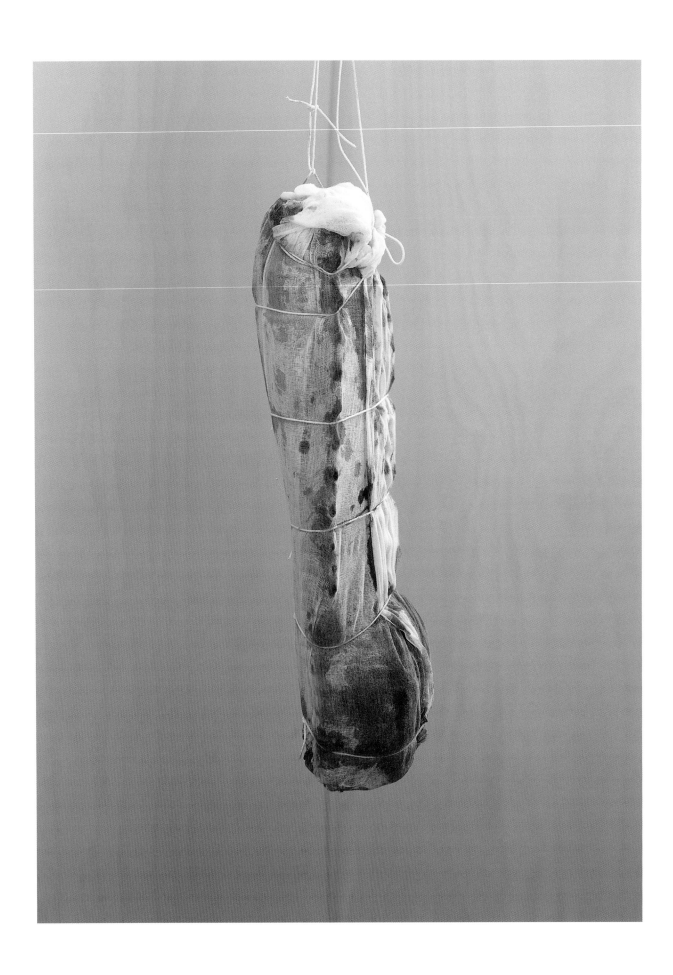

Venison is farmed in ever-increasing numbers and is regarded as a healthy red meat, low in fat, calories and cholesterol and is a good source of protein and iron. Some of the best available free-range venison is reared in New Zealand and South Africa, where the deer graze on grasslands in two of the purest environments in the world. Their diet is free of feed-additives and growth promotants and the mild climate in these countries enable the deer to live outdoors all year round, making it virtually organic.

In most recipes I use the saddle of venison, which I buy whole on the bone and hang for two weeks before butchering. It is the tenderest cut of venison and, being on the bone, it retains its full flavour. It has a thin layer of fat and sinew and gives a good yield with very little wastage and requires minimum cooking.

VENISON

When butchered, the two fillets are removed, trimmed and tightly rolled in clingfilm, giving them a neat, cylindrical shape. Then they are frozen to be used for carpaccio. The two loins are used for tartare and also for roasting. The bones from the saddle are chopped and roasted to make a rich gelatinous stock in the same way as veal stock (basic recipe 23, page 196), with the addition of juniper berries, black peppercorns and bay leaves. The stock is further reduced and turned into a sauce to serve with the venison.

Venison is a very rich meat and can be paired with big flavours such as aged balsamic jus (basic recipe 30, page 198), pepper and chocolate sauces and full-bodied wine reductions made with Shiraz and Cabernet Sauvignon. It is also one of the only meats to serve with fruit, for example, a rare roasted loin of venison with black figs macerated in aged balsamic and Port or, roasted rack of venison with grapes steeped in Marc de Bourgogne.

CARPACCIO AND TARTARE OF VENISON WITH TRUFFLE DRESSING

Serves 4

CARPACCIO OF VENISON

150 g	Fillet of venison, sinew removed
5 ml	Truffle oil
20 g	Deep-fried parsnip chips (basic recipe 47, page 202)
4	Quail egg yolks
24	Mâche leaves (lamb's lettuce)
24	Chive tips

TARTARE OF VENISON

300 g	Venison loin, sinew removed
2	Small gherkins, finely chopped
2	Cocktail onions, finely chopped
1 tsp	Rinsed and finely chopped capers
1 tsp	Sliced chives
1 tsp	Chopped curly parsley
1	Large free-range egg yolk
¼–½ tsp	Dijon mustard to taste
	Dash of Tabasco to taste
	Dash of Worcestershire sauce to taste
1 tsp	Tomato ketchup
	Dash of brandy to taste

CELERIAC RÉMOULADE

1	Small bulb celeriac
150 ml	Mayonnaise (basic recipe 10, page 192)
5 g	Chopped truffle
1 tsp	Julienne of flat-leaf parsley
1	Lemon

POTATOES AND MUSHROOMS

15 ml	Truffle oil
32	Pieces sautéed potato (basic recipe 66, page 206)
24	Small shimiji mushrooms
24	Small oyster mushrooms
60 ml	Truffle dressing (basic recipe 8, page 192)
	Salt
	Freshly ground pepper

Prepare the carpaccio: Roll the fillet of venison in several layers of clingfilm and tightly secure the ends. Freeze for 12 hours before slicing.

An hour before serving, cut four pieces of greaseproof paper 7 cm x 7 cm and brush each sheet with a thin layer of truffle oil. Remove the clingfilm from the frozen venison and slice as thinly as possible. Place overlapping slices of venison to cover the surface of the paper and return to the freezer.

Prepare the tartare of venison: To retain maximum colour, texture and taste do not prepare the tartare more than 20 minutes before serving. Prepared too far in advance, the meat will oxidise and discolour.

Set up a stainless steel bowl half-filled with ice and place a smaller bowl into it. Finely dice the venison using a large, sharp chopping knife. Place the meat into the bowl and mix through the gherkins, cocktail onions, capers, sliced chives, chopped parsley and egg yolk. Add the mustard, Tabasco, Worcestershire sauce, tomato ketchup and brandy to taste, depending on the spiciness required. Season to taste with salt and freshly ground pepper. Refrigerate the tartare until ready to serve.

Prepare the celeriac rémoulade: Peel the celeriac, removing the thick outer layer, and slice as thinly as possible on a mandolin. Cut the slices into julienne, place in a bowl and bind with the mayonnaise. Mix in the chopped truffle and julienne of flat-leaf parsley. Season to taste with salt, freshly ground pepper and a squeeze of lemon.

Heat 15 ml truffle oil in a large cast-iron pan and add the potatoes. Season with salt and freshly ground pepper and sauté the potatoes for 6 minutes, tossing frequently until tender. Add the shimiji and oyster mushrooms and continue to sauté until golden brown. Drain the potatoes and mushrooms, transfer to a bowl and add 40 ml truffle dressing. Lightly season with salt and freshly ground pepper and keep warm.

Remove the carpaccio from the freezer and, using a sharp, long-bladed knife, trim the sides of the carpaccio to shape each one into a square. Peel off the greaseproof paper and place the carpaccio off-centre on a large, chilled plate. Place a 3 cm pastry ring in the centre of the carpaccio and fill with the celeriac rémoulade. Gently remove the pastry ring and sprinkle the carpaccio with the parsnip chips.

Place a 6 cm pastry ring beside the carpaccio and spoon in the tartare, pressing down with the back of the spoon to form a smooth round. Remove the pastry ring and spoon around the sautéed potatoes and mushrooms. Set a quail egg yolk in the centre of the tartare. Dress the mâche with the remaining truffle dressing and arrange the leaves on the sautéed potatoes and mushrooms. Garnish with the chive tips.

LOIN OF VENISON WITH BRAISED RED CABBAGE AND MACERATED FIGS

Serves 4

100 ml	**Sugar syrup**
	(basic recipe 76, page 209)
25 ml	**Port**
25 ml	**Aged balsamic vinegar**
1	**Stick cinnamon**
2	**Star anise**
4	**Black figs**
360 g	**Venison loin**
10 ml	**Vegetable oil**
6	**Kipfler potatoes, or similar**
	waxy potatoes
25 ml	**Clarified butter**
1	**Clove garlic, crushed**
1	**Sprig fresh thyme**
15 g	**Whole, unsalted butter**
320 g	**Braised red cabbage**
	(basic recipe 59, page 205)
1 tsp	**Raisins**
100 ml	**Port wine jus**
	(basic recipe 28, page 197)
12	**Chive tips**
12	**Sprigs fresh chervil**
	Salt
	Freshly ground pepper

Mix together the sugar syrup, Port, balsamic vinegar, cinnamon and star anise in a heavy-based saucepan and bring to the boil. Lower the heat to a simmer and reduce the liquid by a quarter. Remove from the heat and allow to cool. Prick the figs all over with a fork, place in the syrup and macerate for 6 hours before removing them from the liquid. Preheat the oven to 200°C.

Season the venison with salt and freshly ground pepper. Heat 10 ml vegetable oil in a heavy-based frying pan over a medium heat and seal the venison until evenly brown. Transfer to the oven and continue to cook for a further 6–8 minutes until medium-rare or longer if the meat is preferred less rare. Remove the venison from the oven and allow to rest for 15 minutes before carving.

While the venison cooks, wash the potatoes under cold running water and cut in half lengthways. Heat the clarified butter in a large cast-iron pan, add the potatoes, garlic and thyme and season with salt and freshly ground pepper. Sauté the potatoes for 6 minutes, transfer to the oven and cook until tender and golden brown. Add the whole butter and continue to cook for a further 2 minutes. Drain the potatoes and remove the garlic and thyme. Check the seasoning and adjust if necessary. Keep warm while preparing the remainder of the dish.

Gently heat the red cabbage in a heavy-based saucepan and stir in the raisins. Check the seasoning and adjust if necessary. Stir occasionally to prevent the cabbage from sticking to the pan.

Cut the figs into quarters, brush with a little of the syrup and warm through in the oven. Heat the Port wine jus. Trim the ends of the venison and carve into 16 even slices. Lightly season with salt and freshly ground pepper.

Place a 6 cm pastry ring in the centre of a warm plate and spoon the red cabbage into it, pressing down with the back of the spoon so that it holds together. Lay four overlapping slices of venison onto the red cabbage to form a circle. Gently remove the pastry ring. Arrange three pieces of potato around the venison and a wedge of fig between each piece of potato. Set a wedge of fig on top of the venison and drizzle the Port wine jus over and around it. Garnish with the chive tips and sprigs of chervil.

LOIN OF VENISON WITH WILTED SPINACH AND MARC DE BOURGOGNE SAUCE

Serves 4

120 g	**Small, seedless black grapes**
40 ml	**Marc de Bourgogne**
400 g	**English spinach**
1	**Large potato**
360 g	**Venison loin**
10 ml	**Vegetable oil**
60 ml	**Red wine jus**
	(basic recipe 27, page 197)
20 g	**Walnuts, roughly chopped**
20 ml	**Clarified butter**
2	**Cloves garlic, crushed**
1	**Sprig fresh thyme**
35 g	**Unsalted butter**
16	**Sprigs fresh chervil**
	Salt
	Freshly ground pepper

Remove the grapes from the stalks, pick out 60 g of the smallest and reserve until ready to use. Place the remaining grapes in a bowl and hand-crush to release their juice. Pour the Marc de Bourgogne over the grapes to macerate, cover with clingfilm and refrigerate for 12 hours.

Pick the spinach, discarding the stalks and wash in several changes of lightly salted cold water to remove any sand. Set aside and allow to drain. Peel the potato and make balls of potato using a small Parisienne scoop (see glossary). Keep in cold water until ready to use. Preheat the oven to 200°C.

Season the venison with salt and freshly ground pepper. Heat 10 ml vegetable oil in a heavy-based pan and seal the venison until evenly brown. Transfer to the oven and continue to cook for a further 6–8 minutes until medium-rare or longer if the meat is preferred less rare. Remove the venison from the oven and allow to rest for 15 minutes before carving.

Add the macerated grapes to the red wine jus and bring to the boil. Reduce the heat and simmer for 5 minutes before passing through a fine sieve into a clean saucepan, pressing down with the back of a ladle to extract as much flavour and colour from the grape skins as possible. Add the reserved whole grapes and the chopped walnuts to the Marc de Bourgogne sauce and gently warm over a low heat.

Drain the potatoes and dry in a clean kitchen cloth. Heat 20 ml clarified butter in a large cast-iron pan and add the potatoes, 1 clove of garlic and the thyme. Season with salt and freshly ground pepper and sauté the potatoes for 4 minutes, tossing frequently. Transfer the potatoes to the oven until tender and golden brown. Add 10 g unsalted butter and continue to cook for a further 2 minutes. Drain the potatoes and discard the garlic and thyme. Check the seasoning and adjust if necessary. Keep warm until ready to serve.

Cover the base of a heavy-based saucepan, large enough to hold all the spinach, with a thin layer of water. Add 1 clove of garlic and 25 g unsalted butter and bring to the boil rapidly. Add the spinach and cook for 2–3 minutes until wilted but still retaining its colour. Drain the spinach in a colander and discard the garlic. Season to taste with salt and freshly ground pepper.

Trim the ends of the venison, carve into four even pieces and lightly season with salt and freshly ground pepper.

Spread the spinach in the centre of a warm plate and place a piece of venison onto it. Spoon the sauce, grapes and walnuts over and around the venison. Arrange the potatoes on top of the venison and garnish with the sprigs of chervil.

RACK OF VENISON WITH GARLIC CHIVE SPÄTZLE AND PORT WINE JUS

Serves 4

TURNIP

75 ml	Chicken stock
	(basic recipe 22, page 195)
75 ml	Port
1–2	Turnips, cut into 20 x 1 cm
	cubes

RACK OF VENISON

| 1 x 800 g | Rib of venison with 4 cutlets |
| 25 ml | Vegetable oil |

GARLIC CHIVE SPÄTZLE

100 ml	Clarified butter
320 g	Garlic chive spätzle
	(basic recipe 72, page 208)

TO SERVE

10 ml	Olive oil or rendered duck fat
	(basic technique 1, page 215)
12	Pieces roasted garlic
	(basic recipe 51, page 203)
100 ml	Port wine jus
	(basic recipe 28, page 197)
4	Pieces herb crust 4 cm x 4 cm
	(basic recipe 74, page 208)
	Salt
	Freshly ground pepper

Prepare the turnip: Mix together the chicken stock and Port in a heavy-based saucepan. Lightly season with salt and freshly ground pepper, bring to the boil and reduce to a simmer. Add the cubed turnips and cook for 15–20 minutes until tender. Remove from the heat and keep warm in the stock until ready to serve. Preheat the oven to 200°C.

Roast the rack of venison: Season the venison with salt and freshly ground pepper. Heat the vegetable oil in a heavy-based pan, add the venison and seal until evenly brown. Transfer to the oven and continue to cook for a further 20–25 minutes until medium-rare or longer if the meat is preferred less rare. Remove the venison from the oven and allow to rest for 20 minutes.

Cook the spätzle: The spätzle is best cooked in batches. Heat sufficient clarified butter to cover the base of a large non-stick frying pan. Add enough spätzle to cover the surface of the pan and sauté until it begins to crisp slightly. Season to taste with salt and freshly ground pepper. Drain the spätzle in a sieve and keep warm until ready to serve.

To serve: Heat the olive oil or rendered duck fat in a heavy-based pan, add the roasted garlic and warm through in the oven. Heat the Port wine jus over a gentle heat. Carve the rib of venison into four cutlets and lightly season with salt and freshly ground pepper. Cover each rib of venison with the herb crust and return to the oven until the crust begins to melt over the meat – take care not to leave it too long as the butter will separate from the herbs. Remove from the oven.

Drain the turnips. Spoon the spätzle into the centre of a warm plate and place a piece of venison onto them. Arrange the turnips and roasted garlic around the venison and drizzle the Port wine jus over and around the garnish.

Squab is young pigeon reared all year round especially for the table. Usually, it has not been fed anything besides 'pigeon milk', which is formed in the crops of both parents, looks like thick custard and is very high in protein. However, improved weight can be achieved by hand-feeding 10 day-old squabs three times a day on a diet of grain, peas, wheat and safflower. This makes their meat succulent, tender and flavourful with a distinctly milder gamey taste than is traditionally associated with game birds.

While there are several breeds and varieties of pigeon available, the most popular and perhaps the best for squab production is the White King, which has a stocky body with a pale yellow skin. It has a well-rounded breastbone and firm breasts with very lean and deep, red flesh. Reared for a period of four to six weeks before being processed, squab weigh approximately 450 g, making an ideal individual serving. They are dry-plucked to prevent any damage to the skin and tender flesh.

SQUAB

Choose whole, plump, fresh squab with the head and feet still attached. Prepare the birds for roasting by removing the head, neck, wings and feet. Discard the head and feet and reserve the neck and wings for stocks and sauces. Remove the wishbone, making it easier to carve the breasts when roasted. The legs have many tough tendons and sinews and will benefit from being confited (basic technique 1, page 215). Roast the breasts whole on the carcass to prevent them from shrinking and drying out during cooking. This will also add flavour to the meat.

Season the cavity of the squab with salt and freshly ground pepper and stuff with a crushed clove of garlic and a sprig of fresh thyme. Seal the squab in a hot, heavy-based pan with a little olive oil for 3–4 minutes until the skin is caramelised and brown, before transferring it to a hot oven to cook for a further 3 minutes. Squab is best served rare to medium-rare, beyond which it becomes dry, tough and tasteless. Allow the squab to rest for 10 minutes before boning the breasts from the carcass. Reserve the carcass for sauces as there is still plenty of flavour left in them.

ROULADE OF SQUAB AND FOIE GRAS WITH WARM POTATO SALAD

Serves 4

1	**Large piece pig's caul (see glossary)**
160 g	**Kipfler potatoes, or similar waxy potatoes**
2	**Squab**
2	**Cloves garlic, crushed**
2	**Sprigs fresh thyme**
40 ml	**Olive oil**
100 g	**Foie gras**
2	**Large outer leaves Savoy cabbage, blanched and refreshed**
25 ml	**Extra virgin olive oil**
24	**Lardons of pancetta**
1	**Large shallot, thinly sliced**
60 ml	**Truffle dressing (basic recipe 8, page 192)**
40 g	**Mesclun leaves**
	Salt
	Freshly ground pepper

Place the pig's caul under cold running water for 30 minutes to remove any traces of blood and until the water runs clear. Scrub the skins of the kipfler potatoes under cold water and cook in salted water over a medium heat until tender. Allow to cool before peeling and slicing into 5 mm thick slices. Refrigerate until ready to use.

Use a sharp boning knife to remove the legs, wings and wishbones from the squab, leaving the breasts on the carcass. The legs can be confited (basic technique 1, page 215) or chopped up and used for making a stock or sauce with the wings and wishbones. Season the skin and cavities of the squab with a generous pinch of salt and freshly ground pepper and stuff each cavity with a crushed clove of garlic and a sprig of thyme.

Heat 20 ml olive oil in a heavy-based pan over a medium heat. Add the squab, skin side down, and seal for 3–4 minutes until the skin is evenly brown. Remove the squab from the pan and place on a wire rack, skin side down. Spoon the pan juices into the cavities. Allow the squab to rest for at least 10 minutes before boning the breasts from the carcass. (Reserve the squab carcasses as they can be chopped up and roasted further to make a sauce.) Remove the wing bone from the squab breasts. Cut each breast three-quarters of the way through to open up like a book, exposing the flesh of the squab. Lightly season the flesh with salt and freshly ground pepper.

Cut the foie gras into batons and lightly season with salt and freshly ground pepper. Divide them down the centre of each squab breast. Close the breasts over into their original shape, making sure that the foie gras is enclosed inside the breasts.

Cut out four rounds of Savoy cabbage with a 9 cm pastry cutter and wrap each squab breast in a piece of the cabbage.

Remove the caul from the water and squeeze dry. Spread out onto a clean work surface and cut out four pieces large enough in which to wrap each squab breast. After wrapping each breast in one layer of caul, trim the sides neatly. Tightly wrap each breast in several layers of clingfilm, forming a cylinder. Refrigerate for 2 hours to allow the foie gras to firm.

Preheat the oven to 200°C. Remove the clingfilm from the squab breasts and lightly season with salt and freshly ground pepper. Heat the remaining 20 ml olive oil in a heavy-based pan, add the squab breasts and cook for 2 minutes until evenly brown. Transfer to the oven and cook for a further minute. Remove the breasts from the oven and allow to rest for 10 minutes. Heat 25 ml extra virgin olive oil in a heavy-based pan, add the lardons of pancetta and sauté until golden brown. Add the shallot and potatoes and sauté until lightly coloured. Lightly season with salt and freshly ground pepper. Remove from the pan, transfer to a sieve and allow the excess oil to drain off. Place the warm potato salad into a bowl and mix through 20 ml of the truffle dressing. Carve each squab breast into six even slices.

Place an 11 cm pastry ring in the centre of a plate and spoon the warm potato salad into it, pressing down with the back of the spoon so that it holds together. Arrange six overlapping slices of the squab to form a neat circle on top of the potato salad. Gently remove the pastry ring. Dress the mesclun with 10 ml of the truffle dressing, lightly season with salt and freshly ground pepper and arrange in the centre of the squab. Drizzle the remaining truffle dressing over and around the squab.

ROAST BREAST AND CONFIT OF SQUAB WITH CELERIAC RÉMOULADE AND SAUCE PERIGEUX

Serves 4

4	**Squab**	
I	**Small bulb celeriac**	
I	**Lemon**	
4	**Cloves garlic, crushed**	
4	**Sprigs fresh thyme**	
20 ml	**Olive oil**	
40 g	**Unsalted butter**	
100 ml	**Sauce Perigeux**	
	(basic recipe 31, page 198)	
150 ml	**Mayonnaise**	
	(basic recipe 10, page 192)	
5 g	**Chopped truffle**	
I tsp	**Julienne of flat-leaf parsley**	
20	**Slices of truffle**	
24	**Sprigs fresh chervil**	
	Salt	
	Freshly ground pepper	

Confit the squab legs 24 hours in advance of serving: Use a sharp boning knife to remove the legs, wings and wishbones from the squab, leaving the breasts on the carcass. Salt the squab legs and confit (basic technique I, page 215). Reserve the wings and wishbones for making a stock or sauce.

Preheat the oven to 200°C. Peel the celeriac, removing the thick outer layer and slice as thinly as possible using a mandolin. Cut the slices into julienne. Place the celeriac into a bowl of lightly salted cold water with a squeeze of lemon added to prevent it from discolouring.

Season the skin and cavities of the squab with a generous pinch of salt and freshly ground pepper and stuff each cavity with a crushed clove of garlic and a sprig of thyme.

Heat the olive oil in a heavy-based pan over a medium heat. Add the squab, skin side down, and seal for 3–4 minutes until the skin is evenly brown. Stand the squab upright in the pan to ensure even cooking of the breasts and transfer to the oven to cook for a further 3 minutes or until medium-rare. Remove the pan from the oven, add the butter and, as it melts, baste the breasts with it. Remove the squab from the pan and place onto a wire rack, skin side down. Spoon the pan juices into the cavities. Allow the squab to rest for at least 10 minutes before boning the breasts from the carcass. (Reserve the squab carcasses as they can be chopped up and roasted further to make a sauce.)

While the squab are resting, return the pan to the heat. Place the squab legs, skin side down, into the pan and cook for 2 minutes until the skin is brown and crisp. Turn the legs over, transfer to the oven and warm through for a further 2 minutes. Remove the legs from the pan and rest with the breasts while preparing the remainder of the dish.

Heat the sauce Perigeux in a heavy-based saucepan over a gentle heat. Drain the celeriac and dry on a clean kitchen cloth. Place the celeriac in a bowl and bind with the mayonnaise. Add the chopped truffle and julienne of flat-leaf parsley and mix through the celeriac. Season to taste with salt, freshly ground pepper and a squeeze of lemon.

Place a 6 cm wide pastry ring in the centre of a plate and spoon the celeriac rémoulade into it, pressing down with the back of the spoon. Gently remove the pastry ring. Place two squab breasts onto the celeriac and two legs on top of the breasts. Garnish with the sliced truffle. Spoon the sauce Perigeux over and around the squab and garnish with the sprigs of chervil.

ROAST SQUAB BREAST WITH ONION RISOTTO AND BALSAMIC JUS

Serves 4

4	**Squab**
2	**Cocktail onions**
5	**Cloves garlic, crushed**
4	**Sprigs fresh thyme**
40 ml	**Olive oil**
50 g	**Whole unsalted butter, chilled and diced**
1 ltr	**Chicken stock (basic recipe 22, page 195)**
½	**Small onion, finely chopped**
250 g	**Arborio rice (see glossary)**
40 g	**Parmesan cheese, freshly grated**
1½	**Spring onions, sliced**
1½ tbsp	**Sliced chives**
120 ml	**Balsamic jus (basic recipe 30, page 198)**
	Vegetable oil, for deep-frying the onion rings
1½ tbsp	**Plain flour, sifted and seasoned**
8	**Chive tips**
	Salt
	Freshly ground pepper

Confit the squab legs 24 hours in advance of serving: Use a sharp boning knife to remove the legs, wings and wishbones from the squab, leaving the breasts on the carcass. Salt the squab legs and confit (basic technique 1, page 215). Reserve the wings and wishbones for making a stock or sauce.

Preheat the oven to 200°C. Peel the cocktail onions and thinly slice into rounds. Separate the rounds into rings and place in a bowl until ready to use.

Season the skin and cavities of the squab with a generous pinch of salt and freshly ground pepper. Stuff each cavity with a crushed clove of garlic and a sprig of thyme.

Heat 20 ml olive oil in a heavy-based pan over a medium heat. Add the squab, skin side down, and seal for 3–4 minutes until the skin is evenly brown. Stand the squab upright in the pan to ensure even cooking of the breasts and transfer to the oven to cook for a further 3 minutes or until medium-rare. Remove the pan from the oven, add 20 g whole butter and, as it melts, baste the breasts with it. Remove the squab from the pan and place onto a wire rack, skin side down. Spoon the pan juices into the cavities. Rest the squab for 20 minutes before boning the breasts from the carcass. (Reserve the squab carcasses as they can be chopped up and roasted further to make a sauce.)

Bring the chicken stock to the boil and reduce to a simmer. Heat the remaining olive oil in a heavy-based saucepan, add a crushed clove of garlic and the onion and sweat without colouring for 2 minutes. Add the rice and seal without colouring for a further 2 minutes. Add a ladle of chicken stock and reduce the heat to a simmer. Continuously stir until the stock is absorbed and to prevent the rice from sticking. Continue to add the stock, one ladle at a time, and cook until absorbed and the rice is al dente. This will take 18–20 minutes.

While cooking the risotto, return the pan in which the squab was cooked to the heat. Place the squab legs, skin side down, into the pan and cook for 2 minutes until the skin is brown and crisp. Turn the legs over, transfer to the oven and warm through for a further 2 minutes. Remove the legs from the pan and rest with the breasts.

To finish the risotto, add the remaining whole butter and stir into the rice until fully incorporated. Add the Parmesan cheese and fold into the risotto. Remove and discard the garlic clove. Season to taste with salt and freshly ground pepper. Remove from the heat and stir in the sliced spring onions and chives. Keep warm while preparing the remainder of the dish.

Heat the balsamic jus in a heavy-based saucepan over a gentle heat. Heat the vegetable oil for deep-frying the onion rings to 180°C. Pass the onion rings through the flour, shaking-off any excess, and place them into the oil to cook until crisp and golden brown. Drain on kitchen paper to absorb any excess oil. Lightly season with salt and freshly ground pepper.

Carve the breasts from the squab and place with the legs in the oven to warm through for 2 minutes. Place a 10 cm pastry ring in the centre of a warm plate. Spoon the risotto into it and smooth with the back of the spoon. Gently remove the pastry ring. Place the squab breasts onto the risotto and two squab legs on top of the breasts. Spoon the balsamic jus over and around the squab and arrange a small stack of onion rings on top of the squab legs. Garnish with the chive tips.

ROAST SQUAB WITH FOIE GRAS TORTELLINI AND RED WINE JUS

Serves 4

FOIE GRAS TORTELLINI

30 g	**Mushroom duxelle**
	(basic recipe 57, page 204)
10 g	**Chopped truffle**
30 g	**Foie gras, diced**
1	**Small bunch chives, sliced**
200 g	**Plain pasta dough**
	(basic recipe 68, page 207)
	Egg wash of 1 free-range egg
	and 15 ml water

SQUAB

4	**Squab**
4	**Cloves garlic, crushed**
4	**Sprigs fresh thyme**
60 g	**Unsalted butter**
12	**Small shallots, peeled**
120 ml	**Red wine jus**
	(basic recipe 27, page 197)
70 ml	**Olive oil**
24	**Lardons of pancetta**
120 g	**Mixed wild mushrooms**
	Salt
	Freshly ground pepper

Prepare the foie gras tortellini: Place the mushroom duxelle into a bowl, add the chopped truffle, diced foie gras, sliced chives and mix together. Season to taste with salt and freshly ground pepper.

Cut the pasta dough into two pieces. Roll out both pieces with a rolling pin on a lightly floured work surface until they are 5 mm thick. Set a pasta machine on the thickest setting and feed through the first piece of pasta twice. Adjust the setting one notch and feed the pasta through twice again. Continue to roll the pasta until it is on the thinnest setting. Roll the second piece in the same way. When all the pasta is rolled, use an 8 cm plain pastry cutter to cut out 12 circles of pasta. Place the pasta on a plate and cover with clingfilm to prevent it from drying out.

Prepare the tortellini one at a time: Spoon 5 g foie gras mix into the centre of each circle of pasta. Brush the edge of each with the egg wash. Fold the pasta to make a semi-circle and press the edges together from one side to the other, pressing out any air from the pocket of pasta. Hold the tortellini in your hand, curl the two tips around the index finger and press together; then press the edges together again to ensure that they are firmly joined. Repeat with the remaining tortellini. Blanche in salted boiling water for 2 minutes and refresh in iced water. Drain well.

Use a sharp boning knife to remove the legs, wings and wishbones from the squab, leaving the breasts on the carcass. (Reserve the squab legs for confit (basic technique 1, page 215) and the wings and wishbones for making stock.) Preheat the oven to 200°C. Season the skin and cavities of the squab with a generous pinch of salt and freshly ground pepper and stuff each cavity with a crushed clove of garlic and a sprig of thyme.

Melt 40 g butter until foaming in a heavy-based pan and add the shallots. Cook until golden brown, season with salt and freshly ground pepper and drain. Bring the red wine jus to the boil, reduce to a simmer and add the shallots. Cook for 15–20 minutes until tender.

Heat 20 ml olive oil in a heavy-based pan over a medium heat. Add the squab, skin side down, and seal for 3–4 minutes until the skin is evenly brown. Stand the squab upright in the pan to ensure even cooking of the breasts and transfer to the oven to cook for a further 3 minutes or until medium-rare. Remove the pan from the oven, add 20 g butter and, as it melts, baste the breasts with it. Remove the squab from the pan and place onto a wire rack, skin side down. Spoon the pan juices into the cavities. Allow the squab to rest for 10 minutes before boning the breasts from the carcass. (Reserve the squab carcasses as they can be chopped and roasted further to make a sauce.)

Sauté the lardons until brown using the pan in which the squab were cooked, and drain on kitchen paper. Heat the remaining olive oil in a heavy-based pan, add the mushrooms and sauté for 3–4 minutes. Season to taste with salt and freshly ground pepper and drain. Reheat the tortellini in salted boiling water for 3–4 minutes and drain. Lightly season with salt and freshly ground pepper. Remove the braised shallots from the red wine jus and pass the jus through a fine sieve. Place two squab breasts side by side in the centre of a warm plate. Arrange three tortellini at equal distances around the squab and spoon the braised shallots, mushrooms and lardons between the tortellini. Drizzle the red wine jus over and around the garnish.

Chocolate has its origins in Central and South America. Since its discovery, pure chocolate has been mixed with many substances to temper its natural bitterness including honey, vanilla, musk, chilli, pepper, cinnamon, cloves, aniseed, alcohol and liqueurs. During the nineteenth century the French added butter, cream and sugar and created the silky, edible confection that we know as chocolate. Contemporary flavours are created by blending many varieties and flavours of cocoa beans.

Harvesting takes place twice a year when the beans in the pods of the cacao tree are split, the contents scraped out and placed in the sun to ferment. Roasted and crushed, the remaining nib is ground to a paste in temperature-controlled mills, causing it to release fat or cocoa butter. The mass emerges from the grinder as chocolate liquor which is cooled and hardened into blocks of unsweetened chocolate. Grinding the residue from the liquor produces cocoa, a highly concentrated powder with an intensely rich chocolate flavour.

CHOCOLATE

There are several types of chocolate: Couverture, Milk, White, Compound and Cocoa. Couverture is the best quality chocolate available. The liquor, together with sugar, milk solids and cocoa butter is refined and put through a process called conching. The chocolate mass is heated and worked backwards and forwards to develop the flavour and reduce moisture. Depending on the desired quality, conching can take anything from a few hours to a week or more.

For best results, use chocolate with a high cocoa butter content (60 per cent or more) to avoid the flavour from being diluted when other ingredients and flavourings are added. To melt chocolate, chop it into small pieces, place in a bowl and melt over gently simmering water. If water or steam comes into contact with the chocolate, the chocolate will seize and be rendered unusable.

Store chocolate in a cool, dry environment and it will keep for several months, even when opened. It can be refrigerated in hot climates and also frozen. Avoid extreme temperature fluctuations to prevent the chocolate from developing a 'bloom' which is unsightly but tasteless, unless the chocolate is stale.

WHITE CHOCOLATE AND HONEYCOMB MOUSSE WITH DRIED FRUIT AND NUTS

Serves 10

100 g	**Honeycomb** (basic recipe 89, page 211)
40	**Pistachio nuts, blanched and peeled (see glossary)**
165 g	**White chocolate, chopped into small pieces**
1	**Leaf gelatine**
25 ml	**Sugar syrup** (basic recipe 76, page 209)
250 ml	**Cream, chilled**
2	**Medium free-range egg whites**
1 tbsp	**Icing sugar, sifted**
30	**Slices semi-dried peach**
30	**Slices semi-dried quince**
20	**Slices semi-dried fig**
20	**Slices semi-dried apricot**
10	**Hazelnuts, skinned**
10	**Macadamia nuts, split in half**
10	**Almonds, skinned and split in half**
100 ml	**Crème anglaise** (basic recipe 80, page 209) **Frangelico to taste (see glossary)**

Prepare the ring moulds: Cover one end of 10 ring moulds, 7 cm wide × 3 cm deep, with clingfilm and set out on a tray. Break the honeycomb into 10 g pieces. Place a piece of honeycomb onto the clingfilm in the centre of each mould. Split 20 pistachio nuts in half and arrange four halves around the honeycomb.

Prepare the chocolate mousse: Melt the chocolate over a *bain-marie*. Soften the gelatine in cold water. Heat the sugar syrup in a small, heavy-based saucepan over a low heat. Squeeze out the gelatine, add to the sugar syrup and stir until dissolved. Remove from the heat and keep warm.

Whisk the cream to ribbon stage and refrigerate until ready to use. Whisk the egg whites to soft peaks with an electric mixer; reduce the speed, add the icing sugar and continue to beat until the mixture becomes shiny. Pass the melted chocolate through a fine sieve into the beaten egg whites, and continue to mix until the chocolate is fully incorporated. Pour in the dissolved gelatine and mix for a further 2 minutes.

Remove the bowl from the mixer and scrape down the sides with a spatula. Fold the cream through the chocolate mix until incorporated. Pour the chocolate mousse over the honeycomb and pistachio nuts to the top of the moulds. Refrigerate the tray of mousses for 3 hours to set.

Invert each mousse into the centre of a chilled bowl plate with the honeycomb and pistachio nuts facing upwards. Remove the clingfilm from the moulds. Run the tip of a sharp knife around the inside of the moulds and gently remove from the mousses. Arrange the semi-dried fruit and nuts around each mousse. Pour the crème anglaise into a stainless steel jug, add the Frangelico to taste and froth with a hand-held blender. Spoon a little of the Frangelico-flavoured crème anglaise over and around the dried fruit and nuts.

CHOCOLATE PITHIVIER WITH PRUNE AND ARMAGNAC ICE CREAM

Serves 6

125 ml	Milk
½	Vanilla bean, split and scraped
1½	Free-range egg yolks
90 g	Castor sugar
2½ tbsp	Plain flour, sifted
	Icing sugar for dusting
55 g	Dark chocolate with at least 60% cocoa solids, chopped
55 g	Softened, unsalted butter
1	Free-range egg
55 g	Almond meal
1 tbsp	Cocoa powder
	Armagnac to taste
700 g	Puff pastry (basic recipe 94, page 212)
	Egg wash of 1 free-range egg yolk and 10 ml milk
50 ml	Chocolate sauce (basic recipe 91, page 211)
6	Round chocolate tuilles, 5 cm in diameter (basic recipe 87, page 211)
360 ml	Prune and Armagnac ice cream (basic recipe 93, page 212)

Prepare the crème pâtissière: Scald the milk and vanilla bean in a heavy-based saucepan over low heat. Whisk together the egg yolks and 35 g castor sugar in a bowl until pale and double in volume. Whisk in the flour and continue to whisk until the mixture is smooth. Pour a third of the scalded milk onto the egg mixture and whisk thoroughly. Pour this back into the saucepan with the remaining milk, return to a low heat and cook for 5–6 minutes, stirring continuously until the crème pâtissière has thickened. Remove from the heat and pass through a fine sieve, discarding the vanilla bean. Sprinkle icing sugar onto the surface of the crème pâtissière to prevent a skin from forming and refrigerate until ready to use.

Prepare the chocolate filling: Melt the chocolate over a *bain-marie*. Cream together the butter and remaining castor sugar and stir in the egg, almond meal and cocoa powder. Add the melted chocolate and mix until the chocolate is fully incorporated. Add the Armagnac to taste. Beat the crème pâtissière into the chocolate mix until smooth. Refrigerate for 1 hour to firm up sufficiently to roll into 60 g balls. Place the chocolate balls on a tray and freeze until ready to use.

Prepare the pastry: Divide the puff pastry into two pieces; one of 300 g and the other of 400 g. Roll out the smaller piece of pastry to a thickness of 2 mm on a lightly floured surface. Use a 9 cm plain pastry cutter to cut out six round bases for the pithiviers. Place the bases on a tray and refrigerate while preparing the tops. Roll out the larger piece of pastry in the same way, but to a thickness of 3 mm. Cut out six tops with an 8 cm plain pastry cutter. Place the tops on the same tray as the bases and rest the pastry for 30 minutes in the fridge before assembling the pithiviers.

Assemble the pithiviers: Assemble the pithiviers one at a time to prevent the pastry from becoming too warm. Place a pastry base onto a lightly floured surface. Put a chocolate ball into the centre of the pastry base and brush the edge of the base with egg wash. Place a pastry top over the chocolate filling and mould it around the chocolate, removing any air pockets between the filling and pastry. Press together the two pieces of pastry to firmly join. The pithivier should be dome shaped with a 1 cm border. Place the 9 cm plain pastry cutter over the base of the pithivier and cut away any excess pastry. Refrigerate while preparing the remaining pithiviers. When all six pithiviers have been assembled, brush with egg wash and refrigerate for 30 minutes before marking.

Mark the border of the pastry at even intervals with the back of a knife. Mark the dome of the pithiviers at even intervals with the tip of the knife, starting each line from the centre of the dome and curving it downwards to the base – take care not to cut too deeply into the pastry. Lightly spray a baking tray with cold water and place the pithiviers onto it. Refrigerate for 30 minutes before baking. Preheat the oven to 220°C.

Bake the pithiviers for 8–10 minutes until crisp and golden. Remove the pithiviers from the oven. Increase the oven temperature to 240°C. Dust the Pithiviers with icing sugar and return to the oven for a further 1–2 minutes until golden and glazed. Fill a plastic squeeze bottle with the chocolate sauce.

Place a pithivier onto a plate with a chocolate tuille beside it. Set a scoop of prune and Armagnac ice cream onto the tuille. Squeeze a line of chocolate sauce onto the plate.

CARAMELISED LEMON TART WITH CHOCOLATE SORBET

Serves 12

CHOCOLATE SORBET

400 ml	Water
100 ml	Milk
150 g	Castor sugar
40 ml	Glucose
30 g	Cocoa powder
100 g	Dark chocolate with at least 60% cocoa solids, chopped
12	Round chocolate tuilles, 8 cm in diameter (basic recipe 87, page 211)

LEMON FILLING

6–8	Lemons
12	Free-range eggs
500 g	Castor sugar
400 ml	Thickened cream

SWEET PASTRY

250 g	Plain flour
200 g	Unsalted butter, diced and softened
100 g	Icing sugar
	Pinch salt
2	Free-range egg yolks, beaten
10 g	Unsalted butter, softened to grease the pastry ring
	Egg wash of 1 free-range egg yolk and 10 ml milk

Prepare the chocolate sorbet 12 hours in advance of serving: Bring the water, milk, castor sugar, glucose and cocoa powder to the boil in a heavy-based saucepan and continuously stir for 2 minutes. Reduce the heat to a simmer. Add the chocolate and stir until melted. Remove from the heat and allow to cool. Pass through a fine sieve and churn in an ice-cream machine until it becomes smooth and creamy. Transfer to a container and freeze until ready to use.

Prepare the lemon filling: Wash all the lemons and grate the zest of four. Cut all the lemons in half and squeeze out the juice. Pass the juice through a fine sieve and measure out 265 ml. Break the eggs into a bowl, add the castor sugar and whisk until pale and double in volume. Stir 265 ml lemon juice and the grated zest into the egg mix. Whip the cream to ribbon stage in a separate bowl and whisk into the egg mix. Refrigerate for 2 hours for the lemon zest to infuse before passing through a fine sieve. Discard the zest.

Prepare the sweet pastry: Sift the flour onto a work surface, make a well in the centre and place the softened butter into it. Sift the icing sugar onto the butter, add the salt and work into the butter with your fingertips. Pour on the egg yolks and mix well. Gradually draw in the flour and mix to a smooth pastry dough. Do not over-work, as it will become elastic. Roll out the pastry between two sheets of greaseproof paper to flatten; this makes it easier to roll out later. Refrigerate for 1 hour to rest before using.

Preheat the oven to 170°C. Brush a pastry ring, 21 cm x 3 cm deep, with softened butter and refrigerate for 10 minutes. Roll out the pastry to a thickness of 6 mm on a lightly floured surface. Place the pastry ring on a cold baking sheet lined with baking parchment and line with the pastry, leaving a slight overhang. Press the pastry into the corners of the pastry ring – take care not to tear it. Rest in the fridge for 10 minutes.

Line the inside of the tart case with greaseproof paper and fill with baking beans. Blind-bake (see glossary) the case for 15 minutes, remove from the oven and allow to cool. Remove the beans and greaseproof paper and inspect the pastry for any holes or cracks. If there are any, fill with the leftover pastry to prevent the filling from seeping out during cooking. Brush the pastry with egg wash and return to the oven for a further 5–6 minutes until it is lightly coloured. Remove the tart case from the oven and again, brush with the egg wash but do not return it to the oven at this stage. Allow the tart case to cool. Reduce the oven temperature to 140°C.

Place the tart case back in the oven, then pour in the lemon filling to the top of the pastry. Cook for 45–50 minutes until the tart is just set, as it will continue to cook in its own heat when removed from the oven. Remove the tart from the oven and allow to cool and set for 4 hours. Do not refrigerate as the pastry will soften. Trim off any excess pastry with the tip of a sharp knife so that the top of the tart is even.

Remove the pastry ring and cut the tart into 12 slices. Generously dust each slice with icing sugar and glaze with a blowtorch until the sugar melts and begins to caramelise. Take care not to burn the sugar as it will become bitter. Dust and glaze the tart a second time for a crisp finish. Place a slice of tart on a plate with a chocolate tuille beside it. Set a scoop of chocolate sorbet onto the tuille.

MONT BLANC WITH POACHED PEAR AND CHOCOLATE SAUCE

Serves 4

8	**Honey tuilles, 18 cm long x 4 cm wide (basic recipe 88, page 211)**
20	**Slices dried pear (basic recipe 95, page 213)**
1	**Fresh pear**
450 ml	**Coffee syrup (basic recipe 79, page 209)**
100 g	**Chestnut purée (basic recipe 90, page 211)**
½	**Vanilla bean, split and scraped**
50 ml	**Milk**
80 ml	**Cream**
50 ml	**Chocolate sauce (basic recipe 91, page 211)**

The honey tuilles and sliced dried pear can be made in advance and kept in separate airtight containers until ready to use.

Peel the fresh pear and place in a heavy-based saucepan. Cover with the coffee syrup and cook for 10 minutes over a very low heat. Allow the pear to cool in the syrup. Refrigerate the pear in the coffee syrup for 8 hours to allow the pear to absorb both the coffee flavour and colour before using.

Place the chestnut purée, vanilla bean, milk and 20 ml cream in a heavy-based saucepan and cook over a medium heat for 20–25 minutes. Stir continuously until the chestnut purée thickens. Pass the purée through a fine sieve into a clean bowl and discard the vanilla bean. Refrigerate until cold.

Whip the remaining cream to ribbon stage and fold through the chestnut purée until fully incorporated. Fit a piping bag with a Mont Blanc nozzle (see glossary) and fill with the chestnut cream. Refrigerate until ready to use.

Melt the chocolate sauce and pour into a plastic squeeze bottle. Remove the pear from the coffee syrup and cut into quarters. Core and slice each quarter into four slices lengthways.

Place a honey tuille in the centre of a plate and pipe a layer of chestnut cream onto it. Place a second tuille on top of the chestnut cream and pipe on another layer. Arrange five slices of dried pear into the top layer of chestnut cream. Arrange four slices of poached pear around the tuille. Squeeze small dots of chocolate sauce around the slices of poached pear.

The dessert menu comes to life from late spring to the end of summer with the arrival of different berries, stone fruit and soft fruit such as figs. For maximum flavour and taste, berries are at their best served whole or simply accompanied by a flavoured cream, light syrup, crisp pastry or a delicate curd. Use light, subtle flavours that won't overpower the berries.

Choose plump, bright, unblemished berries. Avoid any that are white around the stalk as they are under-ripe and will be hard, dry and tasteless. Once picked, the softer berries such as raspberries, white and red currants, wild Alpine strawberries, blackberries and mulberries will deteriorate quickly. Remove them from their punnets and refrigerate uncovered on a cloth-lined tray. If the berries need to be washed, plunge them quickly into cold water before they are hulled to prevent any water from getting into the fruit. Place on a clean kitchen cloth to absorb the excess water.

BERRIES

Check the insides of raspberries for tiny maggots that often burrow into them. Over-ripe and slightly blemished fruit bought cheaply can be turned into various inexpensive desserts. Once picked through and trimmed they can be puréed and used in coulis, sorbets, ice creams and bavarois.

Cook in a double boiler with a sprinkling of sugar over a very low heat for the berries to release their juice. Strain the juice, chill and serve with a selection of freshly sliced summer fruit such as white peaches, nectarines, plums and figs, and serve with a creamy mascarpone or fromage blanc sorbet.

Steep blackberries or raspberries in brandy, sugar and white wine vinegar for a sharp and intense berry vinegar (basic recipes 5 & 6, page 191). Add nut oils, mustard and seasoning to transform it into a dressing for warm game salads.

Berries, especially strawberries and raspberries, are ideal for jelly and jam-making because they are high in pectin.

MINESTRONE OF FRESH FRUITS WITH MASCARPONE SORBET

Serves 4

BERRY JUICE (makes I ltr)

I kg	**Ripe strawberries**
200 g	**Raspberries**
150 g	**Castor sugar**
750 g	**Ripe fruit and berries such as peaches, plums, black figs, raspberries, blueberries, blackberries and strawberries**
100 ml	**Champagne (optional)**

MASCARPONE SORBET (makes 750 ml)

500 g	**Mascarpone**
250 ml	**Sugar syrup (basic recipe 76, page 209)**
	Zest of ½ lime
	Juice of I lime

Prepare the berry juice: Remove and discard the stalks from the strawberries and roughly chop the flesh. Place in a bowl with the raspberries and the castor sugar. Mix together and cover with clingfilm. Place the bowl over a pot of simmering water and leave for I hour over a low heat. Remove from the heat and refrigerate for a further hour.

Line a sieve with a double layer of muslin cloth and place over a clean bowl. Pour the berry mix into the muslin cloth and allow the berry juice to filter through until only the dried berry pulp remains. Discard the pulp.

Prepare the mascarpone sorbet: Place the mascarpone in a bowl with the sugar syrup and grated lime zest. Gently mix together – take care not to over-beat or the mascarpone will become grainy. Transfer to an ice-cream machine and churn until firm and creamy. Add the lime juice and churn for a further minute. Transfer to a container and freeze until ready to use.

Prepare the fruit: Cut the peaches and plums in half, remove the stones and cut each half into four wedges. Cut the figs into six wedges. Clean the berries if necessary and hull. Arrange the fruit and berries in four chilled bowl plates. Stir the champagne through the berry juice and pour over the fruit. Make a quenelle of mascarpone sorbet using an oval ice-cream scoop and place in the centre of the fruit.

CHAMPAGNE CHIBOUST WITH RASPBERRY JELLY

Serves 8

RASPBERRY JELLY (makes 250 ml)

400 g	**Over-ripe raspberries**
200 g	**Over-ripe strawberries**
50 g	**Castor sugar**
2	**Leaves gelatine**

CHAMPAGNE CHIBOUST

50 ml	**Cream, chilled**
1½	**Leaves gelatine**
250 ml	**Champagne**
290 g	**Castor sugar**
5	**Free-range egg yolks**
20 ml	**Water**
3	**Free-range egg whites**
½ tbsp	**Icing sugar**
40 ml	**Raspberry coulis (basic recipe 82, page 209)**
80	**Raspberries, freshly hulled**

Prepare the raspberry jelly: Remove and discard the stalks from the raspberries and strawberries, roughly chop the flesh and place in a bowl with the castor sugar. Mix together and cover with clingfilm. Set the bowl over a pot of simmering water on a low heat and leave for 1 hour until the berries have released all their juices. Remove the bowl from the heat and refrigerate for 1 hour. Pass the juice through a double layer of muslin cloth and discard the pulp.

Soften the gelatine in cold water. Gently heat 50 ml berry juice in a small saucepan. Squeeze out the gelatine, add to the warm berry juice and stir until dissolved. Mix together both berry juices. Line a small, shallow tray with clingfilm and pour in the jelly to a depth of 1 cm. Refrigerate the jelly for 4 hours until set.

Prepare the Champagne Chiboust: Whip the cream to ribbon stage and refrigerate until ready to use. Soften the gelatine leaves in cold water.

Bring the champagne to the boil in a heavy-based saucepan. Remove from the heat and pour 50 ml of the champagne into a separate saucepan. Squeeze out the gelatine, add to the champagne and stir until dissolved. Keep in a warm place until ready to use.

Whisk together 100 g castor sugar and the egg yolks in a bowl until pale and double in volume. Pour the remaining 200 ml champagne onto the egg yolk mix. Cook over a very low heat in a heavy-based saucepan, stirring continuously with a wooden spoon for 10–12 minutes until the custard coats the back of the spoon. Stir in the champagne and gelatine, remove from the heat and pass through a fine sieve. Allow to cool.

Place the remaining castor sugar and 20 ml water in a heavy-based saucepan and heat to 121°C (use a sugar thermometer to gauge the temperature).

Place the egg whites and icing sugar in an electric mixer and whisk to firm peaks. Reduce the speed, slowly pour in the 121°C sugar syrup and continue to whisk until fully incorporated. Remove the bowl from the mixer, fold the egg and champagne mix through the meringue, and continue to mix until cool. Fold in the whipped cream and pour the Chiboust into 100 ml dariole moulds and refrigerate for 2 hours until set.

Fill a plastic squeeze bottle with raspberry coulis. Turn out the jelly onto a clean chopping board and cut out small cylinders of jelly using a 1 cm round plain pastry cutter. Run the tip of a knife around the inside of the Chiboust and invert into the centre of a plate. Surround the Chiboust with the jellies and fresh raspberries. Pipe small dots of the coulis between the jellies and raspberries.

MILLE-FEUILLE OF STRAWBERRIES WITH PISTACHIO CREAM

Serves 4

100 g	**Pistachio crème pâtissière** **(basic recipe 81, page 209)**
½	**Leaf gelatine**
5 ml	**Sugar syrup** **(basic recipe 76, page 209)**
150 ml	**Cream, chilled**
76	**Small strawberries**
70 ml	**Strawberry coulis** **(basic recipe 83, page 210)**
12	**Pistachio tuilles 7 cm x 7 cm** **(basic recipe 86, page 210)**
1 tsp	**Pistachio nuts, blanched, peeled** **and roughly chopped** **(see glossary)**
10 ml	**Pistachio syrup** **(basic recipe 77, page 209)**

Place the pistachio crème pâtissière into a bowl. Soak the gelatine in cold water to soften. Put the sugar syrup into a small heavy-based saucepan and warm over a low heat. Squeeze out the gelatine, add to the sugar syrup and stir until dissolved. Remove from the heat and whisk it into the pistachio crème pâtissière.

Whip the cream to ribbon stage and fold through the pistachio crème pâtissière until smooth — take care not to over-beat. Transfer the cream to a piping bag fitted with a 5 mm nozzle and refrigerate until ready to use.

Cut four strawberries into small dice and set aside until ready to use. Cut off the bases of the remaining strawberries so that they are all the same height. Place 50 ml strawberry coulis into a bowl, add the strawberries and lightly coat them with the coulis.

Squeeze a dot of the pistachio crème pâtissière in the centre of a plate and place a tuille on top of it to prevent it from sliding. Pipe a thin layer of pistachio crème pâtissière over the tuille to cover the entire surface. Arrange nine strawberries into three rows onto the tuille. Place a second tuille on top of the strawberries and pipe over a second layer of pistachio crème pâtissière. Arrange another nine strawberries onto the tuille. Top with a third tuille.

Spoon diced strawberries and chopped pistachio nuts around the mille-feuille. Drizzle small drops of the remaining strawberry coulis and pistachio syrup between them.

VANILLA CRÈME BRÛLÉE WITH BLACKBERRIES AND FIGS

Serves 6

15	**Free-range egg yolks**
105 g	**Castor sugar**
150 ml	**Milk**
900 ml	**Cream**
2	**Vanilla beans, split and scraped**
150 g	**White chocolate, chopped**
	Icing sugar for dusting
4	**Black figs**
48	**Blackberries**
100 ml	**Blackberry coulis**
	(basic recipe 84, page 210)
	Candied lemon peel of I lemon
	(basic recipe 96, page 213)

Prepare the crème brûlée 24 hours in advance of serving to allow it to set.

Preheat the oven to 95°C. Line a 15 cm wide x 24 cm long x 3 cm deep stainless steel tray with clingfilm. Place the egg yolks and castor sugar in a bowl and whisk together until pale and double in volume. Place the milk, cream and vanilla beans in a heavy-based saucepan and scald over a medium heat. Pour the milk and cream onto the egg yolks and castor sugar and whisk together. Remove the vanilla beans and pass the custard through a fine sieve into the clingfilm-lined tray. Place the tray into a roasting pan. Pour sufficient hot water into the roasting pan to come three-quarters of the way up the side of the custard tray to create a *bain-marie*. Cook the custard for 50–60 minutes until it reaches setting point. Gently shake the tray; the custard should be slightly soft in the centre. If it appears too runny, return it to the oven for a further 10 minutes before checking again. Carefully remove the *bain-marie* from the oven and allow the custard to cool in the *bain-marie*. Remove the cooled custard from the *bain-marie*, cover with clingfilm and refrigerate.

Place the chocolate in a bowl and melt over a pot of simmering water. Turn out the set custard onto a clean chopping board, trim 5 mm off the sides and spread the melted chocolate over the surface using a palette knife. Return it to the fridge for the chocolate to harden. Invert the set custard so that the chocolate forms the base and cut into six squares, 7 cm x 7 cm.

Generously dust the tops with icing sugar and glaze each square with a blowtorch until the sugar caramelises – take care not to burn the sugar as it will become bitter. Dust and glaze the crème brûlée a second time for an extra crisp glaze. Quarter the figs and place in a bowl with the blackberries and 50 ml blackberry coulis and gently coat the fruit with the coulis. Place the crème brûlée in the centre of a chilled plate and spoon the fruit around it. Drizzle a little more coulis over and around the fruit and garnish with the strips of candied lemon peel.

Citrus is a great all-year round fruit with many different varieties popping in and out of season. It has endless uses, particularly for seasoning and flavouring different foods; from a simple squeeze of fresh juice, to a sauce such as a fish velouté, a hollandaise sauce or beurre blanc. By drying and grinding the zest to a powder and mixing with Maldon sea salt it can be used as a sharp, tangy seasoning for fish and shellfish like pan-fried scallops, red mullet and John Dory. It is also used to season chicken, duck and guinea fowl. Citrus is commonly found in Asian cuisine, especially in Thai and Vietnamese dishes.

Use the zest to infuse oils and vinaigrettes such as lemon oil (basic recipe 16, page 193), lemon à la Grecque (basic recipe 2, page 191) and escabèche or, when marinating meats to confit, or fish for soups and stews such as bouillabaisse.

CITRUS

Citrus also plays a big role in the pastry kitchen; a dessert or tangy sorbet made from citrus fruit such as pink grapefruit, blood orange or lime is a refreshing and light way to end a meal.

Before using the zest, remove the pith, which is very bitter. Use a swivel peeler to yield wide strips of peel and use the tip of a knife to remove the layer of white pith.

Syrups and crème anglaise can be infused with zest to make citrus-flavoured custards, curds, bavarois, crème brûlée and ice creams. Blanche in several changes of water to remove the bitterness of the zest and cook in sugar syrup (basic recipe 76, page 209). Then dip into either sugar or chocolate to make delicious, inexpensive petits fours. Grate the zest into tuille mixes or batter to make orange tuilles or lemon financiers.

LIME BAVAROIS WITH CITRUS SALAD

Serves 8

LIME BAVAROIS

315 ml	**Crème anglaise** (basic recipe 80, page 209)
3	**Limes, grated zest and juice**
2	**Leaves gelatine**
250 ml	**Cream, chilled**
75 ml	**Sugar syrup** (basic recipe 76, page 209)

CITRUS SALAD

24	**Lime segments**
24	**Ruby grapefruit segments**
24	**Orange segments**
150 ml	**Sugar syrup** (basic recipe 76, page 209)
20 ml	**Crème de Menthe (see glossary)**
20 ml	**Campari (see glossary)**
20 ml	**Grand Marnier (see glossary)**

Prepare the ring moulds: Cover one end of eight ring moulds, 6 cm wide × 3 cm deep, with clingfilm and set out on a tray.

Pour the crème anglaise into a bowl, add the lime zest and juice and whisk into the crème anglaise. Cover with clingfilm and refrigerate for 4 hours to allow the lime to infuse before passing through a fine sieve, discarding the lime zest. (The anglaise will be sharp at this stage but will become diluted once the cream is added.)

Soften the gelatine in cold water. Whip the cream to ribbon stage and refrigerate until ready to use. Place the sugar syrup in a small saucepan, bring to the boil and reduce to a simmer. Squeeze out the gelatine, add to the sugar syrup and stir until dissolved. Remove from the heat and stir into the lime-flavoured crème anglaise. Fold the cream through the crème anglaise and pour the bavarois to the top of the moulds. Refrigerate for 6–8 hours until set.

Place the three different citrus fruit segments into separate bowls and pour 50 ml sugar syrup over each one. Add the Crème de Menthe to the lime segments. Add the Campari to the grapefruit segments. Add the Grand Marnier to the orange segments. Refrigerate and allow the segments to soak up the flavour and colour of the alcohols while the bavarois are setting. Drain the segments from the syrup and lay on a clean kitchen cloth to absorb excess syrup.

Place the bavarois mould in the centre of a chilled bowl plate. Remove the clingfilm, run the tip of a knife around the edge of the mould and gently remove from the bavarois. Arrange three overlapping segments of each citrus fruit around the bavarois; starting with the orange, followed by grapefruit and finally, the lime. Spoon in the orange syrup to cover the surface of the bowl plate.

RAVIOLI OF PINEAPPLE WITH LIME SORBET AND PASSION FRUIT JELLY

Serves 4

PASSION FRUIT JELLY

175 ml	**Fresh passion fruit pulp**
50 ml	**Orange juice, freshly squeezed and passed through a fine sieve**
2¼	**Leaves gelatine**
125 ml	**Sugar syrup (basic recipe 76, page 209)**
	Cointreau to taste (see glossary)

PINEAPPLE RAVIOLI

1	**Fresh pineapple**
320 ml	**Lime sorbet (basic recipe 92, page 212)**

GARNISH

	Pulp of 1 passion fruit
50 ml	**Lime syrup (basic recipe 78, page 209)**
1	**Banana**
1	**Wedge of watermelon, cut into 8 balls with a Parisienne scoop (see glossary)**
12	**Fresh Raspberries**
8	**Fresh cherries, pitted and halved**

Prepare the passion fruit jelly: Place the passion fruit pulp in a blender and blend for 45 seconds. Pass through a fine sieve over a bowl to catch the juice and discard the seeds. Measure 150 ml passion fruit juice into a bowl, add the orange juice and whisk together.

Soften the gelatine in cold water. Bring the sugar syrup to the boil and reduce to a simmer. Squeeze out the gelatine, add to the sugar syrup and stir until dissolved. Remove from the heat. Pour the sugar syrup and gelatine into the passion fruit and orange juice and whisk together. Add the Cointreau to taste. Line a small, shallow tray with clingfilm and pour the jelly into it to a depth of 1 cm. Refrigerate for 4 hours until the jelly is set.

Prepare the pineapple ravioli: Peel the pineapple and cut 16 thin slices. Allow four slices for each ravioli. Line four small, rounded espresso cups or a mould of similar shape with clingfilm. Arrange three overlapping slices of pineapple to cover the entire inner surface of the mould, making sure that there are no gaps and that there is sufficient over-hang to enclose the lime sorbet.

Cut out the remaining four slices of pineapple with an appropriate-sized, fluted pastry cutter for the ravioli bases. Remove the lime sorbet from the freezer and work it with a spoon until smooth. Fill each pineapple mould to the top with the sorbet. Fold the overhang of pineapple over to enclose the sorbet and place in the freezer while preparing the jelly and fruit.

Prepare the garnish: Turn out the passion fruit jelly onto a clean chopping board and cut into 1 cm cubes. Mix the passion fruit pulp into the lime syrup. Slice the banana into eight pieces.

Place the pineapple base for the ravioli in the centre of a chilled bowl plate. Invert the pineapple ravioli, remove the clingfilm and set in the centre of the pineapple base. Arrange the fruits and passion fruit jelly around the pineapple ravioli. Spoon the passion fruit and lime syrup over and around the fruit.

CITRUS SORBETS WITH MACERATED FRUIT

Serves 4

CITRUS GARNISH

16	**Orange segments**
5 ml	**Cointreau (see glossary)**
16	**Ruby grapefruit segments**
5 ml	**Campari (see glossary)**
	Pulp of 1 passion fruit

ORANGE SORBET

150 ml	**Sugar syrup**
	(basic recipe 76, page 209)
100g	**Castor sugar**
	Grated zest of 1 orange
750 ml	**Orange juice, freshly squeezed**

GRAPEFRUIT SORBET

350 ml	**Sugar syrup**
	(basic recipe 76, page 209)
100 g	**Castor sugar**
	Grated zest of 1 grapefruit
750 ml	**Grapefruit juice, freshly squeezed**

LEMON SORBET

200 ml	**Water**
550 ml	**Sugar syrup**
	(basic recipe 76, page 209)
	Grated zest of 1 lemon
225 ml	**Lemon juice, freshly squeezed**

TUILLES

4	**Tuilles (basic recipe 85, page 210)**

Prepare the citrus garnish: Macerate the orange segments in the Cointreau and the grapefruit segments in the Campari. Refrigerate until ready to use.

Prepare the orange sorbet: Place the sugar syrup and castor sugar in a heavy-based pan over a medium heat and stir until the sugar has dissolved. Remove the syrup from the heat and add the grated orange zest to infuse. When cold, whisk the orange juice into the syrup and pass through a fine sieve, discarding the zest. Churn the orange syrup in an ice-cream machine until it becomes soft and icy. Transfer the sorbet to a container and freeze until ready to use.

Prepare the grapefruit sorbet in the same way as the orange sorbet.

Prepare the lemon sorbet: Bring the water and sugar syrup to the boil and follow the same method as for the orange and grapefruit sorbet.

Strain the orange and grapefruit segments from the alcohol and drain on kitchen paper to absorb excess juice. Place a tuille in the centre of a chilled plate. Arrange four grapefruit segments on one side of the tuille and four orange segments on the other side. Spoon the passion fruit pulp over the orange segments. Make quenelles of each sorbet using an oval ice-cream scoop. Set the lemon sorbet onto the tuille, the orange sorbet onto the orange segments and the grapefruit sorbet onto the grapefruit segments. Serve immediately.

MILLE-FEUILLE OF RASPBERRIES WITH LEMON CURD

Serves 4

3	**Lemons**
1½	**Free-range eggs**
55 g	**Castor sugar**
40 ml	**Cream, chilled**
9	**Sheets ready-made filo pastry** **(see glossary)**
20 ml	**Clarified butter**
	Icing sugar for glazing
48	**Raspberries**
40 ml	**Raspberry coulis** **(basic recipe 82, page 209)**

Wash the lemons under cold water and grate the zest of 1 into a bowl. Juice the lemons and pass the juice through a fine sieve into a separate bowl. Measure 50 ml lemon juice and add to the zest. Whisk together the eggs and castor sugar until pale and double in volume and whisk in the lemon zest and juice. Whisk the cream to ribbon stage and stir into the egg mix. Cover with clingfilm and refrigerate for 2 hours to allow the lemon flavour to infuse the curd. Pass the lemon curd through a fine sieve and discard the zest.

Preheat the oven to 90°C. Line the bottom of four moulds, 4 cm wide x 4.5 cm deep, with clingfilm, and again with aluminium foil. Place the moulds into a small roasting pan and fill each one to the top with 50 ml lemon curd. Pour sufficient warm water into the tray to come three-quarters of the way up the side of the moulds to create a *bain-marie*. Place the *bain-marie* into the oven and cook the lemon curd for 1 hour 40 minutes until the curd is just set. Carefully remove the *bain-marie* from the oven and allow the curd to cool in it. Remove the curds from the *bain-marie* and refrigerate until ready to use.

Adjust the oven to 170°C. Spread out three sheets of the filo pastry on a clean work surface. Brush each sheet with clarified butter and cover each with a second sheet of filo pastry. Brush the second sheet with clarified butter and cover with a third sheet of filo pastry. Cut out four circles from each of the filo pastries using an 8.5 cm plain pastry cutter. Cut a circle from each of the 8.5 cm filo pastry circles using a 4 cm plain pastry cutter – leave a half-moon shape that will perfectly wrap around the lemon curds.

Dredge the filo pastry with a heavy layer of icing sugar and transfer onto a lightly buttered baking tray. Cover the filo pastry with a second baking tray of the same size to keep the pastries flat while baking. Place in the oven and bake for approximately 5 minutes until the pastries are crisp and golden. Remove the glazed pastries from the oven and transfer to a wire rack until cool. Store the pastries in an airtight container until ready to use.

Place the raspberries in a bowl and coat with 25 ml raspberry coulis. Pour the remaining coulis into a small plastic squeeze bottle. Place a filo pastry disc in the centre of a plate, glazed side up. Set the lemon curd in the cut-out area with the aluminum foil facing up; remove the foil and the clingfilm from the mould. Run the tip of a sharp knife around the inside of the mould and carefully remove. Place six raspberries neatly around the filo pastry. Set a second pastry disc on top of the raspberries. Arrange another six raspberries onto the pastry and top with a third pastry disc, glazed side up. Squeeze a line of small dots of raspberry coulis around the filo pastry.

BASIC RECIPES

Basic Recipe 1

À LA GRECQUE
Makes 500 ml

100 ml	Champagne vinegar
250 ml	Water or chicken stock (basic recipe 22, page 195)
150 ml	Extra virgin olive oil
	Juice of 1 lemon
1	Pinch saffron threads
1	Sprig fresh rosemary
1	Sprig fresh thyme
1	Bay leaf
4	Cloves garlic, crushed
20	White peppercorns
20	Coriander seeds
	Pinch Maldon sea salt

Combine all the ingredients in a heavy-based saucepan and simmer over a low heat for 20 minutes. Remove from the heat and allow to cool. Remove the rosemary, thyme, bay leaf and garlic and discard. Store the à la Grecque in a parfait jar and refrigerate until ready to use.

Basic Recipe 2

LEMON À LA GRECQUE
Makes 20 portions

5	Lemons
100 ml	À la Grecque (basic recipe 1, this page)

Wash the lemons under cold water. Remove the peel with a swivel peeler to obtain wide strips. Remove all the pith from the peel using a sharp, thin-bladed knife. Trim the sides of the peel and cut into 5 mm dice. Place the diced lemon peel in a heavy-based pan and add the à la Grecque. Cook over a very low heat for about 1 hour until the lemon peel softens. Remove from the heat and allow to cool. Leave the lemon in the vinaigrette. Store the lemon à la Grecque in a parfait jar and refrigerate until ready to use.

Variation: Slice the lemons into thin rounds. Leave the skin on and cook in the same way.

Basic Recipe 3

MUSHROOM À LA GRECQUE
Makes 250 g

200 ml	À la Grecque (basic recipe 1, this page)
25 ml	Olive oil
150 g	Button mushrooms
50 g	Oyster mushrooms
50 g	Shimiji mushrooms
1 tsp	Sliced chives
1 tsp	Chopped tarragon
1 tsp	Chopped flat-leaf parsley
	Salt
	Freshly ground pepper

Warm the à la Grecque in a heavy-based saucepan over a low heat. Heat the olive oil in a heavy-based pan and sauté all the mushrooms until golden brown. Drain the mushrooms, transfer to a bowl and pour over the warm à la Grecque. Season to taste with salt and freshly ground pepper. Store the mushroom à la Grecque in a parfait jar and refrigerate until ready to use. Add the herbs just before serving to prevent them from discolouring. In addition to the varieties listed, any type of mushroom can be used such as cep, morel or trompette des morts.

Basic Recipe 4

SAUCE BOIS BOUDRAN
Makes 400 ml

75 ml	Walnut oil
75 ml	Peanut oil
50 ml	Cabernet Sauvignon vinegar
85 g	Tomato ketchup
5 ml	Worcestershire sauce
	Tabasco sauce to taste
100 g	Shallots, chopped
	Salt
	Freshly ground pepper

Whisk together the walnut and peanut oils. Add the Cabernet Sauvignon vinegar, tomato ketchup, Worcestershire sauce, Tabasco and the shallots. Season to taste with salt and freshly ground pepper.

Basic Recipe 5

BLACKBERRY VINEGAR
Makes 750 ml

1 kg	Frozen blackberries
750 ml	White wine vinegar
130 ml	Brandy
85 g	Sugar

Defrost the blackberries and divide in half. Blend half the blackberries into a purée and pass through a fine sieve, discarding the seeds. Cover the purée and refrigerate until ready to use. Macerate the remaining blackberries in the white wine vinegar, brandy and sugar for 12 hours. Place the whole, macerated blackberries and the purée in a heavy-based saucepan and bring to the boil. Reduce the heat to a simmer and cook for 1 hour or until the blackberries have reduced by half. Skim frequently to remove any impurities that float to the surface. Line a sieve with a layer of muslin cloth and place over a bowl. Pour the blackberries into it and leave the vinegar to filter through until the pulp in the sieve is dry. Discard the blackberry pulp. Store the blackberry vinegar in a parfait jar until ready to use.

Basic Recipe 6

BLACKBERRY AND WALNUT VINAIGRETTE
Makes 1 ltr

40 g	Dijon mustard
50 g	Hot English mustard
25 ml	Champagne vinegar
25 ml	Sherry vinegar
150 ml	Blackberry vinegar (basic recipe 5, this page)
600 ml	Walnut oil
150 ml	Hazelnut oil
2	Cloves garlic, peeled
	Salt
	Freshly ground pepper

Place the Dijon and English mustards in a bowl. Whisk in the champagne, sherry and blackberry vinegars followed by the walnut and hazelnut oils. Season to taste with salt and freshly ground pepper. Pour the vinaigrette into a bottle and add the garlic. Refrigerate the blackberry and walnut vinaigrette until ready to use. Shake well to re-emulsify the vinaigrette before using and discard the garlic cloves.

Basic Recipe 7

BEETROOT VINAIGRETTE
Makes 550 ml

1	Small, cooked beetroot (basic technique 7, page 216)
1 tsp	Dijon mustard
1¼ tsp	Hot English mustard
50 ml	Champagne vinegar
50 ml	Sherry vinegar
175 ml	Walnut oil
150 ml	Grapeseed oil
2	Cloves garlic, peeled
	Salt
	Freshly ground pepper

Peel the beetroot, cut into small pieces and blend to a purée. Pass the beetroot purée through a fine sieve over a bowl. Press down to extract as much juice and flavour as possible. Place the Dijon and English mustards in a bowl. Whisk in the champagne and sherry vinegars and the beetroot juice, followed by the walnut and grapeseed oils. Season to taste with salt and freshly ground pepper. Pour the vinaigrette into a bottle and add the garlic. Refrigerate the beetroot vinaigrette until ready to use. Shake well to re-emulsify the vinaigrette before using and discard the garlic cloves.

Basic Recipe 8

TRUFFLE DRESSING
Makes 500 ml

150 ml	Veal stock (basic recipe 23, page 196)
125 ml	Extra virgin olive oil
25 ml	Truffle juice
125 ml	Aged balsamic vinegar
50–75 ml	Truffle oil
20 g	Chopped truffle
	Salt
	Freshly ground pepper

Blend together the veal stock and the extra virgin olive oil using a hand-held blender. Add the truffle juice and balsamic vinegar. As truffle oil has an intense flavour, slowly add it to taste. Stir in the chopped truffle and season to taste with salt and freshly ground pepper. Pour the truffle dressing into a bottle and refrigerate until ready to use. The dressing will solidify in the fridge. Bring the truffle dressing back to pouring consistency by standing the bottle in warm water for 30–60 seconds and shake well before using.

Basic Recipe 9

VIETNAMESE DRESSING
Makes 150 ml

10 ml	Sesame oil
1	Small shallot, finely chopped
15 g	Pickled ginger, chopped
10 g	Fresh ginger, chopped
¼	Small fresh chilli, de-seeded and chopped
35 ml	Rice wine vinegar
40 ml	Sugar syrup (basic recipe 76, page 209)
40 ml	Dashi
10 ml	Kikkoman light soy sauce
15 ml	Pickled ginger juice
10 ml	Nam pla
2	Limes, juiced

Heat the sesame oil in a heavy-based pan and sweat the shallots, gingers and chilli without colouring. Add the rice wine vinegar and reduce by a third. Add the sugar syrup, dashi and soy sauce and bring to the boil. Reduce the heat and simmer for 30 minutes. Remove from the heat and add the pickled ginger juice, nam pla and fresh lime juice to taste. Allow the Vietnamese dressing to cool before using.

Basic Recipe 10

MAYONNAISE
Makes 500 ml

2	Free-range egg yolks
¾ tsp	Dijon mustard
30 ml	White wine vinegar
500 ml	Peanut oil
1	Lemon
	Salt
	Freshly ground pepper

Whisk the egg yolks, mustard and vinegar in a bowl until pale and double in volume. Add the peanut oil to the egg yolks in a slow, steady stream. Continue to whisk until all the oil is fully incorporated. Season to taste with salt, freshly ground pepper and a squeeze of lemon. If the mayonnaise is too thick, thin with a dash of cold water. Cover with clingfilm and refrigerate the mayonnaise until ready to use.

Basic Recipe 11

SAUCE GRIBICHE
Makes 300 ml

2	Free-range hard-boiled egg yolks
1 tsp	Dijon mustard
250 ml	Vegetable oil
25 ml	White wine vinegar
30 g	Capers, rinsed and finely chopped
30 g	Gherkins, finely chopped
1 tsp	Chopped herbs, equal quantities of parsley, chive, tarragon and chervil
1	Lemon
	Salt
	Freshly ground pepper

Place the hard-boiled egg yolks and mustard in a bowl and mix to a paste. Pour in the oil in a slow, steady stream, whisking until fully incorporated. Add the vinegar and fold in the capers, gherkins and chopped herbs. Season to taste with salt, freshly ground pepper and a squeeze of lemon. Refrigerate the sauce gribiche until ready to use.

Basic Recipe 12

TAPENADE
Makes 150 g

125 g	Pitted, ripe black olives
10 g	Marinated anchovy fillets
20 g	Capers, rinsed
½	Clove garlic, crushed
10–15 ml	Extra virgin olive oil
1 tsp	Chopped flat-leaf parsley
	Freshly ground pepper

Blend the olives, anchovies, capers and garlic to a smooth paste in a food processor. Add the extra virgin olive oil. Remove the tapenade from the food processor and only season with the freshly ground pepper as the anchovies and capers are very salty. Store the tapenade in an airtight jar. Cover the tapenade with a thin layer of extra virgin olive oil and refrigerate. Spoon out as required and add freshly chopped parsley to taste just before serving.

Basic Recipe 13

PESTO
Makes 250 ml

40 g	**Fresh basil leaves**
40 g	**Pine nuts, toasted**
25 g	**Garlic, finely chopped**
50 g	**Parmesan cheese, freshly grated**
125 ml	**Extra virgin olive oil**
1	**Lemon**
	Salt
	Freshly ground pepper

Blanche the basil leaves in boiling water for 15 seconds and refresh in iced water. Drain the basil and dry on a clean kitchen cloth. Blend together the pine nuts, garlic and Parmesan cheese in a food processor until it is a fine mix. Add the basil and continue to blend. Pour in the oil in a steady stream until it becomes a smooth purée. Season to taste with salt, freshly ground pepper and a squeeze of lemon. Store the pesto in an airtight parfait jar. Cover the pesto with a thin layer of extra virgin olive oil to avoid discolouration and refrigerate.

Note: The ratio of pine nuts and garlic to basil in this recipe is deliberately high as the flavours will be diluted when mixed through the potato for the Swordfish Niçoise dish. If making for another purpose, reduce pine nuts and garlic to taste.

Basic Recipe 14

PESTO OIL
Makes 125 ml

40 g	**Fresh basil leaves**
25 g	**Pine nuts, toasted**
10 g	**Garlic, finely chopped**
25 g	**Parmesan cheese, freshly grated**
125 ml	**Extra virgin olive oil**
1	**Lemon**
	Salt
	Freshly ground pepper

Blanche the basil leaves in boiling water for 15 seconds and refresh in iced water. Drain the basil and dry on a clean kitchen cloth. Blend together the pine nuts, garlic and Parmesan cheese in a food processor until a fine mix is achieved. Add the basil and continue to blend. Pour in the oil in a steady stream until it becomes a smooth purée. Season to taste with salt, freshly ground pepper and a squeeze of lemon. Pour the pesto into a sieve lined with a double layer of muslin cloth set over a bowl to collect the oil; discard the pulp. Store the pesto oil in a sealed bottle and refrigerate until ready to use.

Basic Recipe 15

BASIL OIL
Makes 400 ml

150 g	**Fresh basil leaves**
350 ml	**Extra virgin olive oil**
2	**Cloves garlic, peeled and finely chopped**
	Lemon juice to taste
	Salt
	Freshly ground pepper

Blanche the basil leaves in boiling water for 15 seconds and refresh in iced water. Drain the basil and dry on a clean kitchen cloth. Pour 50 ml olive oil into a blender and, with the motor running, add the garlic and blend to a purée. Feed the basil into the blender, pour in the remaining oil and continue to blend until smooth. Season to taste with salt, freshly ground pepper and a squeeze of lemon. Pour the basil purée into a sieve lined with a double layer of muslin cloth set over a bowl to collect the oil; discard the pulp. Store the basil oil in a sealed bottle and refrigerate until ready to use.

Basic Recipe 16

LEMON OIL
Makes 1 ltr

20	**Lemons**
1 tsp	**Salt**
1 tbsp	**Sugar**
500 ml	**Grapeseed oil**
500 ml	**Extra virgin olive oil**

Wash the lemons and remove the zest over a large bowl to catch all the spray released from the peel. Dissolve the salt and sugar in the juice of two lemons in a heavy-based pot. Add the oils and lemon zest. Place over a very low heat and gently warm the oil. Remove from the heat and allow the lemon zest to infuse in the oil for 24 hours. Pass the oil through a sieve lined with a double layer of muslin cloth. Discard the zest. Store the lemon oil in a sealed bottle and refrigerate until ready to use.

Basic Recipe 17

TOMATO OIL

Makes 600 ml

300 ml	Extra virgin olive oil
2	Cloves garlic, finely chopped
1/2	Small onion, finely chopped
2	Shallots, finely chopped
1	Stick celery, finely chopped
1/2	Head fennel, finely chopped
1	Small leek, white part only, finely chopped
1/2	Split chilli, de-seeded and finely chopped
40 g	Tomato paste
2	Sprigs fresh thyme
1/2	Bay leaf
1	Sprig fresh rosemary
4	White peppercorns, crushed
6	Coriander seeds, crushed
300 ml	Grapeseed oil
1	Medium bunch basil, roughly chopped
	Salt
	Freshly ground pepper

Heat 50 ml extra virgin olive oil in a heavy-based pan and add the chopped vegetables. Sweat for 5 minutes until tender without colouring. Add the tomato paste, thyme, bay leaf, rosemary, peppercorns and coriander seeds and continue to cook for a further 5 minutes. Stir to prevent the tomato paste from sticking. Add the remaining olive oil and 300 ml grapeseed oil and continue to cook over a very low heat for 1 hour. Remove the oil from the heat and refrigerate to cool before adding the basil. Allow the basil to infuse the oil for 24 hours. Pass through a sieve lined with a double layer of muslin cloth set over a bowl to collect the oil. When the oil has drained, discard the vegetables. Adjust the seasoning if necessary. Store the tomato oil in a sealed bottle and refrigerate until ready to use.

Basic Recipe 18

CRUSTACEAN OIL

Makes 750 ml

700 g	Fresh prawn or lobster shells and heads, uncooked
750 ml	Extra virgin olive oil
100 g	Tomato paste
2	Cloves garlic
2	Star anise
2	Red chillies, split and de-seeded
12	White peppercorns, crushed
12	Coriander seeds, crushed
2	Sprigs fresh thyme
2	Sprigs fresh tarragon
2	Dried bay leaves
	Pinch Maldon sea salt
	Freshly ground pepper

Preheat the oven to 130°C. Clean and chop the shells into small pieces. Heat 50 ml extra virgin olive oil in a roasting tray and add the shells. Transfer to the oven and roast the shells for 1–1½ hours. Stir frequently until they become dry, brittle and deeply coloured. Stir the tomato paste into the shells. Return to the oven and continue to roast for a further 15 minutes. Stir from time to time to prevent the paste from burning. Remove from the oven and add the garlic, star anise, chillies, peppercorns, coriander seeds, herbs, Maldon salt and freshly ground pepper; mix through the roasted shells. Spoon the mix into a sterilised kilner jar and pour the extra virgin olive oil over the shells to fill the jar.

Place the sealed jar in a large pot and surround with a kitchen cloth to prevent it from knocking against the side. Pour in enough water to reach the lid of the jar. Bring the water to the boil, reduce to a simmer and cook for 45 minutes. Remove the jar from the water and allow to cool before refrigerating. The longer the crustacean oil is refrigerated, the more intense the flavour and colour. When ready to use, pass the oil through a sieve lined with a double layer of muslin cloth set over a bowl to collect the oil. Discard the shells.

Note: For an intensely coloured and flavoured oil, fresh crustacean shells are preferable. However, cooked shells may also be used, which will result in a less intense flavour and colour.

Basic Recipe 19

BRINE FOR SNAILS

Makes 1.2 ltr

100 ml	Port
20 ml	Vegetable oil
1	Onion, finely chopped
1/2	Carrot, peeled and finely chopped
1	Small leek, white part only, finely chopped
1	Clove garlic, finely chopped
65 ml	Cabernet Sauvignon vinegar
350 ml	Red wine
900 ml	Water
1	Bay leaf
2	Sprigs fresh rosemary
1	Sprig fresh thyme
10	White peppercorns
	Salt
48	Pre-cooked snails (see glossary)

Reduce the Port by half and set aside. Heat the vegetable oil in a heavy-based pan and sauté the onion, carrot, leek and garlic until golden brown. Remove from the heat and drain. Put the sautéed vegetables into a heavy-based saucepan and add the remaining ingredients, except the snails. Bring to the boil and reduce the heat to a simmer. Add the reduced Port and cook for 45 minutes, then transfer to a stainless steel container. Refrigerate and allow the brine to cool. Add the pre-cooked snails and marinate for 12 hours before using.

Basic Recipe 20

PARSLEY STOCK
Makes 1.5 ltr

50 ml	Olive oil
100 g	Leeks, white part only, finely chopped
100 g	Celery, finely chopped
100 g	Onions, finely chopped
100 g	Shallots, finely chopped
2	Cloves garlic, finely chopped
500 g	Parsley stalks
2 ltr	Water or chicken stock (basic recipe 22, this page)
2	Bay leaves
12	White peppercorns, crushed
	Salt
	Freshly ground pepper

Heat the olive oil in a heavy-based pan over a medium heat. Add the chopped leeks, celery, onions, shallots and garlic and sweat for 5 minutes without colouring. Add the parsley stalks and continue to sweat for a further 5 minutes without colouring. Pour in the water or chicken stock and bring to the boil. Reduce the heat to a simmer. Skim the stock and add the bay leaves, crushed peppercorns and a large pinch of salt and cook for 20 minutes. Pass the stock through a fine sieve and press down on the parsley stalks to extract as much flavour and colour as possible – adjust the seasoning if necessary. Pour the parsley stock into a stainless steel container and refrigerate to solidify any fat, which will rise to the surface. Remove the fat before using.

Basic Recipe 21

MUSHROOM STOCK
Makes 2 ltr

2 kg	Button mushrooms
6	Large field mushrooms, gills removed
50 ml	Vegetable oil
1	Clove garlic, crushed
4	Shallots, peeled and sliced
300 ml	Madeira
3 ltr	Water or chicken stock (basic recipe 22, this page)
4	Sprigs fresh thyme
6	Sprigs flat-leaf parsley
6	Sprigs fresh tarragon
50 g	Dried cep mushrooms
	Salt
	Freshly ground pepper

Clean all the mushrooms by wiping them with a damp cloth, then finely slice. Heat the oil until smoking in a large cast-iron pan. Add the button and field mushrooms, garlic and shallots and sauté until golden brown. If the pan is not large enough, sauté the mushrooms in two batches as it is important that the pan maintains heat otherwise the mushrooms will release their juice and end up boiling in it, losing colour and much of the flavour. When golden brown, add the Madeira and continue to cook until it has reduced by three-quarters. Remove the pan from the heat and lightly season the mushrooms with salt and freshly ground pepper. Transfer the mushrooms to a heavy-based saucepan, cover with the water or chicken stock and bring to the boil. Reduce the heat to a simmer and skim off any impurities that float to the surface. Add the fresh herbs and dried cep mushrooms and simmer for 45 minutes. Check the seasoning and adjust if necessary. Pass the stock through a fine sieve, pressing down on the mushrooms to extract as much flavour and colour as possible. Adjust the seasoning if necessary. Pour the mushroom stock into a stainless steel container and refrigerate to solidify any fat, which will rise to the surface. Remove the fat before using.

Basic Recipe 22

CHICKEN STOCK
Makes 4 ltr

4.5 kg	Raw chicken carcasses
7.5 ltr	Cold water
¼	Head celery, roughly chopped
1	Large leek, white part only, roughly chopped
1	Large onion, roughly chopped
250 g	Button mushrooms, sliced
½	Head garlic, roughly chopped
4	Sprigs fresh thyme
4	Sprigs parsley
2	Bay leaves
12	White peppercorns, crushed
	Salt

Remove any excess fat from the chicken carcasses, roughly chop them and place in a large saucepan covered with cold water. Bring to the boil, reduce the heat and simmer for 30 minutes, skimming frequently to remove the impurities that float to the surface. Add the chopped vegetables, herbs, crushed white peppercorns and a large pinch of salt and continue to cook for a further 1½ hours. Continue to skim the stock frequently. Adjust the seasoning if necessary. Pass the chicken stock through a fine sieve into a stainless steel container and refrigerate to solidify any fat, which will rise to the surface. Remove the fat before using.

Basic Recipe 23

VEAL STOCK

Makes 2.5 ltr

6 kg	Fresh veal bones
1	Calves hooves, split
50 ml	Vegetable oil
8 ltr	Cold water
1	Onions, roughly chopped
1	Carrots, peeled and roughly chopped
1	Sticks celery, roughly chopped
125 g	Button mushrooms, sliced
1	Leek, white part only, roughly chopped
½	Heads garlic, halved
50 g	Tomato paste

Preheat the oven to 200°C. Coat the bones and hooves in half the oil and roast in a hot oven until brown, turning the bones frequently to ensure even colouring. When the bones are roasted, drain and place in a heavy-based pot and cover with the cold water. Bring to the boil, reduce the heat to a simmer and cook for 30 minutes, skimming frequently to remove the impurities that float to the surface. Pour the remaining oil into the same tray in which the bones were roasted. Add the vegetables and return to the oven to cook for 20 minutes until caramelised. Stir the vegetables and loosen the sediment left behind by the bones. Mix the tomato paste through the vegetables and continue to cook for a further 10 minutes. Add the vegetables to the stock and continue to cook for a further 6–8 hours or until the stock has reduced by two-thirds, skimming frequently. Pass the stock through a coarse sieve to remove the bones and vegetables. Again, pass the stock through a fine sieve into a clean stainless steel container and refrigerate to solidify any fat, which will rise to the surface. Remove the fat before using.

Basic Recipe 24

FISH STOCK

Makes 1 ltr

2 kg	Fresh white fish bones, such as Blue Eye Cod or John Dory
1	Medium onion, roughly chopped
1	Medium leek, white part only, roughly chopped
1	Stick celery, roughly chopped
1	Small bulb fennel, roughly chopped
2	Cloves garlic, crushed
50 ml	Olive oil
100 ml	Noilly Prat (see glossary)
200 ml	Dry white wine
2 ltr	Cold water
12	White peppercorns, crushed
1	Bay leaf
2	Sprigs fresh thyme
2	Sprigs fresh parsley

Chop the fish bones into small pieces and wash under cold running water to remove all traces of blood. When the water runs clear, drain the bones in a colander. Wash the chopped vegetables in cold water and drain. Heat the olive oil in a heavy-based saucepan over a medium heat. Add the onion, leek, celery, fennel and garlic and sweat without colouring for 5 minutes. Add the fish bones and continue to sweat for a further 3 minutes without colouring. Add the Noilly Prat and white wine and cook until the alcohol has evaporated. Pour 2 litres cold water over the bones and bring to the boil. Reduce the heat to a simmer and remove any scum that floats to the surface. When the stock is clear and the fish bones have settled on the bottom, add the peppercorns, bay leaf, thyme and parsley and continue to cook the stock for a further 15 minutes. Remove the stock from the heat and pass through a fine sieve into a clean saucepan. Discard the bones and vegetables. Put the stock back onto the heat and reduce to 1 litre to concentrate the flavour. Once again, pass the reduced stock through a fine sieve into a stainless steel container and refrigerate to solidify any fat, which will rise to the surface. Remove the fat before using the stock. The fish stock will keep for 2 days in the fridge.

Basic Recipe 25

SHELLFISH STOCK

Makes 1.25 ltr

700 g	Fresh lobster shells and heads, uncooked
50 ml	Olive oil
2	Carrots, peeled and roughly chopped
1	Small bulb fennel, roughly chopped
1	Onion, roughly chopped
1	Stick celery, roughly chopped
1	Small leek, white part only, roughly chopped
2	Cloves garlic, crushed
1 tbsp	Tomato paste
6	Plum tomatoes, de-seeded and roughly chopped
	Pinch saffron threads
	Pinch cayenne pepper
2	Strips orange peel
2	Star anise
150 ml	Noilly Prat (see glossary)
50 ml	Pernod (see glossary)
25 ml	Brandy (see glossary)
1.5 ltr	Water or fish stock (basic recipe 24, this page)
3	Large sprigs fresh tarragon
2	Large sprigs fresh basil
	Salt
	Freshly ground pepper

Clean and chop the lobster shells and heads into small pieces. In a heavy-based saucepan, heat the olive oil, add the shells and gently roast until they become deep red. Stir in the vegetables and continue to cook until softened and lightly coloured. Add the tomato paste, chopped tomatoes, a pinch of both saffron threads and cayenne pepper, the orange peel and star anise and cook for 5 minutes. Stir to prevent sticking to the bottom of the pan. Deglaze with Noilly Prat, Pernod and brandy and allow the alcohol to evaporate. Cover the shells with the water or fish stock and cook over a low heat for 30 minutes, skimming frequently. Pass the stock through a coarse sieve, pressing down on the shells with the back of a ladle to extract as much flavour as possible. Season to taste with salt, freshly ground pepper and more cayenne pepper if necessary. Again, pass the stock through a fine sieve. Allow the stock to cool and add the tarragon and basil to infuse. Pour the stock into a stainless steel container and refrigerate to solidify any fat, which will rise to the surface. Remove the fat before using. When ready to use, pass the stock through a fine sieve, and discard the herbs. The shellfish stock will keep for 2 days in the fridge.

Basic Recipe 26

VEAL JUS
Makes 500 ml

50 ml	Vegetable oil
500 g	Beef trimmings, diced
2	Shallots, sliced
150 g	Button mushrooms, sliced
2.5 ltr	Veal stock (basic recipe 23, page 196)
1	Sprig fresh thyme
	Salt
	Freshly ground pepper

Heat 25 ml vegetable oil in a heavy-based frying pan, add the beef trimmings and cook over a medium heat until evenly brown. Drain the beef trimmings in a colander. Return the pan to the heat and add the remaining oil. Add the shallots and mushrooms and sauté until golden brown and then drain into the same colander with the beef trimmings. Place the beef trimmings, mushrooms, shallots, veal stock and thyme into a heavy-based saucepan and bring to the boil. Reduce the heat to a simmer and cook for 1½ hours, skimming the surface frequently to remove any impurities that float to the surface. Pass the sauce through a sieve lined with a double layer of muslin cloth into a clean saucepan and reduce to 500 ml over a medium heat. Skim the surface frequently and season to taste with salt and freshly ground pepper. Again, pass the stock through a fine sieve lined with muslin cloth into a clean stainless steel container. Refrigerate to solidify any fat, which will rise to the surface. Remove the fat before using the veal jus.

Basic Recipe 27

RED WINE JUS
Makes 500 ml

10 ml	Vegetable oil
3	Shallots, sliced
1	Clove garlic, sliced
750 ml	Red wine
325 ml	Port
1	Sprig fresh thyme
500 ml	Veal jus (basic recipe 26, this page)
	Salt
	Freshly ground pepper

Heat the oil in a heavy-based saucepan over a medium heat. Add the shallots, garlic and a pinch of salt and sweat without colouring until the shallots have softened. Pour in the red wine and Port and add the thyme. Cook over a medium heat and reduce by three-quarters. Pass the reduction through a fine sieve. In a clean saucepan, bring the veal jus to the boil and add the red wine reduction to taste. The sauce will be a deep, rich colour. Season to taste with salt and freshly ground pepper before passing the red wine jus through a sieve lined with a double layer of muslin cloth.

Basic Recipe 28

PORT WINE JUS
Makes 500 ml

10 ml	Vegetable oil
3	Shallots, sliced
1	Clove garlic, sliced
750 ml	Port
325 ml	Red wine
1	Sprig fresh thyme
500 ml	Veal jus (basic recipe 26, this page)
	Salt
	Freshly ground pepper

Heat the oil in a heavy-based saucepan over a medium heat. Add the shallots, garlic and a pinch of salt and sweat without colouring until the shallots have softened. Pour in the Port and red wine and add the thyme. Cook over a medium heat and reduce by three-quarters. Pass the reduction through a fine sieve into a clean saucepan. Bring the veal jus to the boil and add the Port reduction to taste. The sauce will be a deep, rich colour. Season to taste with salt and freshly ground pepper before passing the Port wine jus through a sieve lined with a double layer of muslin cloth.

Basic Recipe 29

SPARKLING SHIRAZ JUS
Makes 750 ml

10 ml	Vegetable oil
3	Shallots, sliced
1	Clove garlic, sliced
750 ml	Sparkling Shiraz
325 ml	Port
1	Sprig fresh thyme
500 ml	Veal jus (basic recipe 26, this page)
	Salt
	Freshly ground pepper

Heat the oil in a heavy-based saucepan over a medium heat. Add the shallots, garlic and a pinch of salt and sweat without colouring until the shallots have softened. Pour in 700 ml sparkling Shiraz, the Port and add the thyme. Cook over a medium heat and reduce by three-quarters. Pass the reduction through a fine sieve. In a clean saucepan bring the veal jus to the boil and add the sparkling Shiraz reduction. The sauce will be a very deep, rich colour. Season to taste with salt and freshly ground pepper before passing the sparkling Shiraz jus through a sieve lined with a double layer of muslin cloth into a clean saucepan. Add the remaining 50 ml sparkling Shiraz just before serving.

Basic Recipe 30

BALSAMIC JUS
Makes 500 ml

10 ml	Vegetable oil
3	Shallots, sliced
1	Clove garlic, sliced
250 ml	Port
50 ml	Aged balsamic vinegar
350 ml	Veal jus
	(basic recipe 26, page 197)
40 g	Unsalted butter, chilled
	and diced
	Salt
	Freshly ground pepper

Heat the oil in a heavy-based pan over a medium heat. Add the shallots, garlic and a pinch of salt and sweat without colouring until the shallots have softened. Pour in the Port and 20 ml balsamic vinegar. Cook over a medium heat and reduce by three-quarters. Pass the reduction through a fine sieve. In a clean saucepan bring the veal jus to the boil and add the reduction. Season to taste with salt and freshly ground pepper before passing through a sieve lined with a double layer of muslin cloth into a clean saucepan. Add the remaining balsamic vinegar to taste just before serving and finish by whisking in the chilled butter piece-by-piece until fully incorporated into the balsamic jus. Adjust the seasoning if necessary.

Basic Recipe 31

SAUCE PERIGEUX
Makes 250 ml

20 ml	Truffle juice
20 ml	Port
20 ml	Madeira
400 ml	Veal jus
	(basic recipe 26, page 197)
25 g	Chopped truffle
40 g	Unsalted butter, chilled
	and diced
	Salt
	Freshly ground pepper

In a heavy-based saucepan reduce the truffle juice, Port and Madeira to a syrup over a medium heat. Add the veal jus and bring to the boil. Reduce the heat to low and continue to reduce the sauce until it coats the back of a spoon. Add the chopped truffle and whisk in the butter piece-by-piece until fully incorporated into the sauce Perigeux. Season to taste with salt and freshly ground pepper.

Basic Recipe 32

FISH VELOUTÉ
Makes 1.4 ltr

1 ltr	Fish stock
	(basic recipe 24, page 196)
375 ml	Noilly Prat (see glossary)
1 ltr	Dry white wine
2 ltr	Cream
25 g	Unsalted butter, diced
4	Shallots, finely chopped
½	Onion, finely chopped
½	Head fennel, finely sliced
3	Cloves garlic, peeled
3	Sprigs fresh thyme
	Lemon juice
	Salt
	Freshly ground pepper

Reduce the fish stock to 300 ml in a heavy-based saucepan. In a separate saucepan reduce the combined alcohols to 400 ml. In a separate saucepan reduce the cream to 750 ml. In a heavy-based saucepan melt the butter until foaming. Add the shallots, onion, fennel, garlic and thyme and sweat for 3 minutes without colouring. Add the reduced alcohol and fish stock and bring to the boil. Add the cream and bring back to the boil. Reduce the heat and cook for 10 minutes. Remove from the heat and pass the fish velouté through a fine sieve. Season to taste with salt and freshly ground pepper and a squeeze of lemon.

Basic Recipe 33

THYME AND RIESLING SAUCE
Makes 1 ltr

25 g	Whole unsalted butter
100 g	Leeks, white part only, sliced
100 g	Shallots, sliced
1	Clove garlic, crushed
150 g	White fish trimmings such as
	Blue Eye Cod or John Dory
375 ml	Riesling, reduced to 150 ml
	(see glossary)
150 ml	Noilly Prat, reduced to 50 ml
	(see glossary)
375 ml	Fish stock, reduced to 150 ml
	(basic recipe 24, page 196)
1 ltr	Cream, reduced to 750 ml
4	Sprigs fresh thyme
	Lemon juice
	Salt
	Freshly ground pepper

Melt the butter over a medium heat in a heavy-based saucepan. Add the leeks, shallots and garlic and sweat for 5 minutes without colouring. Add the fish trimmings and continue to sweat for a further 3 minutes. Pour in the reduced alcohols and fish stock and bring to the boil. Add the reduced cream and bring back to the boil. Reduce the heat and continue to cook for a further 12 minutes. Remove the sauce from the heat, add the thyme and allow to infuse for 15 minutes before passing the thyme and Riesling sauce through a fine sieve. Season to taste with salt, freshly ground pepper and a squeeze of lemon.

Basic Recipe 34

CEP CREAM SAUCE
Makes 350 ml

175 g	Dried cep mushrooms
50 ml	Port
50 ml	Madeira
150 ml	Veal jus (basic recipe 26, page 197)
375 ml	Cream
	Salt
	Freshly ground pepper

Soak the ceps in the Port and Madeira for 4 hours, then place in a heavy-based saucepan and bring to the boil. Lower the heat and reduce the alcohol by three-quarters. Add the veal jus and reduce by half. Pour in the cream and continue to cook until the sauce coats the back of a spoon. Season to taste with salt and freshly ground pepper. Remove from the heat and allow the sauce to stand for 1 hour to allow the dried ceps to infuse the sauce with their flavour. Pass the cep cream sauce through a fine sieve, pressing down on the ceps to extract as much flavour and colour as possible. Adust the seasoning if necessary.

Basic Recipe 35

MOREL CREAM SAUCE
Makes 350 ml

175 g	Dried morel mushrooms
50 ml	Port
50 ml	Madeira
150 ml	Veal jus (basic recipe 26, page 197)
375 ml	Cream
	Salt
	Freshly ground pepper

Soak the morels in the Port and Madeira for 4 hours, then place in a heavy-based saucepan and bring to the boil. Lower the heat and reduce the alcohol by three-quarters. Add the veal jus and reduce by half. Pour in the cream and continue to cook until the sauce coats the back of a spoon. Season to taste with salt and freshly ground pepper. Remove from the heat and allow the sauce to stand for 1 hour to allow the dried morels to infuse the sauce with their flavour. Pass the morel cream sauce through a fine sieve pressing down on the morels to extract as much flavour and colour as possible. Adjust the seasoning if necessary.

Basic Recipe 36

SAUCE SOUBISE
Makes 250 ml

70 g	Whole, unsalted butter
250 g	Onions, sliced
100 ml	Cream
	Salt
	Freshly ground pepper

Melt the butter over a low heat in a heavy-based saucepan, add the sliced onions and lightly season with salt and freshly ground pepper. Sweat for 10 minutes without colouring until the onions are tender. Add the cream and continue to cook over a medium heat for 20 minutes. Remove the saucepan from the heat, transfer the contents to a food processor and blend to a purée. Pass the sauce Soubise through a fine sieve. Taste the sauce and adjust the seasoning if necessary. If the sauce Soubise is too thick, thin with a little milk.

Basic Recipe 37

SWEETCORN AND BASIL SAUCE
Makes 1 ltr

4	Fresh cobs of corn
100 g	Whole unsalted butter, diced
1	Clove garlic, finely chopped
200 g	Onions, finely chopped
1.5 ltr	Water or chicken stock (basic recipe 22, page 195)
50 ml	Cream
1	Bunch basil, roughly chopped
	Salt
	Freshly ground pepper

Prepare a corn stock: Peel and remove all the outer leaves and the stalks from the cobs of corn. Slice the corn kernels from the cobs using a sharp knife and keep separate until ready to use. Cut the cobs in half. In a heavy-based saucepan melt 50 g butter until foaming over a medium heat. Add the chopped garlic and half the chopped onion and sweat for 3 minutes without colouring. Add the cobs and a large pinch of salt and continue to sweat without colouring for a further 3 minutes. Pour 1.5 litres cold water or chicken stock over the cobs, bring to the boil and reduce the heat to a simmer. Continue to simmer the stock for 30 minutes, skimming frequently. Remove from the heat and allow the stock to infuse for a further 30 minutes. Pass the sauce through a fine sieve and discard the cobs, onion and garlic.

Prepare the sweetcorn and basil sauce: Melt the remaining butter until foaming, in a heavy-based saucepan. Add the remaining chopped onion and sweat for 3 minutes without colouring. Add the corn kernels and a large pinch of salt and continue to sweat without colouring for a further 3 minutes. Pour the corn stock over the corn and bring to the boil. Reduce the heat to a simmer and continue to cook for 25–30 minutes until the corn kernels are tender. Add the cream and cook for a further 5 minutes. Remove the sauce from the heat, place in a food processor and blend until smooth. Pass through a fine sieve into a stainless steel bowl, pressing down hard on the corn to extract as much flavour and colour as possible. Season to taste with salt and freshly ground pepper. Refrigerate the sauce until cooled to lukewarm and add the chopped basil to infuse the sauce for 2 hours. Again, pass through a fine sieve and reheat the sweetcorn and basil sauce over a low heat. Adjust the seasoning if necessary.

Basic Recipe 38

FENNEL EMULSION
Makes 220 ml

55 g	Fennel herb
85 g	Bulb fennel, thinly sliced
120 ml	Extra virgin olive oil
1	Small shallot, finely chopped
1	Clove garlic, crushed
30 ml	Pernod reduction (basic recipe 44, page 201)
100 ml	Water or chicken stock (basic recipe 22, page 195)
	Lemon juice
	Salt
	Freshly ground pepper

Blanche the fennel herb in boiling water for 30 seconds and then refresh in iced water. Lift out of the water and drain on a clean kitchen cloth. Heat 40 ml extra virgin olive oil in a heavy-based saucepan over a medium heat. Add the chopped shallot and garlic and sweat without colouring for 2 minutes. Add the fennel bulb and continue to sweat for a further 2 minutes. Pour in the Pernod reduction and bring to the boil. Add the water or chicken stock, a pinch of salt and freshly ground pepper and cook until the fennel is tender. This will take about 5 minutes. Remove from the heat and pour into a clean bowl. Set over a larger bowl half-filled with ice and stir to cool the fennel as quickly as possible and to retain colour. Remove the clove of garlic.

When the fennel is cold, blend to a purée in a food processor. Add the fennel herb and continue to blend until it becomes a smooth, green purée. Pass the fennel purée through a fine sieve into a clean bowl. Whisk in the remaining olive oil in a slow, steady stream until fully incorporated. Season to taste with salt, freshly ground pepper and a squeeze of lemon. Refrigerate until ready to use. When serving, do not reheat the fennel emulsion, rather, serve it at room temperature.

Basic Recipe 39

PARMESAN CREAM
Makes 500 ml

10 ml	Vegetable oil
50 g	Button mushrooms, sliced
100 g	Shallots, finely chopped
25 g	Celery, finely chopped
25 g	White of leek, finely chopped
250 ml	Chicken stock, reduced to 125ml (basic recipe 22, page 195)
250 ml	White wine, reduced to 125 ml
500 ml	Cream, reduced to 250 ml
100 g	Parmesan rind
40 g	Parmesan cheese, freshly grated
	Lemon juice
	Salt
	Freshly ground pepper

Heat the vegetable oil in a heavy-based saucepan, add the chopped vegetables and sweat without colouring until softened. Add both the reduced chicken stock and white wine and bring to the boil. Pour in the reduced cream and bring back to the boil. Reduce the heat to a simmer. Add the Parmesan rind and cook for 25 minutes. Add the grated Parmesan and cook for a further 5–8 minutes until the sauce has reduced and coats the back of a spoon. Season to taste with salt, freshly ground pepper and a squeeze of lemon before passing the Parmesan cream through a fine sieve.

Basic Recipe 40

BEURRE BLANC
Makes 250 ml

100 ml	Dry white wine
50 ml	White wine vinegar
2	Small shallots, sliced
1	Sprig fresh thyme
1	Bay leaf
6	White peppercorns, crushed
50 ml	Cream
225 g	Unsalted butter, chilled and diced
	Lemon juice
	Salt
	Freshly ground pepper

Place the white wine, vinegar, shallots, thyme, bay leaf and crushed peppercorns in a heavy-based saucepan and, over a medium heat, reduce by three-quarters. Add the cream and bring to the boil, allowing the cream to reduce by half. Reduce the heat and whisk in the butter piece-by-piece, until it is fully incorporated into the cream. Remove from the heat and season to taste with salt, freshly ground pepper and a squeeze of lemon. Pass the beurre blanc through a fine sieve and keep warm. Do not re-boil as the sauce will separate. If the sauce gets too cold the butter will solidify.

Basic Recipe 41

TRUFFLE HOLLANDAISE
Makes 300 ml

100 ml	White wine vinegar
50 ml	Dry white wine
6	White peppercorns, crushed
1	Sprig fresh thyme
2	Shallots, finely chopped
20 ml	Truffle juice
3	Free-range egg yolks
225 ml	Clarified butter, at room temperature
15 g	Chopped truffle
	Salt
	Freshly ground pepper

Place the white wine vinegar, white wine, crushed peppercorns, thyme and chopped shallots into a heavy-based saucepan and, over a medium heat, reduce by half. Remove from the heat and pass the liquid through a fine sieve into a clean stainless steel bowl and allow to cool. When cold, add the truffle juice and egg yolks. Place the bowl over a pot of simmering water and vigorously whisk to a sabayon until the eggs double in volume. Take care that the eggs don't become too hot or they will scramble. Remove the eggs from the heat and whisk in the clarified butter in a slow, steady stream until it is fully incorporated and the sauce has thickened. Season to taste with salt and freshly ground pepper. Pass the sauce through a fine sieve into a clean bowl and add the chopped truffle. Cover the bowl with clingfilm and keep the truffle hollandaise in a warm place until ready to use as the butter will solidify if the sauce becomes cold. If too hot, the butter will separate from the eggs.

Basic Recipe 42

HERB BUTTER
Makes 150 g

125 g	Whole unsalted butter, diced
6	Cloves garlic confit, puréed and passed through a fine sieve (basic recipe 52, page 203)
15 g	Flat-leaf parsley, finely chopped
10 g	Chives, finely sliced
1 tsp	Finely chopped tarragon
	Lemon juice
	Salt
	Freshly ground pepper

Allow the butter to soften at room temperature. Place the garlic confit and herbs in a food processor and blend. Add the butter gradually until all of it has been added and the herbs and garlic are fully incorporated. Remove the butter and season to taste with salt, freshly ground pepper and a squeeze of lemon. Place the herb butter in the fridge and allow to firm up before using.

Basic Recipe 43

DEEP-FRIED HERB BUTTER
Makes 8 pieces

150 g	Herb butter (basic recipe 42, this page) Egg wash of 1 free-range egg and 10 ml milk
50 g	Fresh breadcrumbs Vegetable oil for frying the butter Salt Freshly ground pepper

Allow the herb butter to soften at room temperature. Make quenelles of the butter using two warm teaspoons and place them on a clingfilm-lined tray. Place the tray in the freezer until the quenelles of butter are frozen. To prepare the quenelles for frying, dip into the egg wash, drain and coat with the breadcrumbs. Repeat the process so that the butter is double-crumbed. Heat the oil to 180°C and deep-fry until the quenelles are golden. Remove the deep-fried herb butter from the oil and drain on kitchen paper. Lightly season with salt and freshly ground pepper. When the oil has cooled, pass it through a fine sieve into a clean container, ready to use again.

Basic Recipe 44

PERNOD REDUCTION
Makes 250 ml

750 ml	Pernod (see glossary)
2	Small shallots, finely sliced
150 g	Fennel, finely sliced
3	Star anise
4	White peppercorns, crushed

Place all the ingredients into a heavy-based saucepan and, over a very low heat, reduce by two-thirds. Remove from the heat and allow to cool. Refrigerate in a parfait jar until ready to use, leaving the vegetables and spices in the liquid to give it a more intense flavour. When all the reduction has been used, discard the vegetables and spices. The pernod reduction is used for flavouring sauces, butters, fish mousse and terrines.

Basic Recipe 45

ARMAGNAC JELLY
Makes 1 ltr

DUCK STOCK
4 kg	Fresh duck bones
50 ml	Vegetable oil
6	Button mushrooms, sliced
6	Shallots, sliced
1	Onion, sliced
1	Sprig fresh thyme
4 ltr	Chicken stock (basic recipe 22, page 195)
300 ml	Armagnac (see glossary)

TO CLARIFY THE STOCK
400 g	Minced duck or chicken thigh meat with skin and fat removed
10 g	Julienne of carrot
5 g	Julienne of leek
5 g	Julienne of celery
2	Button mushrooms, sliced
250 ml	Free-range egg whites
	Salt
	Freshly ground pepper

Prepare the duck stock: Remove any excess fat from the duck bones and render down for another use (basic technique 1, page 215). Chop the bones into small pieces. Heat half the vegetable oil in a large, heavy-based frying pan over a medium heat, add the bones and cook until evenly brown. Drain in a colander. Place the same frying pan back on the heat and add the remaining vegetable oil. Add the sliced mushrooms, shallots and onion and sauté until golden brown. When ready, drain in the same colander as the duck bones.

Place half the cooked duck bones and half the vegetables into a heavy-based saucepan. Add the fresh thyme and chicken stock and bring to the boil. Reduce the heat and simmer the stock for 1–1½ hours, skimming frequently to remove any scum that floats to the surface. Pass the stock through a fine sieve discarding the bones and vegetables. Refrigerate the stock and allow to cool. Remove any fat that has set on the surface.

Place the remaining cooked bones and vegetables in a clean, heavy-based saucepan and pour over the cold duck stock to make a double duck stock, which will impart a more intense flavour to the finished jelly. Bring to the boil, reduce the heat and simmer the stock for 1 hour, frequently skimming to remove any scum that floats to the surface. Again, pass the stock through a fine sieve, discarding the bones and vegetables, and refrigerate to cool. Remove any fat that has set on the surface. Place the Armagnac in a small saucepan and reduce to 100 ml. Set aside until ready to use.

To clarify the stock: Place the minced poultry, carrot, leek, celery, button mushrooms and egg whites into a bowl and beat together. Lightly season with salt and freshly ground pepper. Pour the cold duck stock and reduced Armagnac into a clean, heavy-based saucepan and beat in the mince mixture to evenly disperse through the stock. Bring to the boil, stirring frequently to prevent sticking on the bottom or around the sides of the saucepan. Reduce the heat to a simmer and cease stirring.

After 10–15 minutes, the minced poultry, vegetables and egg whites will rise to the surface, bringing all the impurities in the stock with them, and will form a crust. Continue to simmer for a further 15 minutes. Use a tablespoon to make a hole in the centre of the crust. Remove from the heat and ladle out the clarified stock, taking care not to break the crust. Pass the stock through a fine sieve lined with a double layer of muslin cloth or coffee filter paper into a clean stainless steel container. Taste the clarified duck stock and adjust the seasoning if necessary. Refrigerate and allow the Armagnac jelly to set.

Basic Recipe 46

SEMI-DRIED TOMATOES
Makes 24 pieces

70 ml	Cabernet Sauvignon vinegar
70 ml	Extra virgin olive oil
1½ tsp	Sugar
1	Sprig basil, roughly chopped
1	Small sprig fresh rosemary
1	Sprig fresh thyme
1	Bay leaf
12	Ripe plum tomatoes
	Salt
	Freshly ground pepper

Mix together the vinegar, oil, sugar and herbs in a bowl and lightly season with salt and freshly ground pepper. Allow to infuse at room temperature for 1 hour.

Preheat the oven to the lowest possible setting. Score the tomatoes and blanche in boiling water for 15 seconds or until the skins start to come away. Refresh in iced water. Peel the tomatoes, cut in half lengthways and remove the seeds using a teaspoon. Place the tomatoes in the marinade for 30 minutes, then remove and drain on a wire rack. Place the rack onto a tray and then into the oven for 2½–3 hours. The tomatoes will have shrunk in size and become more intense in flavour but should still be moist. It is important that the tomatoes are dried at a low temperature. If too hot, they will become overly dry, discolour and lose flavour. If not using immediately, cover the tomatoes with extra virgin olive oil and refrigerate. Add a crushed clove of garlic and a few sprigs of basil until ready to use.

Basic Recipe 47

DEEP-FRIED PARSNIP CHIPS
Makes 8 portions

2	Medium parsnips
	Vegetable oil for deep-frying
	Salt
	Freshly ground pepper

Peel the parsnips, top-and-tail them and thinly slice on a mandolin. In a heavy-based saucepan, heat the oil to 180°C. Add the parsnips and, stirring frequently, deep-fry until they are crisp and golden brown. Remove from the heat and use a slotted spoon to lift the deep-fried parsnip chips out of the oil. Place on kitchen paper to absorb any excess oil. Season to taste with salt and freshly ground pepper. When the oil has cooled, pass it through a fine sieve into a clean container, ready to use again.

Basic Recipe 48

DEEP-FRIED CHILLI
Makes 8 portions

4	Medium chillies
	Vegetable oil for deep-frying
	Salt
	Freshly ground pepper

Cut the chillies in half, remove the stalks and seeds and slice thinly. Heat the oil to 170°C in a heavy-based saucepan. Add the sliced chillies and cook until crisp, stirring frequently. Remove from the heat and lift the chillies out of the oil using a slotted spoon. Drain on kitchen paper to absorb excess oil. Season to taste with salt and freshly ground pepper. When the oil has cooled, pass it through a fine sieve into a clean container, ready to use again.

Basic Recipe 49

DEEP-FRIED SHALLOTS
Makes 4 portions

	Vegetable oil for deep-frying
4	Shallots, sliced
	Salt
	Freshly ground pepper

Heat the oil to 170°C in a heavy-based saucepan. Add the shallots and cook until crisp and golden, stirring frequently. Remove from the heat and lift out the shallots using a slotted spoon. Drain on kitchen paper to absorb excess oil. Season to taste with salt and freshly ground pepper. When the oil has cooled, pass it through a fine sieve into a clean container, ready to use again.

Basic Recipe 50

SHALLOT CONFIT
Makes 500 g

500 g	Shallots, finely chopped
1	Sprig fresh thyme
	Clarified butter or rendered duck fat to cover (basic technique 1, page 215)
	Salt
	Freshly ground pepper

Place the shallots and thyme in a heavy-based saucepan. Season with salt and freshly ground pepper. Cover with either clarified butter or duck fat. Gently cook the shallots until tender over a very low heat for 25–30 minutes. Remove from the heat and allow to cool in the fat. Refrigerate until ready to use. The fat will solidify. The shallots can be stored for up to a week in the fridge before using.

Basic Recipe 51

GARLIC CONFIT
Makes 24 pieces

24	Cloves garlic, peeled
1	Sprig fresh thyme
	Clarified butter or rendered duck fat to cover (basic technique 1, page 215)
	Salt
	Freshly ground pepper

Place the garlic and thyme in a heavy-based saucepan and season with salt and freshly ground pepper. Cover with either clarified butter or duck fat. Gently cook the garlic until tender over a very low heat for about 30–35 minutes. Remove from the heat and allow to cool in the fat. Refrigerate until ready to use. The fat will solidify. The garlic cloves can be stored for up to a week in the fridge before using.

Roast Garlic: To roast, drain the garlic from the fat. Heat a little of the fat in a heavy-based pan. Add the garlic and cook until golden brown. Lightly season with salt and freshly ground pepper. Drain the garlic on kitchen paper before using.

Basic Recipe 52

GARLIC PURÉE
Makes 150 ml

24	Garlic cloves, peeled
1	Sprig fresh thyme
	Clarified butter or rendered duck fat to cover (basic technique 1, page 215)
	Salt
	Freshly ground pepper

Place the garlic and thyme in a heavy-based saucepan and cover with either clarified butter or duck fat. Gently cook the garlic until tender over a very low heat for about 30–35 minutes. Drain and pass through a fine drum sieve. Season to taste with salt and freshly ground pepper. If not using the garlic purée immediately, place in a bowl and cover with a thin film of extra virgin olive oil to prevent it from discolouring. Pass the clarified butter or duck fat through a fine sieve into a clean container, ready to use again.

Basic Recipe 53

FENNEL PURÉE
Makes 250 ml

150 g	Unsalted butter
100 g	Shallots, sliced
3	Medium heads fennel, finely sliced
50 ml	Pernod (see glossary)
50 ml	Chicken stock (basic recipe 22, page 195)
50 ml	Cream
30 g	Whole unsalted butter, chilled and diced
	Salt
	Freshly ground pepper

Melt 150 g butter in a heavy-based saucepan and sweat the shallots for 5 minutes without colouring. Add the fennel and continue to sweat over a low heat for a further 10–15 minutes without colouring until the fennel is tender. Pour in the Pernod and reduce until it has evaporated. Add the chicken stock and reduce by half. Add the cream and reduce by half. Blend to a purée in a food processor and emulsify with the chilled butter. Season with salt and freshly ground pepper and pass the fennel purée through a fine sieve.

Basic Recipe 54

PARSLEY PURÉE

Makes 500 ml

400 g	Sebago potatoes, skin on, or similar baking potatoes
200 g	Flat-leaf parsley
500 ml	Water or chicken stock (basic recipe 22, page 195)
20 ml	Garlic purée (basic recipe 52, page 203)
25 ml	Truffle oil
	Salt
	Freshly ground pepper

Preheat the oven to 180°C. Wash the potatoes under cold running water. Place on a tray in the oven and bake until tender for 70–90 minutes, depending on their size. When cooked, remove the potatoes from the oven and allow to cool. Cut the potatoes in half, scoop out the flesh with a spoon and discard the skins. Pass the potato through a fine drum sieve to produce a smooth purée.

Wash the parsley in several changes of cold water and drain. Blanche the parsley in boiling water for 15 seconds and refresh in iced water. Drain the parsley and dry on a clean kitchen cloth. Put the parsley into a food processor with 100 ml water or chicken stock and blend on a medium speed. Continue to add more water or chicken stock as necessary and blend until a smooth, thick purée is achieved. Place a piece of muslin cloth over a bowl and secure with a piece of string. Pour the parsley purée into the muslin and allow to drain. When the liquid has drained off remove the purée from the muslin and place in a bowl. Gradually add the potato purée; the purée should remain firm and have an intense, deep, green colour. Add the garlic purée and truffle oil to taste and season with salt and freshly ground pepper. Cover with clingfilm and refrigerate until ready to use. Use the parsley purée within 48 hours, as it will begin to lose flavour and colour.

Basic Recipe 55

PARSNIP PURÉE

Makes 500 ml

50 g	Unsalted butter
¼	Small onion, finely chopped
250 g	Parsnips, peeled, topped-and-tailed and sliced
250 ml	Cream
	Salt
	Freshly ground pepper

Melt the butter in a heavy-based saucepan over a low heat. Add the onion and sweat for 5 minutes without colouring. Add the parsnips and sweat for a further 5 minutes without colouring. Pour in the cream and season to taste with salt and freshly ground pepper. Bring to the boil, reduce the heat and simmer for 20 minutes until the parsnips are tender. Transfer the parsnips to a food processor and blend to a smooth purée. Pass the purée through a fine sieve into a clean saucepan. If the purée is too thick, thin with a little milk and adjust the seasoning if necessary.

Basic Recipe 56

LYONNAISE ONIONS

Makes 300 g

1.5 kg	Brown onions
75 g	Unsalted butter
	Salt
	Freshly ground pepper

Peel the onions, cut in half and slice as thinly as possible. Melt the butter in a heavy-based saucepan; when foaming, add the onions and cook for 2½–3 hours over a very low heat until all the juice has evaporated. The onions will caramelise and take on a deep, golden brown colour. Season to taste with salt and freshly ground pepper. If not using immediately, spread the onions on a tray and refrigerate to cool. Reheat over a very low heat when ready to use. Adjust the seasoning if necessary.

Basic Recipe 57

MUSHROOM DUXELLE

Makes 250 g

25 g	Dried cep mushrooms
200 g	Button mushrooms
50 ml	Extra virgin olive oil
1	Clove garlic, crushed
4	Sprigs fresh thyme
1	Small shallot, finely chopped
	Salt
	Freshly ground pepper

Soften and reconstitute the dried cep mushrooms in warm water for 4 hours. Remove from the water and drain. Trim the stalks of the button mushrooms, wipe with a damp cloth and cut into quarters. Heat the extra virgin olive oil until smoking in a cast-iron pan. Add the button and cep mushrooms, garlic, thyme and shallot and sauté until golden brown. Season with salt and freshly ground pepper. (Sauté the mushrooms in two batches if the pan is not large enough. It is important that the pan maintains the heat otherwise the mushrooms will release their juice and end up boiling in it, losing colour and flavour.) Drain the mushrooms and remove the garlic and thyme. When cold, chop the mushrooms very finely – almost to a purée. Adjust the seasoning if necessary.

Basic Recipe 58

CREAMED SPINACH

Makes 4 portions

1.5 kg	Fresh English spinach
140 ml	Cream
1	Clove garlic, crushed
25 g	Shallot confit (basic recipe 50, page 203)
	Salt
	Freshly ground pepper

Pick the spinach and discard the stalks. Wash the spinach in several changes of cold water to remove any grit or sand and blanche in salted boiling water for 1 minute. Plunge into iced water to stop the cooking process. Drain the spinach, squeezing out the water and finely chop. Place the cream in a saucepan with the crushed garlic and lightly season with salt and freshly ground pepper. Reduce by two-thirds, remove from the heat and pass through a fine sieve, discarding the garlic. To serve, reheat the cream in a saucepan, add the spinach and shallot confit and gently warm through. Season to taste with salt and freshly ground pepper.

Basic Recipe 59

BRAISED RED CABBAGE

Makes 500 g

1 x 500 g	Red cabbage
½	Stick cinnamon
6	Juniper berries
325 ml	Cabernet Sauvignon
50 ml	Port
125 ml	Cabernet Sauvignon vinegar
	Juice of 1 orange
25 g	Demarara sugar
100 g	Unsalted butter
	Salt
	Freshly ground pepper

Remove any wilted or damaged leaves from the cabbage. Cut into quarters and remove the core. Slice the cabbage as thinly as possible with a sharp knife and place in a deep tray. Tie up the cinnamon and juniper berries in a piece of muslin cloth and add to the cabbage. Add the remaining ingredients except the butter and mix well. Cover with clingfilm and marinate in the fridge for 12 hours.

Preheat the oven to 140°C. Drain the cabbage and reserve the liquid. Melt the butter in a heavy-based saucepan, add the cabbage and sweat without colouring until it wilts. Add the reserved liquid and bring to the boil. Cover the saucepan with a lid, transfer the cabbage to the oven and cook for 2½–3 hours until the cabbage is tender and the juices have reduced to a syrup. Stir every 30 minutes. Remove the muslin bag from the cabbage and discard. Adjust the seasoning if necessary and check whether more Cabernet Sauvignon vinegar is required. The cabbage can be kept covered in the fridge for 4–5 days before using.

Basic Recipe 60

ROASTED PARSNIPS

Makes 20 pieces

1	Large parsnip, peeled, topped-and-tailed
10 ml	Olive oil
20 g	Unsalted butter
1	Large sprig fresh thyme
1	Clove garlic, crushed
	Salt
	Freshly ground pepper

Preheat the oven to 180°C. Cut the parsnips into 5 cm long pieces; slice the pieces across into 1 cm slices and trim the sides. Slice into 1 cm thick batons. Heat the olive oil in a cast-iron pan and add the parsnips. Season with salt and freshly ground pepper and cook until they are evenly caramelised. Transfer the pan to the oven and continue to cook for a further 4–5 minutes or until the parsnips are tender. Turn the parsnips so that they become evenly coloured. Add the butter, thyme and garlic for the last 2 minutes of cooking. Remove the parsnips from the oven, drain and remove the thyme and garlic. Adjust the seasoning if necessary.

Basic Recipe 61

POTATO PURÉE

Makes 500 g

600 g	Large Sebago potatoes, skin on
70 ml	Cream
70 ml	Milk
50 g	Whole, unsalted butter, diced
	Salt
	Freshly ground pepper

It is preferable to bake the potatoes rather than boil them so that they do not absorb any moisture during the cooking process. This allows more cream and butter to be absorbed, which results in a smoother and creamier potato purée. Preheat the oven to 180°C. Scrub the potatoes under cold running water and place on a baking tray. Cook in the oven for 70–90 minutes until tender, depending on their size. Check the potatoes to ensure that they are cooked through by inserting the tip of a knife. Cut the cooked potatoes in half, scoop out the flesh with a spoon and discard the skins. Pass the potato through a drum sieve set over a large bowl. Bring the cream and milk to the boil and work it into the potato. Add the butter piece-by-piece until fully incorporated into the potato. Season to taste with salt and freshly ground pepper.

Garlic Potato Purée: Follow the recipe as described above and add two crushed garlic cloves to the milk and cream as it is brought to the boil. Remove from the heat and allow to infuse for 10 minutes before passing the milk and cream through a fine sieve to remove the garlic before adding to the potatoes.

Basic Recipe 62

COLCANNON

Makes 600 g

12	Slices pancetta
400 g	Potato purée (basic recipe 61, page 205)
120 g	Savoy cabbage, stalks removed, chopped and blanched
60 g	Spring onions, sliced
1	Small shallot, sliced
5 g	Julienne of flat-leaf parsley
	Salt
	Freshly ground pepper

Preheat the oven to 180°C. Lay the slices of pancetta on a tray and cook in the oven for 4–5 minutes until crisp. Drain on kitchen paper to absorb any excess fat. Break the pancetta into small pieces. Place the potato purée into a heavy-based pot and add the savoy cabbage, spring onions, shallot and pancetta and warm through over a gentle heat. Season to taste with salt and freshly ground pepper. Just before serving the colcannon, fold through the julienne of parsley.

Basic Recipe 63

CRUSHED POTATOES

Makes 4 portions

500 g	Bintje potatoes or similar waxy potatoes, skin on
50 ml	Extra virgin olive oil
	Lemon juice
1 tsp	Chives, sliced
	Salt
	Freshly ground pepper

Scrub the potatoes under cold running water, then cook in a steamer for 15–20 minutes until tender, depending on their size. Remove from the steamer and peel when cool enough to handle. Warm the extra virgin olive oil over a low heat in a heavy-based saucepan and add the potatoes, crushing with a fork into small pieces. Season with salt, freshly ground pepper and a squeeze of lemon. Remove from the heat and cover with clingfilm until ready to serve. Fold through the sliced chives just before serving to prevent them from discolouring.

Basic Recipe 64

CELERY CRUSHED POTATO

Makes 4 portions

400 g	Bintje potatoes or similar waxy potatoes, skin on
50 ml	Extra virgin olive oil
100 g	Celery, peeled, thinly sliced and blanched
	Lemon juice
1 tsp	Sliced chives
	Salt
	Freshly ground pepper

Scrub the potatoes under cold running water, then cook in a steamer for 15–20 minutes until tender, depending on their size. Remove from the steamer and peel when cool enough to handle. Warm the extra virgin olive oil over a low heat in a heavy-based saucepan and add the potatoes, crushing with a fork into small pieces. Add the blanched celery and warm through. Season with salt, freshly ground pepper and a squeeze of lemon. Remove from the heat and cover with clingfilm until ready to serve. Fold through the sliced chives just before serving to prevent them from discolouring.

Basic Recipe 65

ROESTI POTATOES

Makes 4 portions

850 g	Large potatoes, washed
100 ml	Clarified butter
50 g	Onion, sliced
100 g	Julienne of bacon
	Salt
	Freshly ground pepper

Simmer the potatoes in their skins in salted water until three-quarters cooked. It is important that they remain slightly firm as they will be grated and cooked a second time. Remove the potatoes from the water and refrigerate before peeling. Heat 20 ml clarified butter in a pan, add the onion and bacon and sweat without colouring. Remove from the pan and allow to cool. Peel the potatoes and grate on the largest blade of the grater to create long strips of potato.

Preheat the oven to 180°C. Gently mix the onion and bacon through the potato and season with salt and freshly ground pepper. Shape the potato into balls of 250 g each, ready to cook the roestis in individual blini pans. Heat 10 ml clarified butter in each of four blini pans and add a ball of potato to each one. Press down on the potato with a palette knife to cover the surface of the pans. Run the palette knife around the side of the pans to prevent the roesti from sticking. Cook the roestis for 6–7 minutes over a gentle heat until crisp and golden brown. Turn the roestis out onto a plate. Wipe out the pans and add another 10 ml clarified butter. Cook the other side of the roestis until crisp and golden brown. Transfer the roestis to the oven and cook for a further 5 minutes. The roestis can be prepared in advance and reheated in the oven before serving.

Basic Recipe 66

SAUTÉED POTATOES

Makes 4 portions

2	Large Sebago potatoes, or similar baking potatoes, washed
100 ml	Clarified butter
1	Clove garlic, crushed
1	Sprig of fresh thyme
25 g	Whole, unsalted butter
	Salt
	Freshly ground pepper

Peel the potatoes, trim into even blocks and cut into 5 mm cubes. Place in a container and run cold water over them for 5 minutes. Drain and dry the potatoes on a clean kitchen cloth. Heat the clarified butter in a large cast-iron pan and add the potatoes, garlic and thyme. Season with salt and freshly ground pepper and sauté the potatoes for 8–10 minutes. Frequently toss until tender and golden brown. Add the whole, unsalted butter and continue to sauté for a further 2 minutes. Drain the potatoes and remove the garlic and thyme. Adjust the seasoning if necessary. The potatoes can be sautéed in advance and reheated in a little clarified butter before serving.

Basic Recipe 67

POTATO GALETTE
Makes 4 portions

3	Large Sebago potatoes, washed, or similar baking potatoes
120 ml	Clarified butter
	Salt
	Freshly ground pepper

Slice off both ends of the potatoes. Punch a 5 cm diameter steel tube or pastry cutter through the potatoes to produce long cylinders from the centre of all three. Slice on a mandolin into 3 mm thick discs. Place on a clean kitchen cloth and pat dry. Lightly season the potatoes with salt and freshly ground pepper.

Melt 30 ml clarified butter in each of four blini pans. Remove the pans from the heat and arrange 36 overlapping slices of potato into each pan to fit tightly. Cook the potato gallettes over a medium heat for 5–6 minutes until crisp and golden. Flip over with a palette knife and cook the other side. Lift the potato gallettes out of the pans and drain on kitchen paper. Lightly season with salt and freshly ground pepper. The potato gallettes can be prepared in advance and reheated in the oven in a little clarified butter before serving.

Basic Recipe 68

PLAIN PASTA DOUGH
Makes 880 g

500 g	Italian '00' pasta flour, sifted twice
300 ml	Egg mix (3 whole free-range eggs plus additional egg yolks)
20 ml	Olive oil
60 ml	Water
	Salt

Place the flour with a large pinch of salt into the bowl of a food processor. Whisk the eggs and egg yolks until liquified. With the motor running, add the egg, olive oil and water in a steady stream. Continue to process until the dough comes away from the sides of the bowl. Turn out the dough onto a work surface and knead for 5 minutes to a smooth ball of pasta. Wrap the pasta in clingfilm and refrigerate for 1 hour before rolling out through a pasta machine.

Basic Recipe 69

SAFFRON PASTA DOUGH
Makes 900 g

250 ml	Water
5 g	Saffron threads
5 g	Saffron powder
500 g	Italian '00' pasta flour, sifted twice
300 g	Free-range egg yolks
20 ml	Olive oil
	Salt

Place the water, saffron threads and powder into a heavy-based saucepan. Reduce to 50 ml over a low heat. Remove from the heat and allow to cool. Pass the saffron liquid through a fine sieve into a clean bowl and press down on the saffron with the back of a spoon to extract as much colour and flavour as possible.

Place the flour with a large pinch of salt into the bowl of a food processor. Whisk the egg yolks until liquified. With the motor running, add the saffron liquid, egg yolks and the olive oil in a steady stream and continue to process until the dough comes away from the sides of the bowl. Turn out the dough onto a work surface and knead to a smooth ball of pasta for 5 minutes. Wrap the pasta in clingfilm and refrigerate for 1 hour before rolling out through a pasta machine.

Basic Recipe 70

SQUID INK PASTA DOUGH
Makes 420 g

250 g	Italian '00' pasta flour, sifted twice
90 g	Egg mix (1 whole free-range egg plus additional egg yolks)
60 ml	Squid ink
10 ml	Olive oil
	Salt

Place the flour with a large pinch of salt into the bowl of a food processor. Whisk together the egg, egg yolks and squid ink. With the motor running, pour in the egg mix and olive oil in a steady stream. Continue to run the motor until the dough comes away from the sides of the bowl. Turn out the dough onto a work surface and knead to a smooth ball of pasta for 5 minutes. Wrap the pasta in clingfilm and refrigerate for 1 hour before rolling out through a pasta machine.

Basic Recipe 71

TRUFFLE GNOCCHI
Makes 800 g

600 g	Large Sebago potatoes or other potatoes suitable for baking, washed
150 g	Plain flour, sifted
60 g	Parmesan cheese, freshly grated
3	Free-range egg yolks
10 g	Chopped truffle
50 ml	Truffle oil
	Salt
	Freshly ground pepper

Preheat the oven to 180°C. Place the potatoes on a baking tray and bake in the oven for 70–90 minutes until tender, depending on their size. Remove from the oven, cut in half, scoop out the flesh with a spoon and discard the skins. Pass the potato through a drum sieve and weigh out 550 g potato purée; place in a bowl, add the flour, Parmesan cheese, egg yolks, chopped truffle and the truffle oil and work into a dough. Season with salt and freshly ground pepper. Turn out the dough onto a lightly floured work surface and knead for 3 minutes. If it feels wet, add a little more flour. The dough should be firm yet soft. Spoon the dough into a piping bag fitted with a 3 cm plain tube and pipe out in lines onto a lightly floured surface. Cut the gnocchi into 3 cm lengths.

Bring a large saucepan of salted water to the boil and cook the gnocchi in several batches. Drop the gnocchi into the water; they will float to the surface within 3–4 minutes when cooked. Lift out of the water and plunge into iced water to refresh. Drain and dry on a clean kitchen cloth. If not using immediately, mix through a little extra virgin olive oil to prevent the gnocchi from sticking together. Cover and refrigerate until ready to use.

Basic Recipe 72

GARLIC CHIVE SPÄTZLE
Makes 600 g

2	Bunches garlic chives
4 tbsp	Sparkling mineral water
4 tbsp	Cream
500 g	Plain flour, sifted
4	Whole free-range eggs, beaten
	Milk for consistency
150 ml	Clarified butter
	Nutmeg, freshly grated (optional)
	Salt
	Freshly ground pepper

Blanche and refresh the garlic chives in iced water. Drain the garlic chives and place in a food processor. Add the mineral water and cream and blend to a purée. Pass the garlic chive purée through a fine drum sieve and set aside until ready to use.

Place the flour, salt and freshly ground pepper in a large bowl. Beat in the eggs and the garlic chive purée. Add enough milk to make a smooth firm batter and beat thoroughly to obtain a thick pouring consistency. Rest the batter in the fridge for 2 hours before cooking.

Cook the spätzle in batches in a large pot of salted boiling water. Place a colander over the water, ladle some spätzle dough into it and force it through the holes with a plastic dough scraper to achieve long, thin strips of spätzle. The spätzle is cooked when it floats to the surface. Remove with a slotted spoon and plunge into iced water to halt the cooking process. Cook the remaining spätzle in the same manner. Drain and dry on a clean kitchen cloth. If not using the spätzle immediately, mix through a little extra virgin olive oil to prevent the spätzle from sticking together. Cover and refrigerate until ready to use.

Cook the spätzle in batches. Heat sufficient clarified butter to cover the base of a large, non-stick frying pan. Add enough spätzle to cover the surface of the pan and fry until golden and slightly crisp. Season to taste with salt, freshly ground pepper and freshly grated nutmeg. Transfer the spätzle to a sieve to drain off any excess clarified butter.

Basic Recipe 73

DUCK AND SWEETCORN HERBED PANCAKES
Makes 11 x 20 cm pancakes and filling for 4

HERBED PANCAKES

275 g	Plain flour, sifted and seasoned
2	Whole free-range eggs
600 ml	Milk
100 ml	Olive oil
2 tsp	Sliced chives
	Salt
	Freshly ground pepper

DUCK AND SWEETCORN FILLING

70 g	Whole, unsalted butter
180 g	Fresh sweetcorn kernels
180 g	Shredded duck confit, skin and bone removed (basic technique 1, page 215)
2 tsp	Julienne of flat-leaf parsley
10 ml	Sparkling Shiraz jus (basic recipe 29, page 197)
	Salt
	Freshly ground pepper

Prepare the pancakes in advance: Place the flour in a food processor, add the eggs, milk and 45 ml olive oil and blend to a smooth batter. Pass the batter through a fine sieve and refrigerate for 1 hour before using. Stir through the sliced chives just before cooking the pancakes. Heat 5 ml olive oil in a 20 cm cast-iron pan over a medium heat and pour in enough batter to thinly cover the base of the pan. Cook the pancake until set on top and golden brown beneath. Turn the pancake and cook the other side until it, too, is golden brown. Turn out the pancake onto a plate. Cook the remaining pancakes in the same way and allow to cool before using.

Prepare the filling: Melt the butter in a heavy-based pan until it begins to foam. Add the sweetcorn and sauté without colouring for 5–6 minutes until tender. Drain, place in a bowl and add the shredded duck confit, julienne of parsley and the Shiraz jus. Mix together and season to taste with salt and freshly ground pepper. Line a 7 cm wide x 3 cm deep pastry ring with a herb pancake – take care not to tear it. Spoon a quarter of the sweetcorn and duck confit mix into the herb pancake and carefully fold it to enclose the filling. Fill the other three pancakes in the same way.

Basic Recipe 74

HERB CRUST
Makes 10 portions

200 g	Unsalted butter
200 g	White breadcrumbs
75 g	Flat-leaf parsley, finely chopped
25 g	Picked tarragon leaves, finely chopped
1	Clove garlic, finely chopped
	Lemon juice
	Salt
	Freshly ground pepper

Blend the butter and breadcrumbs in a food processor until they resemble a crumble mixture. Add the chopped herbs and garlic and continue to blend until it is an even green-coloured crumb mixture. Lightly season with salt, freshly ground pepper and a squeeze of lemon. Pour out the mixture onto a sheet of greaseproof paper and cover with another sheet of greaseproof paper. Roll out the herb crust until roughly 1 cm thick. Place in the freezer to firm up, after which it can be cut to the required shape and size.

Basic Recipe 75

SCALLOP MOUSSE
Makes 600 g

300 g	Fresh scallop meat, with muscles removed
1	Free-range egg white
5 ml	Pernod reduction (basic recipe 44, page 201)
300 ml	Chilled cream
	Salt
	Freshly ground pepper

Chill the bowl of a food processor in the freezer for 15 minutes before making the scallop mousse. Place the scallop meat on a clean kitchen cloth to extract any moisture. Dice the scallop meat, add a pinch of salt and freshly ground pepper and blend until smooth in the chilled food processor. Add the egg white, Pernod reduction and chilled cream in a slow, steady stream. When fully incorporated, transfer the mousse to a clean bowl and refrigerate for 30 minutes. Set a clean bowl over a larger bowl half-filled with ice. Pass the chilled mousse through a fine drum sieve into the bowl, keeping it chilled throughout the process. Test the mousse (basic technique 11, page 217). Cover the mousse with clingfilm and refrigerate until ready to use.

Basic Recipe 76

SUGAR SYRUP
Makes 200 ml

100 g	Castor sugar
100 ml	Water

Mix together the sugar and water in a heavy-based saucepan and stir until dissolved over a medium heat. Skim off any scum that rises to the surface. Pass through a fine sieve into a clean bowl and allow to cool. Store the sugar syrup in a sealed container in the fridge.

Basic Recipe 77

PISTACHIO SYRUP
Makes 550 ml

500 ml	Sugar syrup (basic recipe 76, this page)
50 g	Pistachio paste

Bring the sugar syrup to the boil in a heavy-based saucepan and whisk in the pistachio paste. Bring back to the boil, reduce the heat to the lowest possible setting and cook for 15 minutes. Remove the pistachio syrup from the heat and stand in a warm place for 2 hours. Pass through a fine sieve and refrigerate until ready to use.

Basic Recipe 78

LIME SYRUP
Makes 500 ml

200 g	Castor sugar
300 ml	Water
	Juice of 3 limes
	Grated zest of 6 limes

Mix the sugar, water, lime juice and zest together in a heavy-based saucepan. Stir over a medium heat until the sugar has dissolved. Bring to the boil, reduce the heat and continue to cook for 3 minutes. Skim off any scum that rises to the surface. Transfer the syrup to a clean bowl and allow to cool. Allow the lime zest to infuse and flavour the syrup. Store in a sealed container in the fridge. Pass the lime syrup through a fine sieve when ready to use and discard the zest.

Basic Recipe 79

COFFEE SYRUP
Makes 450 ml

350 ml	Sugar syrup (basic recipe 76, this page)
100 ml	Strong espresso coffee

Bring the sugar syrup and coffee to the boil in a heavy-based pan. Reduce the heat and simmer for 5 minutes. Pass the coffee syrup through a fine sieve into a sealed container and refrigerate until ready to use.

Basic Recipe 80

CRÈME ANGLAISE
Makes 400 ml

½	Vanilla bean
250 ml	Milk
3	Free-range egg yolks
65 g	Castor sugar

Split and scrape the seeds from the vanilla pod. Scald the milk, vanilla bean and seeds in a heavy-based saucepan. Remove from the heat and allow the vanilla to infuse in the milk for 15 minutes. Beat together the egg yolks and castor sugar in a bowl until pale and double in volume and the sugar has dissolved. Pour half the milk onto the egg yolk mix and whisk together. Pour the mixture back into the saucepan with the remaining milk and whisk. Cook the crème Anglaise over a very low heat until it thickens, stirring continuously with a wooden spoon. It is ready when it coats the back of a spoon and your finger leaves a clear path when run through the crème Anglaise. Remove the saucepan from the heat and pass the crème Anglaise through a fine sieve into a clean bowl. Set the bowl over a larger bowl half-filled with ice to cool the crème Anglaise as quickly as possible. Stir from time to time to prevent a skin from forming.

Basic Recipe 81

PISTACHIO CRÈME PÂTISSIÈRE
Makes 900 g

500 ml	Milk
60 g	Pistachio paste
6	Free-range egg yolks
125 g	Castor sugar
40 g	Plain flour, sifted
	Icing sugar to dust

Scald the milk and the pistachio paste in a heavy-based saucepan. Whisk together the egg yolks and castor sugar in a bowl and beat until pale and double in volume and the sugar has dissolved. Beat the flour into the egg mix. Pour the scalded milk onto the egg mix and whisk until fully incorporated. Pour into a clean saucepan and return to a low heat. Continuously stir with a wooden spoon until thick. Transfer the pistachio crème pâtissière into a clean bowl and dust with icing sugar to prevent a skin from forming on the surface. Cover the pistachio crème pâtissière with clingfilm when cool and refrigerate until ready to use.

Basic Recipe 82

RASPBERRY COULIS
Makes 250 ml

400 g	Raspberries
50 ml	Sugar syrup (basic recipe 76, this page)
	Icing sugar to taste
	Lemon juice

Cook the raspberries and sugar syrup in a heavy-based pan for 5 minutes over a low heat. Blend to a purée in a food processor and pass through a fine sieve. Add icing sugar and a squeeze of lemon to taste. Thin with a little mineral water if the purée is too thick. Refrigerate the raspberry coulis until ready to use.

Basic Recipe 83

STRAWBERRY COULIS
Makes 250 ml

400 g	Strawberries
50 ml	Sugar syrup
	(basic recipe 76, page 209)
	Icing sugar to taste
	Lemon juice

Cook the strawberries and sugar syrup in a heavy-based pan for 5 minutes over a low heat. Blend to a purée in a food processor and pass through a fine sieve. Add icing sugar and a squeeze of lemon to taste. Thin with a little mineral water if the purée is too thick. Refrigerate the strawberry coulis until ready to use.

Basic Recipe 84

BLACKBERRY COULIS
Makes 300 ml

300 g	Blackberries
30 ml	Sugar syrup
	(basic recipe 76, page 209)
	Icing sugar to taste
	Lemon juice

Cook the blackberries and sugar syrup in a heavy-based pan for 5 minutes over a low heat. Blend to a purée in a food processor and pass through a fine sieve. Add icing sugar and a squeeze of lemon to taste. Thin with a little mineral water if the purée is too thick. Refrigerate the blackberry coulis until ready to use.

Basic Recipe 85

TUILLE MIX
Makes 24–30 pieces

30 g	Unsalted butter
40 g	Free-range egg whites
35 g	Plain flour, sifted
60 g	Icing sugar, sifted

Melt the butter over a low heat and set aside until ready to use. Lightly beat the egg whites. Blend together the flour and icing sugar in a food processor and add the egg whites, then the melted butter. Continue to process until all the ingredients are fully incorporated and form a paste. Transfer the tuille mix to a clean bowl, cover with clingfilm and refrigerate for 2 hours to allow the mix to firm up before using.

Preheat the oven to 170°C. Place teaspoonfuls of the mix onto a baking tray lined with parchment paper. Leave a 6 cm gap between each tuille as they will spread during cooking. Smooth out the tuille mix with a palette knife dipped in cold water. (Use a stencil to get even-sized and shaped tuilles or a pastry cutter to cut them into shape as they come out of the oven.) Bake the tuilles for 6–7 minutes until lightly golden. Remove from the oven and allow the tuilles to cool for 1 minute. Lift them off the tray with a palette knife, place onto a wire rack or, drape them over a rolling pin to create curved tuilles and allow to cool and become crisp. Store the tuilles in an airtight container. If not using all the mix immediately, tightly cover with clingfilm and refrigerate. Beat the tuille mix before using again.

Basic Recipe 86

PISTACHIO TUILLES
Makes 24–30 pieces (7 cm x 7 cm)

150 g	Unsalted butter
7	Free-range egg whites
175 g	Plain flour, sifted
300 g	Icing sugar, sifted
50 g	Pistachios, blanched, peeled and finely chopped
3 ml	Vanilla extract (see glossary)

Melt the butter over a low heat and set aside until ready to use. Lightly beat the egg whites. Blend the flour and icing sugar in a food processor, add the chopped pistachios, egg whites, vanilla extract and then the melted butter. Continue to process until all the ingredients are fully incorporated and form a paste. Transfer the pistachio tuille mix to a clean bowl, cover with clingfilm and refrigerate for 2 hours to allow the mix to firm up before using.

Preheat the oven to 170°C. Place teaspoonfuls of the mix onto a baking tray lined with parchment paper. Leave a 6 cm gap between each tuille as they will spread during cooking. Smooth out the tuille mix with a palette knife dipped in cold water. (Use a stencil to get even-sized and shaped tuilles or a pastry cutter to cut them into shape as they come out of the oven.) Bake the tuilles for 6–7 minutes until lightly golden. Remove from the oven and allow the tuilles to cool for 1 minute. Lift them off the tray with a palette knife, place onto a wire rack or, drape them over a rolling pin to create curved tuilles and allow to cool and become crisp. Store the tuilles in an airtight container. If not using all the mix immediately, tightly cover with clingfilm and refrigerate. Beat the pistachio tuille mix before using again.

Basic Recipe 87

CHOCOLATE TUILLES
Makes 55–60 pieces

50 g	Unsalted butter, softened
55 g	Free-range egg whites
85 g	Castor sugar
125 g	Cocoa powder, sifted

Melt the butter over a low heat and set aside until ready to use. Beat the egg whites and sugar to soft peaks with an electric mixer. Reduce the speed, add the butter in a steady stream and continue to mix until it is fully incorporated into the egg whites and sugar. Add a tablespoon of cocoa powder and mix until it is fully incorporated and continue to add a tablespoon at a time until all the cocoa powder is used. Transfer the chocolate tuille mix to a clean bowl, cover with clingfilm and refrigerate for 2 hours to allow the mix to firm up before using.

Preheat the oven to 170°C. Place teaspoonfuls of the mix onto a baking tray lined with parchment paper. Leave a 6 cm gap between each tuille as they will spread during cooking. Smooth out the tuille mix with a palette knife dipped in cold water. (Use a stencil to get even-sized and shaped tuilles or a pastry cutter to cut them into shape as they come out of the oven.) Bake the tuilles for 4–5 minutes until crisp. Remove from the oven and allow the tuilles to cool for 1 minute. Lift them off the tray with a palette knife, place onto a wire rack or, drape them over a rolling pin to create curved tuilles and allow to cool and become crisp. Store the tuilles in an airtight container. If not using all the mix immediately, tightly cover with clingfilm and refrigerate. Beat the chocolate tuille mix before using again.

Basic Recipe 88

HONEY TUILLES
Makes 55–60 pieces

25 g	Unsalted butter
125 g	Icing sugar
25 ml	Honey
200 g	Plain flour, sifted
1 tsp	Ground cinnamon

Cream together the butter and icing sugar with an electric mixer and beat until light and airy. Add the honey, then the flour and cinnamon and mix until fully incorporated. Transfer the tuille mix to a clean bowl, cover with clingfilm and refrigerate for 2 hours to firm up before using.

Preheat the oven to 170°C. Roll out the tuille mix between two sheets of silicon paper to a thickness of 2 mm. Return to the fridge to firm-up before baking. Grease a baking tray. Peel off the silicon paper and place the tuille mix on the baking tray. Place in the oven and bake for 6 minutes until golden. Remove the tuille from the oven and cut to the desired shape with a sharp, heavy knife. If the tuille is too hard and brittle to cut, return it to the oven for 15 seconds to soften. Allow 10 g of mix per tuille.

Basic Recipe 89

HONEYCOMB
Makes 200 g

165 g	Castor sugar
25 ml	Honey
60 g	Glucose
30 ml	Water
7 g	Bicarbonate of soda

Line a baking tray with parchment paper. Place the castor sugar, honey, glucose and water in a large, heavy-based saucepan. Cook over a medium heat until the mixture is a caramel colour. Add the bicarbonate of soda and quickly whisk. The mixture will double in volume. Pour out onto the paper. Allow the honeycomb to cool and set for 15 minutes before storing in an airtight container.

Basic Recipe 90

CHESTNUT PURÉE
Makes 1 kg

300 ml	Milk
750 g	Sweetened chestnut purée
1	Vanilla bean, split and scraped
75 ml	Cream

Bring the milk, chestnut purée, vanilla bean and seeds to the boil over a low heat. Continuously stir until the mixture thickens. Add the cream and bring back to the boil. Remove from the heat, pass through a fine sieve and discard the vanilla bean. Transfer the chestnut purée to a clean bowl, cover with clingfilm and refrigerate until ready to use.

Basic Recipe 91

CHOCOLATE SAUCE
Makes 250 ml

150 ml	Milk
50 ml	Cream
30 g	Castor sugar
250 g	Dark chocolate, with at least 60% cocoa solids, chopped
30 g	Whole unsalted butter, diced

In a heavy-based saucepan bring the milk, cream and sugar to the boil over a medium heat. Remove from the heat and allow to cool slightly. Add the chopped chocolate, return to the heat until melted and whisk in the diced butter. When fully incorporated pass through a fine sieve. If the chocolate sauce should solidify, reheat in a bowl over a pot of simmering water.

Basic Recipe 92

LIME SORBET
Makes 1 ltr

6	Limes
550 ml	Sugar syrup (basic recipe 76, page 209)
225 ml	Water

Wash the limes, grate the zest and place in a heavy-based saucepan with the sugar syrup. Bring to the boil and reduce to a simmer for 2 minutes. Remove from the heat and cool, allowing the zest to infuse the sugar syrup. Cut the limes in half and squeeze out the juice. Measure 225 ml lime juice and add it to the water. Pass the zest-infused lime syrup through a fine sieve into the lime juice and water and whisk. Transfer to an ice-cream machine and churn until firm. Place in a container and freeze.

Basic Recipe 93

PRUNE AND ARMAGNAC ICE CREAM
Makes 600 ml

12	Plump, semi-dried prunes
100 ml	Armagnac (see glossary)
250 ml	Milk
250 ml	Cream
2	Vanilla beans, split and scraped
6	Large free-range egg yolks
100 g	Castor sugar

Place the prunes in a bowl. Heat the Armagnac over a gentle heat and pour over the prunes. Cover with clingfilm and macerate overnight. Drain off the Armagnac and reserve it to flavour the ice cream. Remove the stones from the prunes and discard. Cut the flesh into small pieces and set aside until ready to use.

Scald the milk, cream, vanilla beans and seeds in a heavy-based saucepan over a gentle heat. Remove from the heat and allow the vanilla to infuse for 15 minutes.

Beat together the egg yolks and castor sugar until pale and double in volume and the castor sugar has dissolved. Pour half the milk onto the egg mix, and whisk together. Pour the mixture back into the saucepan with the remaining milk and whisk. Cook the crème Anglaise over a low heat until it thickens, stirring continuously with a wooden spoon until it coats the back of a spoon and your finger leaves a clear path when run through it. Remove the saucepan from the heat and pass the crème Anglaise through a fine sieve into a clean bowl. Set the bowl over a larger bowl half-filled with ice to cool the crème Anglaise as quickly as possible. Stir from time to time to prevent a skin from forming. When the crème Anglaise is cold, add the Armagnac to taste.

Transfer the Armagnac-flavoured crème Anglaise to an ice-cream machine and churn until firm. Add the chopped prunes, fold through the ice cream and remove from the machine. Transfer to a clean container and freeze until ready to serve.

Basic Recipe 94

PUFF PASTRY
Makes 1.4 kg

675 g	Strong plain flour, sifted
	Large pinch salt
85 g	Whole unsalted butter, chilled and diced
15 ml	White wine vinegar
270 ml	Water
565 g	Whole unsalted butter, rolled into a 10 cm x 10 cm square, chilled
	Salt
	Egg wash of 1 free-range egg and 10 ml milk

Place the flour and a large pinch of salt onto a work surface. Make a well and add 85 g butter, working it into the flour with your fingertips. Add the vinegar and water and mix until a dough is formed; knead for 5 minutes until smooth and shiny. Roll the dough into a ball and score a cross across the top. Place in a bowl, cover with clingfilm and refrigerate for 1 hour.

Roll out the pastry into a neat square, 30 cm x 30 cm, on a lightly floured surface, keeping the edges straight. Roll out the four corners a little more thinly than the centre of the pastry. Place the chilled square of butter into the centre of the pastry and fold over the four sides to completely enclose. Press the edges together to seal and prevent any butter seeping out when it is rolled. Refrigerate for 30 minutes.

Roll out the pastry into a rectangular shape 20 cm x 60 cm, three times as long as it is wide. Take care that none of the butter seeps through. Fold down the top third of the pastry and then fold the bottom third over it (like folding a letter). Lightly dust the work surface with flour. Give the pastry a quarter turn so that it lies lengthways. Roll out again in exactly the same way. Fold again in thirds and wrap the pastry in clingfilm. Refrigerate the pastry to rest for a further hour.

After 1 hour, roll out the pastry and fold it twice more in exactly the same way as before. Roll in the same direction as before. Wrap in clingfilm and return to the fridge for a further hour.

Roll out the pastry and fold it once more as before. Cut the pastry into three even pieces and wrap each piece in clingfilm. Refrigerate the pastry until ready to use or store in the freezer.

To roll out the puff pastry, work on a lightly floured surface and roll out to a thickness of 5 mm. Place the rolled pastry on a baking sheet and refrigerate for 30 minutes before cutting and baking. Spray a clean baking sheet with water and place the cut pastry onto it. Egg wash the pastry – take care that it does not run down the sides, which will prevent it from rising evenly. Refrigerate for 30 minutes before baking.

Preheat the oven to 200°C. Place the baking tray in the oven and bake the pastry for 7–8 minutes until golden. Reduce the oven temperature to 180°C and continue to cook for a further 2–3 minutes until the centre of the pastry is cooked through.

Basic Recipe 95

SLICED DRIED PEAR

1	Large, firm pear
	Icing sugar

Preheat the oven to 85°C. Ensure that the pear is unblemished and slice it as thinly as possible – the best result is obtained with an electric slicing machine. The pear should yield 18–24 slices, depending on the size. Lay a silpat mat on a baking sheet and cover it with a dusting of icing sugar. Arrange the sliced pear onto the icing sugar in rows. Dust the exposed sides of the pear with icing sugar to completely cover and cook in the oven for 2 hours until crisp and golden. Gently remove the sliced pears with a palette knife and allow to cool. Store in an airtight container until ready to use.

Basic Recipe 96

CANDIED LEMON PEEL

2	Lemons
	Water to cover
150 ml	Sugar syrup
	(basic recipe 76, page 209)

Wash the lemons and cut wide strips of peel from them with a swivel peeler. Remove the pith from the peel with the tip of a knife. Square up the peel with a knife and cut the rind into julienne. Cover the peel with cold water, bring to the boil and strain. Once again, cover with cold water and repeat the blanching process five times to remove the bitterness from the citrus peel.

Place the softened peel in a wide-based pan and cover with sugar syrup. Bring to a simmer over a low heat and continue to cook for 45 minutes to 1 hour until the peel is translucent. Remove the peel from the pan, place onto a wire rack in a single layer and cover with a cloth. Store in a cool place and allow to dry for a few days. The peel can be rolled in sugar or dipped in chocolate and served as petits fours.

BASIC TECHNIQUES

Basic Technique 1

PREPARING AND COOKING CONFIT

The word confit means to preserve or conserve. The process of making confit involves cooking meat very slowly in fat, until it literally falls off the bone. The most common fats used for confit are duck, goose and chicken. These are available commercially, but to make them is a very simple process.

Poultry legs like quail, squab, guinea fowl, pheasant, turkey and duck are most suitable for confit as they can be tough and contain sinew that is broken down during the slow cooking process. Other meats with a low fat content that also benefit from being confited are loin of pork and rabbit.

Rendering Fat

To produce 1 litre of rendered fat, begin with 2 kg of raw fat. Place the fat in a heavy-based saucepan with 100 ml cold water to prevent it from sticking to the saucepan – the water will evaporate during cooking. Add 2 sprigs rosemary, 2 sprigs thyme, 2 crushed cloves garlic and 12 each crushed white peppercorns and coriander seeds. Render the fat over a very low heat for 6–8 hours. When the fat has melted and is crystal clear, pass it through a fine sieve into a stainless steel container, removing any solids that remain. The fat can be used immediately or refrigerated in a covered container where it will solidify and will keep for several months. When ready to use, melt the fat over a very low heat.

Salting Confit

Salt and refrigerate the meat for a couple of hours or overnight, depending on the size; quail, squab legs and duck gizzards will only need 2 hours while larger pieces like duck or chicken legs will take 12 hours. The salt will extract moisture from the meat, which enables it to be stored in its fat for several months.

TO SALT 2 KG OF MEAT

175 g	Coarse salt
2	Star anise
12	Coriander seeds
12	White peppercorns
1	Stick cinnamon
1	Bay leaf
2	Sprigs fresh thyme
6	Cloves garlic, crushed
	Zest of ½ orange

Using a pestle and mortar, crush the salt, star anise, coriander seeds, white peppercorns and cinnamon stick. Transfer to a bowl and add the bay leaf, thyme, garlic and orange zest. Rub the salt mix into the meat and place onto a perforated tray with another tray beneath it to collect the moisture released from the meat.

Cooking Confit

Preheat the oven to 120°C. Rub the salt off the legs with a clean cloth. Place in a heavy-based saucepan, cover with rendered fat and heat to simmering point. Cover the pot with a lid, transfer to the oven and cook the meat until tender and comes away from the bone. Duck legs will take 3–3½ hours depending on their size and smaller pieces of meat such as duck gizzards will take 45–60 minutes. It is important that the temperature of the fat stays constant during cooking; if it gets too hot, the result will be fried, stringy and dry meat. Remove the pot from the oven and allow the confit to sit in the fat for an hour to cool slightly.

Storing Confit

Carefully lift the confit piece-by-piece out of the fat using a perforated spoon, and place in a clean stainless steel or earthenware dish. Gently layer the pieces on top of one another. Pass the fat through a fine sieve to completely cover the meat. Store the confit in the fridge for up to 3 months where the fat will solidify and form an airtight seal.

Pressing Confit

This process is optional and is usually done for presentation purposes (see Roast Breast and Confit of Duck with Seared Foie Gras and Sauce Soubise, page 136). Carefully lift the confit, piece-by-piece, out of the fat using a perforated spoon and place onto a clean tray. Allow the confit to cool sufficiently to be handled. Carefully extract the bones by gently twisting and pulling – they will come away easily from the meat.

Place the confit on a greaseproof paper-lined tray, with space between each piece. When the tray is full, cover with a second sheet of greaseproof paper. Place another tray on top with a 5 kg weight evenly dispersed across the tray to press the confit. Refrigerate for at least 3 hours before removing the weight. When the confit is cold, trim the sides to form even squares of confit.

Basic Technique 2

BLANCHING CALVES SWEETBREADS

For 4 portions

4 x 100 g	Calves sweetbreads from the pancreas
1	Small leek, washed and sliced
1	Carrot, peeled and sliced
1	Onion, peeled and chopped
1	Large stick celery, sliced
2	Cloves garlic, peeled and crushed
1	Sprig fresh thyme
1	Bay leaf
1	Large sprig parsley
100 ml	Dry white wine
1 ltr	Cold water
	Pinch sea salt
10	White peppercorns, crushed

Place the sweetbreads into a stainless steel bowl and run cold water over them until there is no trace of blood and the water runs clear.

Prepare a court bouillon by placing the remaining ingredients in a heavy-based saucepan. Bring to the boil, reduce the heat and simmer for 30 minutes. Add the sweetbreads and blanche for 5 minutes in the simmering court bouillon. Remove the sweetbreads from the court bouillon – they will have firmed slightly but should remain soft in the centre – cover with a damp cloth and refrigerate until cold. Peel off the thin membrane layer and any fat or gristle that is attached. Now the sweetbreads are ready to be pan-fried.

Basic Technique 3

SHUCKING OYSTERS

Select live oysters with the shells firmly closed and at all cost, avoid pre-shucked specimens. Oysters should be opened at the last minute before serving using a specially designed oyster knife.

Place the oyster onto a damp cloth, cupped side down. This is the side of the shell that holds the oyster meat and juice. Fold the cloth over the top of the oyster to hold it steady and to protect your hand from the shell.

Insert the tip of the oyster knife between the joint of the two shells at the narrow end of the oyster. Put some pressure on the knife and gently twist the blade until the two shells separate. Take care not to push the tip of the blade too far in, to avoid puncturing the oyster. Gently pull the lid off the oyster and use the tip of the knife to separate the oyster from the muscle that attaches it to the shell. When shucked, discard the lid and place the oyster in its shell into an empty egg carton to keep the oyster upright and prevent the juice from spilling out of the oyster shell.

Basic Technique 4

COOKING AND PICKING FRESH CRAB

Buy live crab as the flesh deteriorates very quickly once they are dead. Fresh crab is also easier to clean and pick and will give a larger yield of meat. Check that both claws and all the legs are still attached to the body. The crab should feel heavy in relation to its size.

Mud crab is preferable as it is large and consequently easy to pick, giving a higher yield of meat. Many recipes call for a court bouillon (see glossary) in which to cook crab, however, to cook them in simmering salted water is acceptable as the flavour of a court bouillon does not necessarily penetrate the thick shell of a mud crab and is more suitable for cooking soft-shell crabs.

Bring a large pot of water to the boil and add 150 g salt for every 5 litres. Reduce the heat to a simmer and plunge the crab into the water. A mud crab weighing between 800 g–1 kg will take 9 minutes to cook and will yield approximately 45 per cent of its body weight in crab meat. Remove the crab from the water and cover with a cold damp cloth. Refrigerate to cool while it continues to steam in its own juices. Allow the meat to firm up. Set a small metal bowl into a larger bowl half filled with ice. The smaller bowl will catch the crab meat as it is picked and ensure that it remains chilled.

To extract the crab meat, begin by breaking down the crab into pieces. Remove both claws and the legs from the body and set aside. Firmly hold the crab and use your thumb to remove the shell from the body of the crab. Remove the stomach sack and gills ('dead man's fingers') from the body and discard, leaving just the body of the crab. Cut the body in half horizontally using a heavy knife, which will allow easier access to the meat. Pick out the meat from the cavities of the body with a skewer.

Place the claws inside a clean cloth and gently crack the shells with the back of a heavy knife or a mallet – take care not to crush the meat. Peel away the shell to expose the meat. Repeat this process with the legs until all the shell is removed.

Again, pick through the crab meat with your fingertips to ensure that no fragments of shell remain.

Basic Technique 5

PREPARING AND COOKING ASPARAGUS

Buy firm, crisp asparagus. Remove the woody base by cutting 2–3 cm off the spear depending on the length. Peel the outer skin from just under the tip down to the base using a swivel peeler and discard the skin. Cook the asparagus in salted boiling water for 1–1½ minutes until tender, depending on the thickness of the asparagus – check with the tip of a knife. If not serving the asparagus immediately, refresh in iced water to stop the cooking process and drain. Place on a clean kitchen cloth and refrigerate until ready to use.

Basic Technique 6

PREPARING AND COOKING ARTICHOKES

Use only the heart of the artichoke and discard the rest. Have a bowl of cold, lightly salted, citric water standing by to drop in the prepared artichoke bottoms, which will prevent them from discolouring. Snap the stalk from the base of the artichoke. If it's fresh, the stalk will be very firm and come away easily. Peel away all the tough outer leaves to reveal the purple inner leaves and the artichoke heart. Using a serrated knife, cut across these leaves at the point where they join the artichoke heart. Cut off 2 mm of the base of the artichoke to reveal the bottom of the artichoke heart. Trim around the sides of the artichoke with a sharp paring knife to remove all the outer leaves. Scoop out the fibrous centre of the artichoke with the tip of a teaspoon. Place in the cold water until ready to cook.

To cook the artichoke hearts, add a squeeze of lemon, coriander seeds, a sprig of fresh rosemary, a sprig of fresh thyme, a bay leaf and a dash of olive oil and cover with greaseproof paper. Simmer in salted water over a low heat for 5–10 minutes until tender depending on their size. Remove from the heat and allow to cool in the poaching liquid. If not serving immediately, refrigerate the artichokes in the poaching liquid.

Basic Technique 7

PREPARING AND COOKING BEETROOT

500 g	Baby beetroot
2 ltr	Cold water
200 ml	Verjuice
50 ml	Champagne vinegar
	Pinch sugar
	Salt
	Freshly ground pepper

Remove the leaves and stalk from the beetroot and wash under cold running water. Bring the water, verjuice and vinegar to the boil and reduce to a simmer. Season with sugar, salt and freshly ground pepper. Add the beetroot and cook until tender for 30–40 minutes, depending on their size. Remove from the heat and allow the beetroot to cool in the cooking liquid before peeling. Pass the cooking liquid through a fine sieve. Refrigerate the beetroot in the cooking liquid for up to 3 days.

Basic Technique 8

BLANCHING CAPSICUM

Heat 1 litre vegetable oil to 120°C in a heavy-based saucepan. Place the capsicum into the oil and, with a long-handled spoon, turn until the skin starts to blister but do not allow it to colour. When the skin is blistered remove the capsicum from the oil, place in a bowl and cover with clingfilm. The capsicum will steam in its own heat and the skin will loosen after 15 minutes. Place the capsicum on a chopping board and, using a sharp knife, cut through the centre to open it up like a book, keeping it in one piece. Remove the stalk and seeds, turn the capsicum over and scrape off the skin with the tip of a knife. Preserve the capsicum in olive oil with fresh herbs and crushed garlic until ready to use. When the vegetable oil has cooled, pass it through a fine sieve into a clean container, ready to use again.

Basic Technique 9

TOMATO CONCASSÉE

Score tomatoes and blanche in boiling water for 10 seconds or until the skin begins to peel away. Refresh in iced water and remove the skin. Cut each tomato into quarters and remove the seeds. Trim the quarters to give even, rectangular pieces of tomato according to the required size. Slice the tomato into even width strips lengthways and cut across at the same width to make tomato concassée. If using the tomato concassée in a cold dish, lightly season with salt, freshly ground pepper and a drizzle of olive oil. If adding the tomato concassée to a hot sauce, do so at the last minute to prevent the tomato from becoming over-cooked, mushy and discolouring the sauce.

Basic Technique 10

TOMATO CONFIT

Makes 650 g

8 kg	Roma tomatoes cored, halved and de-seeded
200 g	Maldon sea salt
1 tsp	Celery salt
1	Small bunch flat-leaf parsley, roughly chopped
1	Small bunch basil, roughly chopped
1	Small bunch tarragon, roughly chopped
6	Sprigs fresh thyme
25 ml	Extra virgin olive oil
4	Cloves garlic, peeled and thinly sliced
	Freshly ground pepper

A 750 ml terrine takes 650 g tomato confit for which 8 kg Roma tomatoes is required. After the tomatoes have been cored, de-seeded, confited, skinned, hung and squeezed they will have reduced by 85–90 per cent in weight; this gives the confit an intense flavour and vibrant colour.

Prepare the tomato confit: Preheat the oven to 140°C. Sprinkle the sea salt and celery salt over a tray and spread the chopped herbs evenly over the salts. Arrange the tomato halves on top of the herbs – packed closely together, flesh side down. Pour over 25 ml extra virgin olive oil and scatter the sliced garlic over the tomatoes. Season the tomatoes with freshly ground pepper, cover with greaseproof paper and then cover the tray with aluminium foil. Bake the tomatoes in the oven for 25–30 minutes, depending on their size. The tomatoes are ready when the flesh has softened and the skins come away easily. Remove from the oven and allow to cool slightly. Brush off any herbs, garlic or salt that have stuck to the tomatoes. Remove and discard the skin while the tomatoes are still warm. Place the tomatoes in a large piece of muslin cloth, tightly tie up the corners and put it into a sieve over a large bowl to catch the tomato water released from the tomatoes. Hang for 24 hours and reserve the tomato water. Remove the tomato confit from the muslin cloth and refrigerate until ready to use.

Basic Technique 11

MOUSSE TEST

To check the consistency and seasoning of a savoury mousse, lightly butter a piece of aluminium foil, spoon a small amount of mousse onto the foil and roll up into a sausage shape. Drop the mousse into a small pot of simmering water and gently poach for 5 minutes. Remove from the heat and leave the mousse in the water for a further 5 minutes. Remove the mousse from the water, unwrap it and taste. Adjust the seasoning if necessary, and if the mousse is too firm, add a little more chilled cream.

Basic Technique 12

BRAISING PIG'S TROTTERS AND OTHER PARTS

To braise pig's trotters, ears, heads, tongues and hocks follow the same technique as described below.

4	Boned pig's trotters
100 g	Carrots, chopped
100 g	Onions, chopped
150 ml	Dry white wine
50 ml	Port
500 ml	Veal stock (basic recipe 23, page 196)

Preheat the oven to 160°C. Hold the trotters with a pair of tongs over a low, open gas flame to remove any hair. Place the trotters (or other parts) in a heavy-based saucepan together with the carrots, onions, white wine, Port and veal stock and gently bring to the boil, skimming off any scum that may rise to the surface. Cover the pot with a lid and transfer to the oven. Braise the trotters (or other parts) for 3–3½ hours until tender, depending on their size – take care that the stock just simmers during cooking.

Remove the trotters (or other parts) from the stock, place on a tray and allow them to cool slightly. Remove any remaining bones from the toes of the trotters with the tip of a sharp knife – take care not to split the skin. Spread out the trotters or pig's ears flat (does not apply to any other parts) on a clingfilm-covered tray and cover again with a second layer of clingfilm. Place another tray on top and refrigerate to chill, which will make the trotters or pig's ears easier to handle. Pass the braising liquid through a fine sieve and discard the vegetables. Reserve the liquid for poaching the stuffed trotters.

GLOSSARY

À LA GRECQUE Foods that are prepared in the Greek style of cooking. Usually for dishes including Mediterranean vegetables, lemon, garlic or mushrooms.

AL DENTE An Italian term used to describe the texture of pasta, risotto or vegetables that are cooked until just tender and retain some resistance in the centre.

ARMAGNAC Brandy originating from Armagnac, France. Aged in oak casks before bottling.

BAIN-MARIE A water bath used for cooking terrines, parfaits, custards and curds.

BALSAMIC VINEGAR Produced in Modena, Italy, it is sold under a label of authenticity making it superior to cheaper factory-produced balsamic that often has added caramel to enhance colour and taste. The must of late-harvested white Trebbiano grapes is boiled until reduced by half and then transferred to, and aged in, wooden casks. During the hot summer months the balsamic evaporates and concentrates and in the colder months it rests and matures. As it ages, it is siphoned from barrel to barrel of decreasing size and different woods, which add a variety of aromas to the vinegar. Ageing can take up to 10 years and as long as 50 years. As it ages it becomes richer, sweeter, syrupy and more expensive. It is used in both sweet and savoury dishes and the older vinegars should be used very sparingly. The sweetness makes it ideal to dress bitter salad leaves such as radicchio and chicory or fresh fruits such as strawberries and figs.

BASTE To spoon over the pan juices or fat to keep poultry, game, meat or fish moist and to add flavour during cooking.

BATONS Uniformly cut sticks of vegetables.

BAVAROIS/BAVARIAN CREAM A flavoured custard mixed with whipped cream and set with gelatine. Usually sweet, it can, however, be flavoured with savoury ingredients such as avocado.

BEIGNET Fritter traditionally made from choux pastry as a sweet rather than a savoury. These are light, crisp, golden brown pieces of batter which, after frying, are drained and dusted with sugar.

BEURRE BLANC A classic white butter sauce made with a wine, vinegar and shallot reduction into which chilled, diced butter is whisked until emulsified. Other flavours can be added to the basic beurre blanc, such as tapenade, herbs or pesto.

BICARBONATE OF SODA/BAKING SODA A leavening agent used in baking. Also used to soften skins of beans or pulses.

BLANCHE To briefly immerse food, such as vegetables and pasta, in large quantities of salted, boiling water to rapidly par-cook while still preserving colour, texture and flavour. Use large amounts of salted, boiling water so that when food is immersed, the boiling point is maintained. The food is then refreshed by plunging it into iced water to stop the cooking process. Bacon is blanched to reduce salt content. Other foods can be blanched in hot oil or in simmering court bouillon, e.g. sweetbreads.

BLIND BAKE To bake a pastry case that is lined with greaseproof paper and filled with baking beans before adding the filling to it and cooking it further. This is done to prevent the sides from falling in during baking.

BRAISE Suited to whole joints and smaller cuts of meat and poultry. First seal to evenly brown, then add aromatic vegetables and seasonings and sufficient flavoured stock to cover. Cook slowly in the oven until tender. The stock will reduce to sauce consistency.

BRANDY A grape-based spirit distilled from wine.

BRINE Used to flavour and preserve a wide variety of foods, e.g. meats, snails, olives and vegetables. Can be flavoured in various ways, from salted water to reduced wine with vegetables, herbs and spices.

BRUNOISE A very fine uniform dice of vegetables.

CARAMELISE The process by which sugar, whether added to or occurring naturally in food, reaches 160°C and begins to brown.

CAMPARI A bitter aperitif flavoured with herbs, roots and the dried peel of Seville oranges.

CANDIED Fruit such as citrus or pineapple that have been simmered in sugar syrup until tender, then dried and rolled in granulated sugar or dipped in chocolate.

CAPERS The flower buds from the *Capparis spinosa*, a Mediterranean shrub. The buds are hand picked before they open, then dried and preserved either in a coarse salt or vinegar. Rinse under cold water before using. The finest capers grow on the islands of Pantellerie and Salina close to Sicily.

CARPACCIO A dish of thinly sliced raw fillet of beef. Also prepared with other meats, e.g. venison, and fillets of fish such as tuna, swordfish and salmon. Meat and fish used for carpaccio should be extremely fresh, trimmed of fat and sinew and refrigerated.

CAUL FAT A web-like sheet of fatty membrane surrounding the pig's intestine. It has a strong smell and must be soaked under cold running water to remove all traces of blood. Squeeze dry before using. Meats wrapped in caul will benefit from being basted, as the caul renders down during cooking and keeps the meat moist.

CAVIAR The processed, salted roe (eggs) of various species of sturgeon. Grading is determined by the size and the colour of the roe. The finest is from sturgeon fished from the Caspian and Black seas by the Iranians and Russians. Caviar production involves extracting the ovaries within 2 hours of the sturgeon being fished. The ovaries are beaten to loosen the eggs and passed through a sieve to remove any fat and membrane surrounding them. Any liquid is drained off and the eggs are salted and sealed in tins. Eggs vary in size from grain size to the size of small peas. Colours vary from black, brown, and green to the more rare grey and golden eggs. Over-fishing, pollution and quota restrictions on wild harvesting have driven up the price of caviar, the highest being for Beluga, Oscietra and Sevruga. Aquaculture of sturgeon has increased especially in France, Uruguay and North America.

CELERIAC A bulbous vegetable also known as celery root, it has a thick, brown, warty skin that, when removed, reveals white flesh that can be eaten either raw or cooked. Celeriac should be firm and feel heavy in relation to its size. Place peeled celeriac in acidulated water to prevent it discolouring. Use celeriac raw in salads, bake, deep-fry, purée and use trimmings in stocks to impart a subtle flavour.

CEP MUSHROOMS (see also Dried Mushrooms) A fleshy wild mushroom of the Boletus family with a pungent flavour and meaty texture. It has a wide, pale brown cap with a large, swollen white stem and should be firm, with the cap securely attached to the stem.

CEVICHE A dish originating from Spanish-speaking countries where thin slices of raw fish are marinated in lemon or lime juice with extra virgin olive oil and spices. The citric acid in the juice partially cooks the fish.

CHAMPAGNE Comes from Champagne, France. Made in the method champinoise from Chardonnay, Pinot Noir and Pinot Meunier grapes. Use authentic champagne for flavouring, but a sparkling wine for sauces will suffice.

CHERVIL A delicate herb with a mild aniseed flavour that diminishes when cooked.

CHIBOUST A pastry cream lightened with Italian meringue and set with gelatine.

CHILLIES Many varieties of chilli are sold fresh or dried. They come in various shapes, sizes and colours, the most common being red and green. Red chillies are sweeter and milder. The smaller the chilli the hotter it will be. Choose firm chillies with shiny skins. When preparing chillies, split them lengthways and remove the stalk and seeds. Avoid touching your skin and wash your hands and any equipment used.

CHIVES Related to the onion and leek family. Chives are a long, thin, deep green herb with hollow stems and a mild onion flavour. Slice thinly rather than chop, which will cause bruising. Garlic chives are a wild herb with a deeper colour and strong garlic flavour and usually can be found in Asian supermarkets.

CLARIFIED BUTTER Melt whole butter over a low heat until the milky solids separate from the fat and sink to the bottom of the saucepan. Pass the clarified butter through a fine sieve and discard the milky solids. Clarified butter can be heated to higher temperatures than whole butter before reaching burning point and will keep longer than whole butter.

CLARIFY A process of removing particles from a stock by cooking over a low heat with the addition of egg whites, minced poultry or fish with vegetables, until it forms a crust that floats to the surface, bringing all the solids and impurities with it and leaving a crystal clear consommé beneath the crust. A small hole is made in the crust and the consommé is gently ladled out without disturbing it.

COATING CONSISTENCY Describes the thickness of a sauce or custard when it coats the back of a metal or wooden spoon. The sauce or custard is ready when a finger is run through, leaving a clear channel.

COCOA POWDER Extracted from the residue left from the grinding of the cocoa nibs, it is used to flavour chocolate desserts. A good cocoa powder will have a deep, rich, dried blood colour.

COGNAC The finest of all brandies produced in Cognac, France.

COINTREAU Cointreau is a double distillation of grape brandy infused with orange peel. It is sweet in taste and colourless. Grand Marnier or Mandarine Napoleon are good substitutes.

COLCANNON An Irish potato dish consisting of mashed potato, butter, milk, finely chopped and cooked onion, cabbage or kale and sliced spring onion.

CONCASSÉE A term used to describe a uniform dice of blanched tomatoes.

CONFIT Preserve or conserve. The process of making confit involves cooking meat, most commonly goose or duck, in its own fat over a very low heat until tender. Confit can be stored in its own fat for several months. Certain vegetables, such as shallots and garlic, can be prepared in the same way.

CONSOMMÉ A clarified broth or stock (see Clarify). A clear, concentrated soup made from meat, game, poultry, fish or vegetables.

CORIANDER A pungent herb with a very distinctive flavour. The whole plant can be used; leaves, stalks and roots. Also known as cilantro, dhania or Chinese parsley. Dry-roast coriander seeds in a frying pan for a few minutes before crushing them to release maximum flavour.

COULIS Puréed savoury or sweet sauce with one prominent ingredient, such as tomatoes or strawberries.

COURT BOUILLON Translated it literally means 'short-boil'. A seasoned cooking liquid used for blanching sweetbreads, or cooking lobsters or whole fish.

CRACKLING Strip of animal or fish skin rendered of all fat and fried or grilled until crisp.

CRÈME ANGLAISE A custard made from egg yolks, milk, sugar and vanilla. Used as a sauce for desserts or as the base for bavarois.

CRÈME DE MENTHE A spearmint-flavoured liqueur used in pastry preparation to flavour creams, custards and mousses and to macerate fruit.

CRÈME FRAÎCHE A thick, slightly soured cream used in both sweet and savoury dishes. It contains less fat than clotted or double cream and is not good to cook with at high temperatures as it separates more easily than other creams.

CRÈME PÂTISSIÈRE A thick pastry cream made with egg yolks, milk, cream, sugar and flour.

CURD Made from the juice of citrus fruits with the addition of eggs, castor sugar and cream. Cooked in a *bain-marie*.

DASHI A Japanese stock made by simmering flakes of dried bonito and kombu (kelp). It has a very delicate flavour and can be used in dressings, or for finishing cream sauces or beurre blanc to be served with fish. Available in powdered or liquid form.

DEGLAZE Adding liquid, usually alcohol, stock or water to loosen the caramelised juices deposited in the base of a roasting or frying pan. Whisk to emulsify the fats and reduce to concentrate the flavour. Pass through a fine sieve for a sauce or gravy.

DICE To cut into small, even-shaped cubes.

DRIED FRUITS Drying fruits intensifies the flavour and sweetness of fresh fruits. Like dried mushrooms, fruits lose much of their weight during the drying process, making the final product expensive.

DRIED MUSHROOMS Mushrooms lose between 80 and 90 per cent of their weight when dried, making them expensive to use. Dried mushrooms, especially ceps and morels, have an intense flavour and are used to add flavour to stocks and sauces. Grind to a fine powder with Maldon sea salt for seasoning meats, poultry, stocks, sauces or risotto. Most commonly used dried mushrooms are ceps, morels, shiitake and trompette des morts.

DUXELLE A mixture of finely chopped button mushrooms and shallots sautéed in olive oil. Used as a garnish or added to stuffing.

ENOKI/ENOKITAKE Long-stemmed mushrooms with tiny white caps. They have a very delicate flavour and are commonly used in Asian cooking for garnishing broths. They grow in clusters and the base needs to be cut away and the mushroom separated before cooking.

EMULSION/EMULSIFY A stable suspension of two liquids that don't normally combine together smoothly, such as oil and water. They are slowly added to each other while being mixed rapidly. This suspends minute droplets of one liquid through the other. Mayonnaise and hollandaise are examples of emulsified sauces.

ESCABÈCHE A preparation of fish fillets, such as sardines, red mullet or shellfish, that have been briefly seared in a hot pan and allowed to cool before being soused for a short time in a warm, flavoured vinaigrette.

FILO/PHYLLO PASTRY Paper-thin sheets of pastry usually stacked in layers. Allow frozen filo pastry to thaw in the fridge. Work one sheet at a time as the pastry dries out quickly. Cover unused pastry with clingfilm and then a damp cloth to prevent the cloth coming into contact with the pastry.

FIVE SPICE An aromatic blend of ground spices commonly used in Chinese cooking, consisting of ground star anise, cloves, fennel seed, cassia (Chinese cinnamon) and Szechuan pepper. Some five-spice mixes may also contain ginger.

FOIE GRAS A French term meaning 'fat liver'. The livers of force-fed geese or ducks that are put through a process called 'gavage'. They are funnel fed a diet of corn, which is poured directly into the stomach, resulting in large amounts of fat being deposited in the livers, causing them to expand. The birds are fattened over a period of 4–5 months, by which time the livers will have expanded up to 10 times their normal size and weigh between 1–1.5 kg. The practice of force feeding is prohibited in many countries around the world.

FOLD To mix with a gentle lifting motion, rather than to vigorously stir, avoiding loss of aeration.

FORESTIÈRE A French term meaning 'forest'. Usually refers to meat, poultry or game bird dishes that are garnished with sautéed potatoes, lardons and wild mushrooms.

FRANGELICO An Italian hazelnut-flavoured liqueur infused with berries and flowers.

GARAM MASALA A mixture of Indian spices ground and blended together. Usually consists of coriander seeds, cumin seeds, cardamom seeds, cinnamon, cloves, nutmeg, mace, black peppercorns and ginger.

GELATINE Available in sheet and powdered form, it is produced from collagen extracted from the skin and bones of young animals. Each sheet usually weighs 2 g and has a long shelf life. Powdered gelatine loses strength once opened, which can make stocks and jellies appear cloudy. Also, it is difficult to weigh accurately in small amounts.

GNOCCHI Italian for dumpling, gnocchi is made with potatoes, flour, eggs and Parmesan or with semolina.

GRAND MARNIER A premium orange-flavoured liqueur made from Cognac and flavoured with the peel of bitter Haitian oranges, spices and vanilla. Cointreau and Mandarine Napoléon are good substitutes.

HAZELNUT OIL Extracted from hazelnuts, it has a potent flavour and is not normally served neat but is used as a flavouring in dressings, sauces and pastries. Buy in small quantities as it has a short lifespan.

HONEY Honey is used as a sweetening agent in many desserts. The taste and colour is influenced by the type of plant from which it has

been collected, such as clover, blue gum, lavender and orange blossom.

INFUSE For ingredients such as herbs and spices to impart their flavour by steeping them in lukewarm liquids.

JULIENNE A term used to describe vegetables that have been cut into very fine strips, the length of a matchstick.

JUS (see also Deglaze) The French word for 'juice', it can refer to fruit and vegetable juices but is also used to describe a dish served with its own natural juices.

LARDON A thin strip of salt pork, bacon or pancetta that is briefly blanched to remove any excess salt and then sautéed. Lardons are sometimes inserted into lean cuts of meat to keep them moist and to add flavour during cooking.

LIQUID GLUCOSE Heavy, thick, clear syrup made from maize starch, it is used as a sweetening agent in place of sugar. It is less sweet and doesn't crystallise as easily as ordinary sugar. Also, it prevents fructose and sucrose from crystallising.

LYONNAISE Denotes the use of caramelised onions as a garnish.

MACADAMIA NUTS From the macadamia tree that originated in northern Australia but now also grows in America, where large amounts of the world's supply are produced. They can be bought salted or unsalted.

MACERATE To soak fruit or other foods in flavoured liquid, usually with the addition of alcohol, to soften and/or flavour.

MADEIRA A fortified wine that ranges in colour from pale blond to deep tawny and varies in style from dry to sweet. An excellent cooking wine, especially for adding to savoury sauces that benefit from a little sweetness.

MANDOLIN A compact, hand-operated stainless steel or hard plastic slicing utensil with various adjustable blades. Used for finely slicing any firm fruit and vegetables.

MARC DE BOURGOGNE Distilled from the skins and pips of wine grapes after the juice has been extracted, the best Marc comes from Burgundy and Champagne. In Italy, Marc is known as Grappa.

MARINATE (see also Verjuice) To soak food such as meat, fish or vegetables in a seasoned liquid, paste or dry rub to flavour and tenderise it.

MARRON A large freshwater crayfish with very sweet flesh found in rivers and streams in western Australia. It has a very distinctive maroon-coloured shell and should be cooked live. Marrons are farmed successfully.

MASCARPONE A fresh cow's milk cream cheese with a high fat content produced in Italy's Lombardy region. It is used mainly in desserts.

MEDALLION A circular portion of food usually used to describe a boneless cut of meat, such as beef or veal.

MESCLUN A salad mix consisting of baby salad leaves and picked herbs.

MILLE-FEUILLE French for 'a thousand leaves', describes layers of cooked puff pastry usually filled with a flavoured pastry cream and seasonal fruits.

MINUTE Describes food that has been quickly fried or grilled. Usually refers to a thin entrecôte steak.

MIREPOIX Large, diced, peeled and washed aromatic vegetables used in stocks and sauce-making usually consisting of carrot, celery, leek and onion. When the stock or sauce is ready and their flavour has been absorbed, sieve and discard the vegetables.

MONT BLANC A dessert of chestnut purée flavoured with sugar, vanilla bean, milk and cream. Alcohol can be added, e.g. brandy. The Mont Blanc can be passed through a potato ricer if you don't have a special nozzle (see below).

MONT BLANC NOZZLE A nozzle punctured with several little holes to create long, worm-like squiggles of chestnut purée for the classic Mont Blanc dessert.

MOREL MUSHROOMS (see also Dried Mushrooms) Morels occur in early spring. They are hollow and cone shaped with a surface of crinkled cavities that trap a lot of dirt. They vary in size and colour from very small to the size of an egg and from tan to dark brown. The French varieties have a more pronounced nutty flavour. Dried morels reconstituted in warm water until soft can replace fresh morels.

MOUSSE French for 'foam'. Mousse is a preparation of aerated egg yolks or whites combined with a purée of the main flavouring ingredient such as fish, chicken, fruit purée or melted chocolate. The addition of chilled cream creates a light, velvety texture.

MUD CRAB Also known as Mangrove Crab, Muddy or Black Crab, it is found in warm tropical waters and mangrove forests. Mud crabs have hard, dark brown or mottled green shells. They can live for three years and weigh up to 3.5 kg. They have a firm texture with delicate, sweet meat. Buy crabs that are alive as they deteriorate rapidly once dead. They should feel heavy in relation to their size and have both claws still attached. Keep live crabs refrigerated, covered with damp newspaper, until ready to cook. Substitute with any other fresh crab meat. Buy pre-cooked, picked crab meat from a reputable fishmonger.

MUSLIN A very fine cloth used to strain impurities from liquid. Coffee filters are a good substitute.

NAGE French for 'to swim'. In the culinary sense, it refers to shellfish that are gently poached and served in a light stock or broth.

NAM PLA A thin, salty, light brown fish sauce made in Asia from the fermented juice of fish such as anchovies and sardines that are salted in barrels and left to dry in the sun. The salt extracts the clear liquid, which is the fish sauce.

NIÇOISE Used to describe dishes consisting of ingredients common in the cuisine of Nice, France, such as olives, garlic, fish, beans, eggs, olive oil and tomatoes.

NOILLY PRAT Dry vermouth produced in the south of France. Dry Martini is a good substitute.

NUTS Pressed to extract oil, ground to make pastes, used as thickening agents for sauces or roasted to add to salads, desserts or as a healthy snack. Nuts quickly become rancid, so buy in small quantities. Refrigerate in an airtight container. Freeze large quantities and defrost just before using.

OLIVE OIL The best is 'cold pressed' from ripe olives. Choose a fruity extra virgin olive oil such as Colonna for olive oil-based dressings and sauces such as sauce vierge or fennel emulsion. Olive oil has a limited shelf life and begins to deteriorate after a year. Refrigerate to prevent it oxidising and bring back to room temperature before using. Use a less expensive and less fruity olive oil for cooking.

OYSTER MUSHROOMS Also known as abalone mushrooms or pleurotus, they grow in clusters and are oyster-shaped. They are delicate and range in colour from beige to light pink. Sauté briefly in olive oil over a high heat.

PANCETTA Italian-style streaky bacon taken from the belly of pork. It is cured for three weeks with aromatics, then air-cured for several months; some varieties are lightly smoked. It is sold either in a roll or a flat slab with a thick rind.

PARCHMENT PAPER Non-stick paper used in baking to line trays; also known as silicone paper.

PARISIENNE SCOOP An implement for cutting out balls of fruit and vegetables.

PARMESAN/PARMIGIANO Italian, hard-grained cow's milk cheese with a pale straw colour, crumbly texture and a salty, nutty flavour that can be aged for up to four years. Parmigiano Reggiano is the finest Parmesan and is used as a seasoning and grated or shaved over food. For cooking, use the less expensive Grana Padano. Reserve the rind and use to infuse oil or to make Parmesan cream sauce.

PASS To put food through a fine sieve or muslin cloth to remove any solids.

PERIGEUX A sauce made with reduced veal stock, Port, Madeira and chopped truffle, and finished with diced, chilled butter, salt and freshly ground pepper. Not to be confused with sauce Périgourdine, which is made the same way as sauce Perigeux but finished with the addition of foie gras.

PERNOD Yellowish liquor with a strong aniseed flavour, used to flavour fish dishes and mousses.

PESTO A paste originating from Genoa made with fresh basil, roasted pine nuts, garlic, Parmesan cheese, lemon juice and olive oil. Many variations of this sauce exist, including different nut-based pestos and different herb-based pestos such as coriander.

PETITS FOURS French for 'little oven'. Bite-size sweetmeats made with pastry, chocolate, nuts and fruits, such as coconut tuilles, chocolate truffles and candied peel. Served with coffee after a meal.

PICKLED GINGER Fresh ginger root peeled, sliced and preserved in brine with rice wine vinegar. Due to a natural chemical reaction the ginger becomes pink.

PIN BONE The fine bones that are found in certain species of fish such as salmon, trout or mackerel. Swordfish and John Dory do not have pin bones. Remove with fish tweezers, pulling them out at an angle and taking care not to rip the flesh.

PISTACHIO (see Nuts) Remove the nut from its thin brown shell. Simmer for 2 minutes in milk to loosen the purple skin covering the nut. Peel away the skin to reveal the vibrant green pistachio nut. Use pistachio pastes and syrups sparingly as they are intense in flavour.

PITHIVIER A classical French dessert made with puff pastry, it is filled with frangipane, a rich almond paste that is sometimes flavoured with liqueur. Pithiviers can also be filled with savoury mixes.

POACH To cook food in barely simmering water, milk, flavoured stock or syrup.

POLENTA Coarsely ground maize or corn commonly used in Italian cuisine. It can be served hot or spread onto a lightly greased tray and set in the fridge before cutting into shapes, and reheated by frying, baking or grilling.

PORT/PORTO A sweet fortified wine usually served after a meal or with the cheese course. Use in sauces, reductions and for deglazing.

PURÉE To blend food in a food processor, then pass through a fine sieve to remove solids, pressing down hard to extract as much flavour as possible from the resulting pulp.

QUENELLE To shape food such as a vegetable purée, soft cheese or ice cream between two spoons into a smooth, three-sided oval shape. Classically, a quenelle is fish or white meat bound with cream and eggs, shaped and gently poached in a flavoured stock.

REDUCE/REDUCTION To boil a liquid over a high heat to reduce and to concentrate the flavour. Different recipes call for varied amounts of reduction to achieve the required strength and consistency.

REFRESH (see Blanche)

RÉMOULADE Describes finely cut raw vegetables; commonly used is raw celeriac and fennel bound with mayonnaise and chopped, or julienne of flat-leaf parsley seasoned with a squeeze of lemon, salt and freshly ground pepper. Can be flavoured with chopped truffle, fresh, picked crab meat or diced, cooked prawns.

RENDER The process of melting animal fat over a low heat to separate it from skin, meat and bones. Rendered pork fat is known as lard.

RESTING MEAT Heat cooks meat from the outside inwards, driving all the moisture into the centre, particularly in larger cuts or whole birds. This causes the meat fibres to tense so it is important to allow it to rest after cooking and before carving. The juices will evenly redistribute and relax the meat fibres, resulting in tenderness. The larger the piece of meat, the longer the resting time. The meat may need to be returned to the oven briefly before serving to bring its temperature back up.

RESTING PASTRY After making pastry, refrigerate to allow the gluten to contract, which would have stretched during mixing. By resting the pastry it will lessen the chance of it shrinking during baking.

RIBBON STAGE To beat cream or eggs and sugar to the stage where, when the whisk is lifted out, the mixture leaves a trail or 'ribbon' that holds its shape for a few seconds before sinking.

RICE WINE VINEGAR Made from fermented rice or other grains such as wheat or millet.

RIESLING Considered to be one of the world's great white wine grapes. Indigenous to Germany, Riesling wines are delicate and characterised by their spicy, fruity flavour and long finish.

RILLETTE Made from meat or poultry slowly cooked in its own fat. All bone is removed and the meat shredded and bound in its own fat with the addition of different flavourings. It is spooned into ceramic pots or moulds and covered with a thin layer of fat or jelly. Pork, rabbit, duck, guinea fowl and pheasant are good meats for rillette.

RISOTTO A slowly cooked, creamy rice dish made with rice that is grown in the Po Valley, Northern Italy. Varieties include Arborio, Vialoni nano, Vialoni nano gigante and Carnaroli. The rice has good absorption and maintains its shape during cooking. It is also very rich in starch which is important to the finished creamy texture of the risotto.

ROAST A method of cooking food such as meat, fish or vegetables in an enclosed space exposed to dry heat without being covered.

ROESTI A mixture of grated, par-boiled potatoes, sliced bacon and onions, shaped into round cakes and shallow-fried until golden brown on both sides.

ROSSINI Named after the nineteenth century Italian composer Gioacchino Rossini, it describes dishes that are garnished with foie gras, truffle and sauce Perigeux.

ROULADE A term used to describe food that has been rolled up.

SAFFRON Contained in the stigmas of the crocus flower, each blossom grows just three stigmas. It takes over 250,000 hand-picked stigmas to yield 500 g, making it the world's most expensive spice. After drying it is sealed in jars whole, or ground into a very fine dark orange powder. Choose saffron originating from Iran, Spain or Kashmir as these countries harvest the finest saffron. Citrus enhances the flavour of saffron. Buy in small quantities and refrigerate in an airtight container away from sunlight and heat.

SAUTÉ To cook food quickly over a high heat in a small amount of fat, while tossing the ingredients around in the pan.

SCORE To make 1 mm shallow incisions in the skin or outer layer of foods such as fish and duck breasts before cooking. It helps food to cook evenly and prevents it from shrivelling and becoming tough during cooking.

SEALING A method of cooking used to brown meat, poultry, game or fish in fat over a high heat in a pan or roasting tray to 'seal' in moisture. Seal fish, poultry and game birds, skin side down, until crisp and golden brown.

SEAR To cook very quickly over a high heat.

SEASONING (see Before Seasoning…, page 9)

SESAME OIL There are two varieties of sesame oil: a light, mild one that is cold pressed from white sesame seeds, and a darker and stronger flavoured one extracted from roasted sesame seeds. It has a distinctive nutty taste and is mainly used in Asian cooking to flavour and is often blended with more neutral oils to dilute its intensity.

SHALLOTS/ESCHALLOTS Used in French and Asian cooking for their milder flavour instead of onion, especially in salads, sauce-making and deep-frying.

SHISO Japanese name for the herb 'Perilla'. It is either green or deep purple and has a slight peppermint flavour. Used in salads or for garnishing.

SIMMER To heat liquid to just below boiling poin;.the surface of the liquid should ripple but the bubbles should not break the surface.

SKIMMING STOCKS AND SAUCES It is necessary to constantly skim stocks and sauces as they cook to remove any impurities and scum that rise to the surface. If not skimmed, the proteins and starches released from bones and vegetables will boil back into the stock, leaving it cloudy and discoloured.

SNAILS Many varieties of snail are cultivated for the table and are fed on a diet of bran and herbs. The most common are Escargot de Bourgogne, also known as the vineyard snail and the smaller Petit Gris, otherwise known as the common garden snail. Rinse and marinate in brine before using.

SORBET Flavoured-water ice. Usually flavoured with something acidic and served as a palette cleanser between courses.

SOUBISE Denotes the use of an onion purée as a garnish.

SOUR CREAM A thickened cream produced by adding a bacterial culture to fresh cream.

SOY SAUCE Made from soya beans fermented with wheat, water and salt in different stages for between six months and up to several years. It is used in Asia like salt is in the west. The Indonesians produce a much thicker and darker soy sauce, Kecap, that is strong and overpowering.

SPÄTZLE Small noodles blanched in water, drained and fried in butter until crisp and golden brown. The batter can be flavoured with herbs or dried and ground wild mushrooms.

STAR ANISE Native to China and Vietnam, as the name suggests star anise is star-shaped. It is tough skinned with a rust colour and has a powerful liquorice-like flavour. Buy whole or powdered.

SQUID INK Contained in little dark silvery sacs in the body of the squid. Remove from the squid and squeeze out the ink. Dilute with a little water and pass through a fine sieve before using. Squid ink can be bought in jars or sachets at good fishmongers or stores. Freeze if not using all at once. Ink is also obtained from cuttlefish and octopus.

SWEAT To cook vegetables in fat over a low heat until tender, extracting moisture and flavour without colouring.

TAPENADE A thick paste of puréed black or green olives, capers, anchovy and parsley blended with olive oil and seasoned with salt, freshly ground pepper and a squeeze of lemon.

TARTARE A dish of finely chopped, high-quality, raw lean meat or fish. Traditionally made from beef with the addition of chopped gherkins, capers, cocktail onions and herbs. Flavour with Dijon mustard, Tabasco, Worcestershire sauce, brandy, salt and freshly ground pepper. Usually shaped into a mound with an indentation in the top, into which is placed a raw egg yolk.

TERRINE A china, earthenware or cast-iron dish with a close-fitting lid, usually loaf-shaped. Also describes what has been cooked in it.

TORTELLINI Small folded pockets of pasta containing various fillings, cooked in salted, boiling water and coated in an appropriate sauce or served as a garnish.

TROMPETTE DES MORTS (see also Dried Mushrooms) Also known as 'horn of plenty'. A very distinctive mushroom; it has a blue-grey colour and is completely black when wet. Unlike other mushrooms it doesn't have a cap but the stem and cap form a continuous hollow. Trim the base before briefly sautéing in olive oil over a high heat. Also available dried.

TRUFFLES The white truffle of Alba in Piedmont and the black truffle of Perigord are the most sought-after and valuable species. The truffle season runs from November to February and they are harvested with the help of specially trained pigs and dogs who detect the aroma of the underground fungus. Dogs are preferred as pigs are reluctant to give up their 'find'. White truffles are creamy beige in colour, have a smooth surface and a pungent aroma and flavour. They are best served raw, thinly sliced and are favoured over the black truffles by connoisseurs. The black truffle has a rough outer skin, varies in colour from deep brown to black and once sliced, reveals a marbled pattern running through it. Black truffles benefit from cooking to release their full flavour. Simmer truffles in a reduction of Madeira, Port and veal stock and allow to cool in the cooking liquid that will become the base for Perigeux sauce. Refrigerate and the cooking liquid will solidify, preserving the truffles and perfuming the stock. The truffles can be spooned out as needed. Fresh truffles stored in raw Arborio rice, polenta or with fresh free-range eggs in sealed containers for 24 hours will impart their aroma and flavour, which then can be turned into dishes like truffle risotto, creamed truffle eggs and

polenta and truffle terrine. Ensure that truffles are clean, with no hidden pockets of mud as they are sold by weight. Avoid any with tiny holes through them, as this is a sign of worms. They should feel heavy and firm in relation to their size. To clean truffles, gently brush them with a hard nail-brush to remove any soil. Preserved truffle pieces are available but do not compare with fresh truffle. Truffle-infused oils are available but avoid those that are chemically enhanced. Use truffle oil with slivers of truffle infusing it and use in moderation as the flavour can be intense and overpowering.

TUILLE Thin, crisp, sweet biscuits made from egg whites, flour, icing sugar and unsalted butter. With the addition of different ingredients the flavour can be easily changed, e.g. almond meal, pistachio, cocoa powder, grated orange or lemon zest, or honey. The tuilles can be shaped on baking sheets before cooking using stencils, or shaped once cooked and still warm by draping them over a rolling pin or cutting out with plain pastry cutters.

VANILLA From the tropical plant *V. planifolia*, belonging to the orchid family. Ensure vanilla beans are moist and have a strong perfume. Store in a sealed container of castor sugar to infuse; use the sugar in desserts like crème brûlée and cakes. To obtain maximum flavour, split the bean lengthways and scrape out the seeds. Whole vanilla beans can be used 3–4 times if washed after using. Ensure that vanilla extract is made from fresh, macerated, chopped vanilla beans and avoid those that have been chemically enhanced.

VELOUTÉ French for 'velvety', a term used to describe a sauce or soup with a smooth texture made with a flavoured stock and finished with the addition of butter and cream.

VERJUICE The juice extracted from unripe fruit, most commonly wine grapes. A premium flavour enhancer and tenderiser, it is a good substitute for lemon juice and vinegar. Its unique balance of sweet and sour adds richness and flavour, making it excellent for dressings, sauces, marinades, poaching and deglazing. It shares the same acid-base as wine, making it compatible with all wine styles. Verjuice has an affinity with nut oils and emulsifies well with mild-flavoured, creamy olive oils.

VICHYSSOISE A classic soup made with a purée of leeks and potatoes and finished with cream and sliced chives. Usually served cold.

WALNUT OIL Produced from walnuts with high oil content. Once harvested, the walnuts are stored for 2–3 months to allow their milky juices to transform into clear oil before being pressed. Not usually served neat, it is used as a flavouring in dressings, sauces and pastries. It has a short shelf life, so buy in small quantities.

YABBY Freshwater crayfish found in Australian waters. Lobster or Dublin Bay prawns can be used as a substitute for yabby, which is best cooked when still alive. Before cooking, the bitter intestinal tract should be removed. This is done by twisting the middle section of the tail and gently pulling it out.

ZEST The peel of citrus fruit used to flavour syrups, custards and curds. Remove the white pith before using as it is bitter.

ZURICHOISE Sautéed thin slices of veal, diced shallots and sliced mushrooms, deglazed with white wine and finished with veal stock and cream. Zurichoise is always served with a wedge of roesti potato.

INDEX

ACKNOWLEDGEMENTS

Season To Taste is a well-travelled book; it began its journey in Australia where I lived for many years and, where the design and food photography were completed; then on to Ireland where it was researched and written. Finally, it arrived at its end destination, South Africa, to be published. Truly the result of international effort, I have many people to thank and acknowledge for its final realisation.

THANKS TO …

… four very special people without whom this book would never have happened: In Sydney – the legendary Geoff Lung, photographer and the ultimate professional and perfectionist; you supported this book a hundred per cent even during times of unavoidable delays. Anne Barton, art director; you kept this book alive, nothing was too much trouble and your uncompromising eye for detail has been unwavering. Warren Turnbull, loyal chef and faithful friend who for six months gave up his precious days off to help put these recipes and photographs together; you are one of the finest people and most talented chefs with whom I have worked. In Cape Town – Janice Botha, who believed in the book from the minute she saw the mock-up; you sprinkled your gold-dust working into the wee hours editing and embellishing my work and enthusiastically tried out the recipes. I am deeply grateful to you all.

Special thanks to Geoff Lung's assistant, Emma Reilly, and his studio crew for their energy and talents. To Judy Pascoe and Greg Slater for their contributions and time spent on *Season To Taste* – a big thank you.

The restaurant brigade at Banc Sydney – lead by Warren Turnbull – is the best with whom I've ever had the privilege to work: Kirsty Hollis; Peter McKenna (Irish); Ciaran Glennon; Collie Mac; Sorren; Greek Willie; 'Galway' John; Grecco; Jo Karmis; Tanya Poles; Liza Noakes; Lisa Ryak; Annette Mudie; Nicholas; Bertie Nom-Nom; Rachel McShane; Princess Olivia; Mark; Steve Canavan and Michael from Winnipeg.

Brilliant young chefs who were part of my team and for whom I have the greatest respect are: Justin North of Becasse, Sydney; Matthew Kemp of Balzac, Sydney; Peter Sheppard of Caveau; Brett Graham of The Ledbury, London; Darrell Felstead, a chef for whom no challenge was ever too big; Sean McBride, Colin Fassnidge and Richard Kindermann; Anthony Flowers and Carlo Morandin.

Great chefs who have inspired and influenced me over the past 20 years are: Tim O'Sullivan of Renvyle House Hotel, Connemara, Ireland; Bruno Enderli of Hotel Central, Zurich, Switzerland; Manfred Kolhn of The Amsterdam Hilton, Amsterdam, The Netherlands; Rene Bajard of Le Mazarin, Pimlico, London; Herbert Berger, the biggest influence of all, of Keats, Hampstead, London and presently of 1 Lombard Street, London; Dietmar Sawyere of Restaurant Forty One, Sydney, Australia; Russell Armstrong, a true friend and the most passionate chef that I have ever met and worked alongside.

Dear friends in Sydney who supported me right to the end: John Stewart, Lexi Collins, Annie Sapsford; Lisa and Brett Patterson; Simon Johnson and David; Serge Dansarau; Peter and Bev Doyle; Greg Doyle; Tony Bilson; John Wilson; Jamie and Barry McDonald; Les Shiratto; Clara Mason; Jane Adams and Sue Farlie-Cunningham.

Tony King, David Stockton, George Banks and the crew at British Airways, London – your support over the years is much appreciated and it is a privilege to be associated with the British Airways Culinary Council.

All the dishes in *Season To Taste* are plated on Wedgwood crockery and I thank John Mohin and Belinda Price from Wedgwood for supplying me with such a beautiful range with which to work.

Stephen Cloughley and his wonderful family – thank you for welcoming me into your home in Philadelphia. To Amar – thanks for the opportunity.

To old and new-found friends in South Africa who have welcomed me to Cape Town: My great friend, Conrad Gallagher – your hospitality knows no bounds and I value our friendship; Kim Maxwell – your friendship and invaluable network opened many doors; Murray Giggins and family – your staunch support, encouragement and incomparable PR services are appreciated; the guys at In House Brand Architects, Lawrence Holmes and his beautiful wife Amanda, Aidan Hart and Michael Miles – your charitable works are your best and most highly recommended; Chris Beagrie – the horse that's always racing; Rob Walker – master of the 'braai' and Deamo of Long Street Café and Maria's – your lamb is incomparable and smashing your plates is always fun; Melvyn Minnaar and Tommy Stephens – your Friday night dinners and conversation are always an adventure; Pete and Elize Goffe-Wood of PGW Eat – your warmth and help make you very special 'Cowboys'; Bruce Robertson – your help is appreciated and your touch of madness refreshing; Jean-Yves Muller, Brendon Crew and the 'real crew' at Caveau – love my new office; Clare O'Donoghue, Sonya Schoeman and all at *Top Billing* – you're the top team; Ingrid Lourens, Debbie Wilsnagh, Catherine Kerswill and Ann Thomas of Coastal Connection Producers – thanks, ladies, for the constant stream of coffee and long-sufferance while I hijacked your boss and disrupted the office routine.

Very special thanks to Steve Connolly, Linda de Villiers, Joy Clack and the team behind the scenes at Struik for taking on *Season To Taste* and putting your weight and energy behind it.

Thanks to Bridie and Seamus of Galway – your consistent feedback on recipes and method descriptions kept my feet firmly on the ground.

The Osborne and Davis families – thank you for your constant support and encouragement.

Love and thanks to my family in Dublin for a year of great food, drink and laughs: my beloved mum, Vera Tomlin; sister, Ann and her partner, Shane; brothers David and Noel and nephew, young Christopher – I miss our fun and memorable Tuesday afternoons. To my relatives, the Tomlins, Keegans, Gibsons, Counihans, Kellys and Shortalls – thank you all.

Finally, my wife Jan, thank you for always being there through thick and thin.